The Destiny of Civilization

Finance Capitalism, Industrial Capitalism or Socialism

Michael Hudson

www.michael-hudson.com
www.islet-verlag.de

Cover design by Miguel Guerra

Index by Ashley Dayman

Typeset by Global University for Sustainability

Hudson, Michael, 1939-
The Destiny of Civilization: Finance Capitalism, Industrial Capitalism
or Socialism

ISBN 978-3-949546-07-5 paperback
ISBN 978-3-949546-06-8 hardback
ISBN 978-3-949546-08-2 ebook

Contents

Foreword by Wen Tiejun

Humanity Shares a Common Prospect: Barbarism or Ecological Civilization

The most important factor affecting the global economy is the increasing strain caused by U.S. hegemony. Its diplomacy has shaped the economic and trading rules enforced by the IMF, World Bank and other international institutions in America's favor after World War II. U.S. leadership reached its peak with its Cold War victory over the Soviet Union in 1991, consolidated by increasingly aggressive military diplomacy over the next twenty years. But since 2008 this U.S. diplomacy has become so aggressive that it is now self-destructive, driving other nations out of the U.S. orbit, leading America's international influence to fall increasingly short of its ambition to siphon off the world's income and wealth for itself despite its own weakening economic power.

The principal conflict in today's world is between the United States and China. This book by Professor Hudson explains this conflict as a process of international transformation, above all in the sphere of economic systems and policy. He explains why the U.S.-China conflict cannot simply be regarded as market competition between two industrial rivals. It is a broader conflict between different political-economic systems – not only between capitalism and socialism as such, but between the logic of an industrial economy and that of a financialized *rentier* economy increasingly dependent on foreign subsidy and exploitation as its own domestic economy shrivels.

Professor Hudson endeavours to revive classical political economy in order to reverse the neoclassical counter-revolution. The essence of 19th-century political economy was its conceptual framework of value, price and rent theory. Its idea of a free market was one free from economic rent – defined as the excess of market price over intrinsic cost-value, and hence unearned income. The classical aim was to free markets from landlords, monopolies and creditors. Yet the reverse has occurred in the West, particularly since the globalization of neoliberal policies in the 1980s.

Historically, the way for industrial nations to gain wealth and power was to make their government strong enough to prevent a landlord class from dominating, and indeed to suppress the *rentier* sector as a whole. To promote industrial prosperity, governments provided public services to reduce the costs of living and doing business. Basic services were provided at subsidized prices that would have been replaced by exploitative monopoly prices if key public infrastructure were turned over to private owners.

Economically, the most important service that all economies need to function smoothly is the provision of money and bank credit. When privatized, it becomes a rent-extracting choke point. That is why 19th-century economists developing the logic of industrial capitalism concluded that money and banking needed to be a public utility, so as to minimize financial overhead unnecessary for industrial production.

Today's anti-classical economics regards financial charges as income earned productively by providing a "service," which is categorized as output and hence part of Gross Domestic Product (GDP). That statistical methodology treats financial profits, along with other forms of economic rent, as additions to GDP, not as an overhead burden. This produces an illusion that the real economy is growing. But what actually is growing is the *rentier* sector, which does not create real economic value, but merely transfers income from debtors, renters and consumers to creditors, landlords and monopolists. This *rentier* takeover is achieved by privatizing the public sector to create rent-extracting means for monopoly capital, organized mainly by the financial sector.

This book by Professor Hudson is based on the lecture series on finance capitalism that he presented for the Global University for Sustainability. The series is directed towards the Chinese audience because he believes that China's mixed economy with its classical industrial policy has best succeeded in avoiding the neoliberal American disease. These lectures explain why the U.S. and other Western economies have lost their former momentum: A narrow *rentier* class has gained control and become the new central planner, using its power to drain income from increasingly indebted and high-cost labor and industry. The American disease of de-industrialization has resulted from the costs of industrial production being inflated by the economic rents extracted by this class under the system of financialized monopoly capitalism that now prevails throughout the West.

The policy question for China is how it can best maintain its advantage and indeed, avoid falling prey to American ideological and diplomatic pressure. Professor Hudson summarizes his prescription as follows: First, national statistics should distinguish the productive sectors that create real value from the financial *rentier* sectors that merely transfer income from the rest of the economy to themselves. A transfer payment is not production. Second, all successful economies have been mixed economies. Money and credit, land, public services and natural resources should be controlled by the government so that they can be provided at cost or on a subsidized basis, thereby lowering the cost of living and doing business in the private sector. Third, the way to prevent unproductive debt overhead is to tax away economic rent so that it will not be financialized and paid out to banks as interest by speculators and buyers of rent-extracting opportunities.

A central point of Professor Hudson's analysis is that U.S. diplomacy is an extension of the neoliberal ideology sponsored by its *rentier* oligarchy. "U.S. exceptionalism" means that the United States can ignore international laws, dictate the policies of other countries, and demand that they relinquish control of potential rent-yielding assets (Such as banking, mineral-resource extraction rights, and high-technology monopolies) to U.S. multinational corporations and those of U.S. economic satellites.

For nearly the entire 75 years since World War II, pro-creditor laws have been imposed on all nations within the U.S. diplomatic orbit. This U.S. drive has imposed austerity on Global South countries when they have not been able to pay their dollarized debts, sacrificing their domestic economy and the well-being of their people to pay foreign bondholders.

What is ironic is that the United States itself is by far the world's largest international debtor. It has turned the dollarized system of international payments into a way to make other countries finance its global military spending by making the foreign reserves of the world's central banks take the form of loans to the U.S. Treasury – holdings of U.S. Treasury securities, U.S. bank deposits and other dollar-denominated assets. That is the buttress of today's debt-based Dollar Hegemony. To break out of this dollar trap, China should stand with other independent nations to develop a new system of international payments and formulate new principles of international law for trade and investment relations. These principles require an overall economic and political doctrine along the lines described in this book.

What I find strange is that despite the West's economic, political, social and cultural problems stemming from its neoliberal anti-classical ideology being obvious for many years, many people in China still look to Western schools and leaders for guidance, as if their own native institutions, civilization and even their own race are inferior. The defeat of a country starts with the defeat of the people's self-confidence in its institutions. Yet as an American scholar, Professor Hudson, who has studied U.S. finance his entire life and worked on Wall Street for decades, recognizes China's institutional advantages. As long as we have the scientific spirit to continue self-reflection, self-correction and self-enhancement, there is no reason not to believe that China's social organization and its ideology of Common Prosperity can lead its society toward a higher form of civilization. The key is to pursue our institutional advantages and abandon the shortcomings of the post-industrial Western *rentier* economies, not follow the Western neoliberal path and fall into dependency on the U.S. hegemony and ideology that has ground prosperity to a halt in most Western economies, subjected as they are to debt-ridden austerity.

Behind today's finance-capitalist crisis is thus a profound civilizational crisis. The world is at a crossroad in which all humanity now shares a common prospect: Barbarism or Ecological Civilization.

Wen Tiejun
Executive Dean, Institute of Rural Reconstruction of China
Southwest University, China

Translated by Alice Chan

Foreword by Lau Kin Chi

How an Economist is Tempered: The Contributions of Michael Hudson to Humanity's Future

A favorite book of my generation was Nicolai Ostrovsky's 1936 novel *How Steel was Tempered*, with the famous quote: "Man's dearest possession is life. It is given to him but once, and he must live it so as to feel no torturing regrets for wasted years, never know the burning shame of a mean and petty past; so live that, dying, he might say: all my life, all my strength were given to the finest cause in all the world – the fight for the Liberation of Mankind." When I was young, I copied this in my diary to remind myself that every moment should be given to the fight for the liberation of mankind. Many friends of my generation were similarly affected.

Starting to write the foreword to Michael Hudson's book *The Destiny of Civilization*, this quote was the first thing that came to my mind. Having come to know Michael as a person and intellectual, working together intensely on his lectures and book projects, I find him to be dedicated with a single mind, not wasting a moment of his life on less relevant matters. I saw from our back-and-forth e-mail correspondence that he often sat writing for 15 hours a day, at the age of 82. This self-discipline stems, I believe, from an adamant will to give all his strength to the finest cause in the world.

Economist on governing the world and caring for the people

Michael is a world-renowned economist. Here's what has been said about him:

David Graeber, author of *Debt: The First 5,000 Years* and co-organizer of the Occupy Wall Street Movement: "Michael Hudson is surely the most innovative, and in my view, the most important economic historian of the last half century. There are few people alive who have taught me more than Michael Hudson."

Steve Keen, author of *Debunking Economics*: "Michael Hudson has consistently been an eloquent, erudite, accurate analyst of the strengths and failings of modern capitalism. He is one of the prescient few who anticipated today's never-ending economic crisis, and one of a smaller number still whose advice about how to end the crisis would actually work."

Paul Craig Roberts, former Under-Secretary of the U.S. Treasury, wrote on February 3, 2016 on *CounterPunch*: "Michael Hudson is the best economist in the world. Indeed, I could almost say that he is the only economist in the world. Almost all of the rest are neoliberals, who are not economists but shills for financial interests."

The above is no exaggeration. I would add that Michael is the world's best economist not only in professional expertise but in moral rectitude *fighting for the liberation of mankind*. By "economist," I would invoke the meaning of the term "economy" as used in classical Chinese. The contemporary Chinese term "economy" (*jingji*, 经 济) is derived from the term *jingshi jimin* 经 世 济 民 used in the 4th to 6th century, literally meaning "governing the world and caring for the people." This classical sense of the term is most appropriate to describe Michael as an "economist," as he has been concerned not with the narrow workings of the status quo of market production and consumption, but with the way the world is governed, and how people take care of themselves and are taken care of. His erudite concerns are presented in this book, aptly entitled *The Destiny of Civilization*.

Eminent scholar and erudite writer

Michael is president of the Institute for the Study of Long-term Economic Trends (ISLET), which he founded in the 1990s to coordinate a joint project with Harvard University's Peabody Museum to create an economic history of the Bronze Age Near East and trace the transformation of economies in their political and social context over the past five thousand years. Like all his work, this has not merely been about understanding the world; his prime motivation has been his endeavor to create a better and fairer world.

One can imagine how a person of integrity, proposing genuine conceptual and practical alternatives to end polarized wealth and power, and, above all, particularly intelligent and competent, would be a threat to corporate and financial interests, their state agents, media propagandists, and mainstream academia. Yet his analysis is so pragmatic and backed by statistics that despite the controversial nature of his critique of mainstream assumptions and theories, Michael remains widely respected for the dozen books he has written. His op-eds have been published in the *Financial Times*, *New York Times*, *Washington Post*, and major European papers, such as the *Frankfurt Allgemeine Zeitung*. His numerous cover stories for *Harper's* magazine gained him international recognition for not only predicting in 2006 the imminent 2007-08 junk-mortgage crisis, but also for diagramming the financial overhang that was causing the crash and leaving debt deflation in its wake, an analysis that he had earlier presented in articles in books published with his colleagues at the University of Missouri at Kansas City (UMKC) and at the Levy Institute at Bard College. He is a frequent guest on a broad range of TV and radio programs, including National Public Radio's *Marketplace* reports, *Democracy Now*, and numerous Russia TV shows. He is on the editorial board of *Lapham's Quarterly*, is a regular contributor to the e-blogs *Naked Capitalism* and *CounterPunch*, and maintains his own website at michael-hudson.com providing access to his frequent public interviews and articles.

Michael has had several books published in Chinese (with more coming soon), and is well known and respected in China. The Chinese Academy of Social Sciences has published numerous articles by him. He has been honorary professor at Huazhong University of Science and Technology in Wuhan, and a professor at the School of Marxist Studies at Peking University. I had read him long before we became acquainted. It was only in May 2016 that we met for the first time, in the company of Samir Amin. Samir and Michael were attending the First World Congress on Marxism held in Beijing. I introduced to Michael the work of the Global University for Sustainability (Global U), of which Samir and I were among the initiators. Michael gracefully accepted to become one of the Founding Members of the Global U. In May 2018, on the occasion when he, Samir and David Harvey were invited as speakers at the Second World Congress on Marxism in Beijing, I interviewed him on his life and thought. (https://our-global-u.org/oguorg/en/michael-hudson/) I was struck by his demeanor of gentleness as a person and poignancy as a thinker. In the one-hour interview, Michael told his story which was simply amazing, explaining how his tempering as an economist is a combination of chance and the logic of the circumstances of his time.

Between music and economics – modulation to a higher overtone key

Chance and contingency shape our lives. We might have seen Michael as a conductor and music theorist, which was his career aspiration as an undergraduate at the University of Chicago, studying for his BA in

Germanic philology and the history of culture. At the same time, independently, he became the master-student of Oswald Jonas, the collaborator of the German music theorist Heinrich Schenker emphasizing counterpoint as driving the structural harmonic progression forward by dissonance resolving itself. To Michael, this unfolding of the overtone system by modulation to a higher key was a musical analog to the dynamic of social evolution.

Michael's decision to shift to economics was dramatic. One evening, after moving to New York planning to publish the works of Schenker, George Lukacs and others, he had dinner with Terence McCarthy, an Irish communist and translator of Karl Marx's *Theories of Surplus Value*. The conversation turned to how changes in water levels caused crop failures in the United States that led to an autumnal drain of money from the stock and bond market, and hence to periodic financial crises. In Michael's words, "to me, these interconnections between production, finance and the overall economy's systemic relationships were so beautiful, so aesthetic in their unfolding – like musical counterpoint leading to modulation to a higher overtone key – that I decided on the spot to become an economist." Ever since, he says, he has been able to achieve in his economic writing what he could not have created in music.

Michael's first training followed his acceptance of the condition Terence McCarthy set to mentor him: that he would read all the works in the bibliography of Marx's *Theories of Surplus Value*. So while taking his graduate degrees and working for Wall Street banks, Michael also worked part-time for the publisher Augustus Kelley to recommend and write introductions to reprints of economic classics. In the process, he acquired a library of books by economists missing from the "normal" history of economic thought.

Childhood and teenage experience – in an adversarial position

Michael's disposition certainly has a lot to do with his family and social background during his formative years. He was born in March 1939 in Minneapolis, Minnesota, into a family of labor activists. Of all the cities in the world, Minneapolis had the strongest Trotskyist influence. Michael's father, Carlos Hudson, had worked with Leon Trotsky in Mexico and had been one of the leaders of the great Minneapolis general strike of 1934 as editor of the *Northwest Organizer*. His father loved Huckleberry Finn, and Michael was called "Huck" by family and friends. But since his father's party name was Jack Ranger, Michael as a boy also was nicknamed "The son of the Lone Ranger."

When Michael was three years old, Carlos Hudson was jailed under the Smith Act as one of the Minneapolis 17. Carlos remarked that his year in prison was the happiest time of his life, being assigned to the library, where he collected a long list of proverbs that Michael reproduced on his blog in June 2017. Reading "Dad's Many Proverbs," one might come to see not only how *J is for Junk Economics* came to be structured, but also where Michael's remarkable sense of humor and witty comments can be traced.

When he was growing up in Chicago, visitors to his house included former German colleagues of Rosa Luxemburg and Karl Liebknecht, and members of the Third International when Lenin was still alive and in power. There was almost constant discussion of socialist doctrine and tactics in the meetings convened in his home. When Michael was 14 years old, in the University of Chicago's high school, he was called a fascist by Stalinists and a communist by fascists. He told me, "I was very happy being in an adversarial position, yet also the reasonable voice avoiding ideology. I liked being hated by the right-wing because it made me a lot of friends and I recruited many members into the socialist youth groups in Chicago."

Getting more confident and stronger when put in an adversarial position probably has been one of the key traits of his life. Michael has never accepted the world as it is, with its frauds, hypocrisy and injustice. Yet it has taken more than self-confidence and a strong spine to become the great economist that he is today. One reason for his brilliance and uniqueness is that he has not been swayed by his academic training in the unrealistic theories of the economics schools in the universities that justify rather than critically challenge the status quo. Michael has developed his analytic ideas through his real-life work experience in many countries, combined with his deep understanding of the history of economic thought.

Wall Street bank experience – countering ideology

While employed by Wall Street banks as a statistical economist to understand how the financialized economy works, Michael studied for a Master's and then a PhD degree in economics at New York University. According to him, most teachers in the master's program at NYU were part-time. The relatively few full-time academics had no experience working in a bank or corporation; their worldview came from textbooks. Michael fortunately found out for himself how the banks worked, starting as a statistical analyst for the Savings Bank Trust for three years, and then as balance-of-payments economist for the Chase Manhattan Bank from 1964 to 1967.

Initially, Michael's job was to trace how savings were recycled into new mortgage loans by New York's savings banks. His research showed that most deposits grew not by new saving, but simply by the accrual of dividends at compound interest. This exponential growth was recycled into new mortgage loans to buyers of real estate, seeking ever larger debt/equity ratios in order to dispose of the surplus finance capital. He saw that commercial banks did not lend money to finance new industrial capital investment, but only lent against existing assets, seeking above all to turn their profits or rents into a flow of interest payments. In short, rents were for paying interest. And increasingly today, so are wages, because payments on bank loans, mortgage loans, student debt and credit-card debt eat away at the disposable income of most families. This is the monthly "nut" that households pay to the Finance, Insurance and Real Estate (FIRE) sector off the top of their paychecks.

Later, at Chase Manhattan, Michael compiled statistics to trace how the export earnings of foreign countries were captured into paying debt service. He also traced statistically how U.S. oil companies made profits by "transfer pricing," selling crude oil production cheaply to tax-free "non-countries" such as Liberia or Panama that used U.S. currency. The oil was then re-sold to refineries in Europe and the USA at a mark-up so high that oil companies had no profits to report, and hence paid no income tax anywhere on their international and domestic operations. To U.S. policy makers, this exploitation was a success story. In 1966 the oil industry had copies of Michael's report placed on the desk of every senator and representative, and obtained special favoritism as a result of the sector's strong contribution to the U.S. balance of payments during the Vietnam War years.

The conflict between this reality and academic orthodoxy struck him in 1968 when he had to retake the money-and-banking part of his PhD orals, because his answers were based on his real-world monetary and financial experience, which was at odds with the Chicago School monetarism and vulgarized Keynesian liberalism that had become the academic norm. That was an era when textbooks still taught of helicopters dropping money on the economy – not acknowledging the principle that Michael has made at many monetary conferences ever since: the central bank's helicopter only flies over Wall Street. Money from this helicopter is lent out to buyers of real estate, stocks and bonds (and to corporate raiders), with little being spent on goods and services. So the effect is asset-price inflation – which Michael has shown leads to debt *deflation* as homeowners need to borrow higher and higher mortgage loans to afford the debt-inflated cost of housing, leaving them with less to spend on real goods and services.

This now-obvious linkage between rising housing costs and debt deflation was deemed heresy in the 1960s. Mainstream economists thought that as families became wealthier homeowners, they would have more to spend – ignoring the debt dimension of how homes were bought on credit that steadily pushed up the cost of obtaining housing. The Finance, Insurance and Real Estate (FIRE) sector was (and still is) treated as if its *rentier* income should be added to the economy's output instead of siphoning it off.

Economic historian – delving into the origins of money and debt

Michael's experience on Wall Street inspired him to set about investigating the origins of money and replacing the individualistic theories of its origin with a more realistic and historically based explanation. His technical articles and monographs are now accepted as documenting how money originated, not in barter among individuals, but as a means of palatial accounting in Bronze Age Mesopotamia, above all to denominate debts owed to the palace, temples and other creditors in grain and silver as common denominators whose units were set as having equal value for fiscal payments to the palace.

Michael also has shown that instead of interest being invented by individuals lending cattle or grain to reflect productivity rates (as Austrian theory imagines), early interest rates were set by the palaces or other civic authorities simply on the basis of ease of accounting, in terms of the local system of fractions – 60ths in Mesopotamia and Egypt, decimals in Egypt and Greece, and the 12-based duodecimal system in Rome (1 troy ounce on the pound per year), increasingly decimalized into 1 percent per month. Finally, he has applied this historical analysis to modern times by showing that throughout history, debts have grown at compound interest faster than the economy is able to pay, leading to foreclosures and economic polarization if the debts are not cancelled. Indeed, for this reason, personal debts were cancelled when new rulers took the throne in Sumer, Babylonia, Egypt and their neighboring lands, in contrast to Greek and Roman oligarchic opposition to debt cancellation and imposition of pro-creditor laws.

Michael's insights into the workings of modern financialized rent-seeking economies, both within the United States and globally, have prompted him to conduct years of research not only into the origins of money and accounting, but into the origins of labor and how it was paid, the origins of land tenure and taxation, and the origins and history of debt. This analysis has led to his well-known proposition that "debts that can't be paid, won't be paid," and to his advocacy that unpayable debts should be cancelled, and *can* be cancelled without causing economic disruption – and indeed that without doing so, economies will polarize and crash.

At the World Social Forums, I had marched with tens of thousands of participants, including Samir Amin and Immanuel Wallerstein, with a banner whose slogan "Don't owe, won't pay" demanded cancellation of debts for impoverished countries of the Global South. However, I sometimes wondered if the slogan was chanted by many from a political position without a deep understanding of *how* the debts were generated. The slogan would be meek if it were only a political position to express the distress of the indebted countries and peoples, without an appreciation of why and how the debts should be cancelled.

Michael's advocacy of debt cancellation does not come from a simplistic political position, though certainly the proposition itself is profoundly political. The proposition comes from his insider knowledge of the operation of banks, oil companies, the government and even the military. This experience informed his understanding of the domestic and global politics of the United States, and of the financial dynamics of debt and the long history of debt cancellation in antiquity. Exempt from academic dogmatism and left-wing infantilism, Michael's economic theories are based on decades of pragmatic statistical and historical inquiry, backed by his earlier training in cultural history as well as his comprehensive reading of Marx's economic works.

Staunch critic of U.S. Super Imperialism

Working for the accounting firm Arthur Anderson, Michael spent a year analyzing the U.S. balance of payments. His statistics showed that the entire payments deficit resulted from military spending on the Vietnam War and elsewhere. Seeking ways to finance that military deficit led the U.S. Government to ameliorate the worsening balance-of-payments deficit by asking U.S. banks to set up branches in offshore banking centers to attract the world's criminal capital, from drug dealings to kleptocratic embezzlement (the world's new "neoliberal" sectors). This outgrowth of oil-industry "flags of convenience" has led to today's crisis of tax enclaves enabling the world's wealthy individuals and corporations to avoid taxation and file fictitious economic statistics. Michael has exposed this in numerous introductions to books and in interviews in documentary films.

Michael's understanding of how the global economy under U.S. hegemony worked enabled him to forecast in *Ramparts* in 1968 that the USA would have to go off gold, which it indeed did in August 1971. Explaining how ending the gold standard had inaugurated the U.S. Treasury-bill standard that obliged foreign governments to finance the U.S. balance-of-payments and domestic budget deficits, his first book, *Super Imperialism: The Economic Strategy of American Empire* (1972), gained him international recognition and has been translated into many languages. He had hoped to help countries resist the system of dollarization that has enabled the United States to obtain a free ride for its foreign military spending and takeover of other economies. But from the very beginning, the U.S. Government used the book as a how-to-do-it manual. Michael was quickly employed by Herman Kahn's Hudson Institute to explain to the White House and the Department of Defense how the new international financial order worked.

The success of Michael's books led many Wall Street and Canadian financial institutions to retain him as a consultant forecasting interest rates and currency exchange rates. The Canadian government invited him as financial advisor to develop the balance-of-payments dimension of what has become Modern Monetary Theory (MMT), showing that Canada did not need foreign loans to finance its provincial and other domestic spending. His book describing why Canada did not need foreign borrowing for its provinces and companies to spend domestically, *Canada in the New Monetary Order* (1978), showed that when Canada borrowed abroad, the central bank still had to create domestic money in any case to be spent locally as a counterpart to the foreign currency inflow. Hardly by surprise, this led to passionate attacks by Canada's banks seeking to profiteer by indebting the economy through their loan underwriting. But it also led to further contracts with Canada's State Department and Science Council.

In the late 1970s, Michael was invited by the United Nations Institute for Training and Research (UNITAR) to become economic advisor on North-South debt and trade. He warned of the coming Latin American debt defaults, which indeed began in 1982 with Mexico. He subsequently has served as economic advisor to numerous governments, agencies and political parties from Latvia to Greece. He has argued for national protectionism and capital controls to resist free-trade imperialism, for domestic money creation to finance domestic spending on less inflationary terms than borrowing foreign currency, and for the need to tax and limit *rentier* gains in real estate and finance.

Academic and theoretical contributions

Michael has worked within academia on sustained intellectual inquiry. For many years he was on the economics faculty of the University of Missouri at Kansas City (UMKC), which became the center of MMT in the early 2000s with Randall Wray, Stephanie Kelton and Bill Black. He was Economic Research Director at the Riga Graduate School of Law (RGSL), where he became Chief of the Committee of Experts for the Renewal Task Force Latvia (rtfl.lv). As for his most well-known academic inquiry, that into the history of debt and money, he was appointed a research fellow in Babylonian economics at the Peabody Museum of Archeology and Ethnology at Harvard University, where he organized a colloquium every few years from 1994 onward. The five volumes of conference colloquia that he has co-edited have rewritten the economic history of the ancient Near East and classical antiquity.

These colloquia were on privatization, land tenure and real estate ownership (which were found to be based on fiscal liability), debt cancellation and economic renewal, the origins of money and accounting, and the origins of labor services (discovered to have arisen to work on public infrastructure and to work off personal debts). The findings of these colloquia and their members refute previous libertarian individualistic theorizing on economic origins, and have now become the new orthodoxy among Assyriologists, Egyptologists and anthropologists, most notably Michael's friend David Graeber, who wrote his book *Debt: The First Five Thousand Years*, largely to popularize Michael's approach.

The essential focus of the colloquium volumes is on how money, interest-bearing debt and land tenure were innovated in the palaces and temples of the ancient Near East, and on how the privatization of money and credit led to the polarization in ownership of land and other wealth in the hands of private oligarchies from classical antiquity to today's Western economies.

As one of the few economists who predicted the 2008 crash, Michael published one of his most important theoretical papers in 2006: "Saving, Asset-Price Inflation, and Debt-Induced Deflation."[1] It accurately explained how the exponential expansion of credit created correspond-

---

[1] In L. Randall Wray and Matthew Forstater, eds., *Money, Financial Instability and Stabilization Policy* (Cheltenham: 2006), pp. 104-24.

ing debt that would lead to the impending financial crash and its aftermath. On September 8, 2009, Dirk Bezemer wrote an article "Why some
economists could see it coming" in the *Financial Times*, which stated
that "Michael Hudson of the University of Missouri wrote in 2006 that
'debt deflation will shrink the 'real' economy, drive down real wages,
and push our debt-ridden economy into Japan-style stagnation or worse.'
Importantly, these and other analysts not only foresaw and timed the
end of the credit boom, but also perceived this would inevitably produce
recession in the US."

That article included the set of charts that helped make Michael
famous for his explanation of why financial crises are endemic and lead
to secular stagnation:

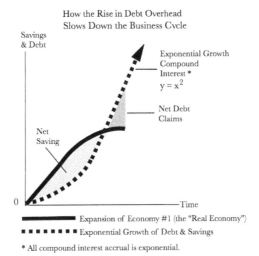

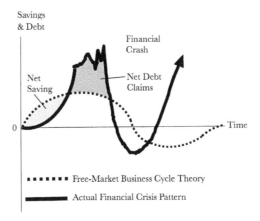

Today, with the world in deep financial crisis, Michael has reiterated his proposition that unpayable or odious debts should be cancelled, and indeed *must* be cancelled in order to avoid a global austerity crisis and economic polarization stemming from chronic debt deflation. One point of clarification here. The United States has become the world's biggest debtor, mainly as a byproduct of the fact that most international debts are denominated in dollars. This poses a basic question: Which debts should be wiped out?

Michael urges that the debts of overindebted households and impoverished countries in the Global South should be written down, but that one debt should *not* be cancelled: the official foreign debt of the U.S. Government. The United States has run up this official foreign debt – like its domestic Treasury debt – without expecting ever to actually pay it off. It has no intention of imposing on itself the austerity that it and the IMF demand of other debtor countries. This asymmetry, along with the U.S. sponsorship of today's New Cold War, has led leading dollar-holding nations such as China and Russia to begin de-dollarizing their economies. This signals the fracturing of the world economy that Michael predicted in his 1977 *Global Fracture*. The United States is forcing other countries to choose between accepting a dollarized and militarized *rentier* austerity, or going their own way by creating mixed public/private growth-oriented economies.

For socialism

For us on the Global U team, it has been a great privilege and honor to be learning from Michael, face to face. He was invited to give lectures in Hong Kong and Macau in November 2019, during which he had a dialogue with Wen Tiejun on economic and financial issues in China. During the Seventh and Eighth South-South Forums on Sustainability in 2020 and 2021, he had further discussions with Wen Tiejun. Michael has a particular concern for China's development, as he feels that China is the leading exception to the U.S.-based neoliberal economic model, not taking the destructive advice of the IMF and World Bank. He has argued that China's economy can be resilient if it organizes its real estate, debt and tax system to avoid the *rentier* financialization process that is destroying the West.

In September 2020, while we were chatting online, I sounded the idea that Michael give a lecture series for Global U. Michael accepted on the spot. I emailed him a proposal of 10 topics, and within five hours he came back with a detailed outline. The lectures were delivered weekly in September-December 2020. Rewriting these lectures to create the current book took another few months.

I sometimes wonder whether Michael would have had second thoughts if he had known that his spontaneous acceptance of my request would take ten months of his time. But fortunately for readers, this became a blessed opportunity to access his central ideas and be guided to his dozen books. The videoed lectures, subtitled in Chinese and divided into 70 episodes, were screened in April-August 2021 in China. The first episode has been watched by over 188,000 viewers, with 30,000 viewers on average for the remaining episodes. The English-subtitled lectures are available on www.michael-hudson.com. What readers now hold in their hand, the book written on the basis of these lectures, presents Michael's dissection of the burning global issues of today, and his explanation of how the industrial capitalism analyzed in the 19th century by Marx and other classical economists has turned into finance capitalism based on debt and rent extraction. This financialized system is polarizing the Western economies and threatening their collapse in a wave of foreclosures and new privatizations by a financial oligarchy.

Most important are Michael's proposed alternatives for de-dollarization and de-privatization to avoid global debt deflation and New Cold War imperialism. Indeed, if civilization is to avoid the destiny of destruction, if humanity is to have a future, socialism is the only way – and that is what Michael has passionately argued in this book.

Lau Kin Chi
Director, Executive Team, Global University for Sustainability
Coordinator, Programme on Cultures of Sustainability, Centre for Cultural Research and Development, Lingnan University, Hong Kong, China

Preface

This book started as a series of lectures in October 2020 on the political economy of globalization and the logic guiding China, Russia and other countries to break free of U.S. Dollar Diplomacy. These lectures were sponsored by the Global University for Sustainability as part of its South-South Dialogue Master Series. The discussion was led by Kin Chi Lau and included Erebus Wong, Tsui Sit and Tung-yi Kho. All are on the faculty of Lingnan University's Centre for Cultural Research and Development in Hong Kong or are associated with it. Ashley Dayman in Australia also participated and has been remarkably helpful in discussing and copy-editing my lectures. Other support came from the Green Ground Eco-Tech Center in Beijing, and the Asian Regional Exchange for New Alternatives (ARENA-Hong Kong).

The discussion quickly came to focus on the difference between today's finance capitalism and the industrial capitalism described by 19th-century classical economists. The historical task of industrial capitalism – and classical political economy – was to free economies from the hereditary landlord class and predatory usurious finance. That seemed to be occurring from the late 19th century to the outbreak of World War I in 1914. But instead of progress into what was considered to be "modern" a century ago, the *rentier* interests have reasserted themselves. Their neoliberal ideology inverts the classical idea of a "free market" from one free *from* economic rent to one free *for* the *rentier* classes to extract rent and gain dominance. In contrast to classical political economy, their ideology promotes tax favoritism for *rentiers*, privatization, financialization and deregulation.

U.S. foreign policy seeks to extend this neoliberal *rentier* program throughout the world, mainly for the benefit of Wall Street, the City of London, Frankfurt, the Paris Bourse and other financial centers. That effort is at the core of today's global fracturing. The resulting dynamics of financialization and debt deflation are polarizing and, as such, are antithetical to widespread industrial prosperity.

The leading beneficiary of neoliberal ideology is the Finance, Insurance and Real Estate (FIRE) sector. That sector is based on the symbiosis of finance and real estate. Rent extraction by that sector, along with the extraction of natural-resource rents from oil and mining, and the monopoly rents resulting from the privatization of public enterprises, has become the central dynamic of the finance capitalism that has expanded to overpower industrial capitalism since World War I. The central role played by mortgage debt is largely the result of land and home ownership being democratized – on credit. Owner-occupied housing has replaced tenancy to a hereditary absentee landlord class living off groundrents. But rent is still being paid – to the banks, whose main source of revenue is mortgage lending.

A drastic phase change occurred with the Reagan-Thatcher revolution of the 1980s with its privatizations, junk-bonding of corporate industry, and dominant financial strategy of "creating wealth" by asset-price inflation ("capital gains"). By 2000 this strategy had led to a merger of investment banking with commercial banking, opening the gates for junk-mortgage lending, commercial bank fraud, speculation in financial and insurance derivatives, and a broad regulatory capture of government by the FIRE sector.

These changes led America to seek gains financially, de-industrializing its economy by asset stripping – using corporate revenue for stock buybacks and dividend payouts instead of new capital investment – and offshoring its labor and production in an attempt to win the race to the bottom. U.S. financialization policy thus provides an object lesson in the economic dynamics that China and other nations need to avoid.

Readers may forgive me for returning repeatedly to the above themes throughout these lectures. My aim is to emphasize the common denominators in today's financialized *rentier* economies, and to show how their polarizing financial dynamics have become universal, threatening China as well as the United States and Europe.

Introduction

Most forecasts of GDP and national income assume that existing trends will continue, with economic product and income growing exponentially at historical rates, *ad infinitum*. But economic reality knows only one form of perpetual exponential growth: that of debt accruing at compound interest. Financial claims expand by mathematical principles independent of the economy's ability to pay. The "real" economy's growth tapers off as its circular flow of income between producers and consumers is drained by debt-overhead charges.

That is the phenomenon of debt deflation. The tendency for debts and savings to grow faster than the underlying economy imposes austerity on labor and industry, and polarizes the distribution of wealth (real estate, stocks and bonds) much more than that of income. In due course financial wealth politicizes itself, aiming to block governments from regulating and taxing creditors, large property owners and monopolists.

The task of today's neoliberal economics is to provide an ideological cover story to rationalize this opposition to public regulation and progressive taxation. What appears at first glance to be a libertarian ideology of minimal government turns out to be a capture of government by increasingly centralized financial interests. The result is an inherently anti-democratic power grab by the One Percent.

Neoliberal ideology diverts attention from the economy's polarizing dynamics

Neoliberal orthodoxy aims to deter governments from public regulation, as if the major problem is not the *rentier* sector's debt and rent overhead, but governments strong enough to prevent predatory rent extraction. Today's national income and GDP statistics depict the Finance, Insurance and Real Estate (FIRE) sector and extraction of economic rent from land, natural resources, monopolies and banking as productive, not as overhead to be minimized.

Government intervention is deemed unnecessary by assuming the operation of supposedly natural tendencies for economies to settle automatically at a stable equilibrium, with wealth and income becoming more fairly and equally distributed, internationally as well as nationally. This fiction is necessary to support the claim that governments should step aside and refrain from "interfering" with free markets. The reality is that neoliberal "free markets" and "free trade" concentrate wealth and income in the hands of creditors and other *rentiers*, polarizing economies domestically and indeed internationally.

Wealth addiction as a polarizing dynamic

The most fatal error that any theory can make is to get the direction of change wrong. But that is what today's mainstream economics does. Its notion of consumer choice assumes diminishing marginal utility, based on the trite observation that as consumers are satiated with food, each additional mouthful gives less pleasure ("utility"). So "demand" is supposed to fall with increasing supply.

A subtle sleight of hand then uses food and other consumables as a proxy for wealth – as if the only purpose of obtaining wealth is to buy consumer goods. The implication is that the richest individuals will become satiated with their wealth and leave more eager and "hungry" newcomers to strive to earn more and catch up.

But Plato, Aristotle and indeed most classical Greek philosophers, poets and dramatists recognized that wealth is addictive, and that creditor demands threaten to disrupt social balance. In their view, the more money one has, the more its possessor falls prone to a money-lust for more. Money and power are not like a diet of bananas making one quickly satiated. Once addicted, one never has enough. And wealth addiction leads to a hubristic use of economic power to gain control of government and use it to facilitate greed and patronage power over clients, debtors and renters. That is the history of classical Greek, Roman and modern oligarchies in a nutshell.

The "abstinence" theory of interest implies that the richest individuals are not greedy but are patient in forgoing consumption and making (or financing) a productive sacrifice to make their wealth. Recipients of interest are depicted as playing a productive role helping economies grow. But most lending today (and indeed, historically) has not been for productive purposes, and most wealth has not been gained by hard work as much as by the *rentier* privileges that go with one's inherited status and assets. (If non-consumption was the key to wealth, starving people would be the richest.)

Mainstream theory also ignores the limited range of choice that confronts most non-affluent people. Consumer spending is depicted as being open to choice: whether to consume now or save up for the future, earning interest, which is seen as a reward for abstaining from consumption. There is no acknowledgement of interest as a form of economic rent obtained by inheritance or privilege, nor that the indebted poor need to pay interest (or rent) as a condition of survival for basic needs. "Your money or your life" is the choice that in reality accounts for most consumer spending, headed by housing, education, health care and emergencies.

Marginalism and centrist politics ignore the structural causes of inequality

Looking at small changes occurring in a given economic and political environment, marginalism focuses on income, consumer spending and investment in the short run, not on the direction in which property and debt relations are moving. Lacking the concepts of wealth addiction, predatory lending and the mathematics of compound interest, marginalist economic theory does not acknowledge that without public checks and balances, economies will polarize as wealthy elites use their power to impoverish the non- *rentier* sectors.

Like marginalism, centrist politics only recognizes problems that can be resolved without challenging the status quo and its vested interests. Centrism assumes that however much the economy is polarizing, life can go on without systemic institutional change. This policy passivity ignores the tendency of economies to polarize as imbalances mount up – imbalances that are largely financial in character, with the FIRE sector's exponential growth of debt being their primary cause. Centrists view the economy as if automatic stabilizers will return life to normal growth in due course. But nothing marginal can save economies from polarizing as a widening swath of the population becomes more indebted while wealth is monopolized.

Assuming that all debts can and should be paid, this centrism opposes reforms that would block the financial sector from indebting the economy and then monopolizing it as defaulters forfeit their homes and businesses. And when indebted cities and states suffer declining tax revenues and budget deficits as a result of debt deflation and economic polarization, they are told to cut back public spending, borrow or sell off public property and infrastructure rights. The effect is to increase the financial sector's power.

"Free-trade imperialism" and that of U.S.-centered finance capital

Fifty years ago, in 1969, I started lecturing graduate economics students at New York's New School on theories of trade, development and foreign debt.[1] From the outset I found a serious problem: If I taught the mainstream trade theory that appeared in the standard textbooks, it was not realistic. If I taught how trade and investment work in reality, it would be the opposite of what the textbook models taught and still teach. A perhaps apocryphal story about an American evangelist expressed the problem. Taunted about his illiteracy, he replied: "What is the sense of knowing such a lot, if what you know isn't so?"

Mainstream theory assumes production functions to be subject to diminishing returns. Yet the reality is increasing returns, thanks to the progress of technology in industry, agriculture and commerce. That perception was the essence of the American School of Political Economy in the 19th century, and of Joseph Schumpeter's "creative destruction" by innovative firms employing new technology to cut costs and thus undersell existing producers. It is one of the principles guiding China's economic rise.

Without tariff protection, production subsidies and related government support, many countries will be unable to develop their industry and agriculture and move toward self-sufficiency in essentials by investing to modernize their technology, and therefore will remain dependent on trade patterns and credit dominated by the lead nations. If China had followed mainstream orthodoxy, it would have left its industry and agriculture to "market forces," meaning the existing productivity gaps. "The market" would have left it with rising trade dependency and hence dollar dependency on U.S. banks and international organizations. That is the policy that the United States and other industrial creditor nations would like all countries to follow instead of funding their own industry and agriculture to become self-sufficient.

The reality is that international productivity and income gaps widen, with increasing returns to scale and rising creditor power benefiting the lead nations. The counterpart to the widening advantage of these nations is obsolescence for economies not keeping pace with improvements in productivity. Free trade theory is a rationale to justify such widening gaps and the resulting trade and financial dependency as the most efficient development policy. But instead of describing how Britain, the United States and Germany industrialized and gained world leadership by protecting their industries in the 19th and early 20th centuries, neoliberal free trade ideology hypothesizes a "what if" world. The so-called "gains from free trade" from buying lower-priced goods abroad

---

[1] *Trade, Development and Foreign Debt: A History of Theories of Polarization v. Convergence in the World Economy* (new ed., Dresden: 2010; Chinese translation, Beijing: 2012).

actually measure the degree of trade dependency resulting from wage and productivity gaps.

The drive by the United States to impose debt and trade dependency is the essence of today's New Cold War shaped by active and often violent U.S. diplomacy. Charley Wilson's famous phrase, "What's good for General Motors is good for the country" has been transmuted into "What's good for Wall Street is good for America." When merged with evangelistic U.S. foreign policy, "What's good for America is good for the world," the logical syllogism is clear: "What's good for Wall Street is good for the world."

Dealing with financial polarization requires systemic across-the-board reforms

Social systems are different from individuals acting by themselves. Changing a social system requires systemic across-the-board reforms, not merely marginal changes. Creating a post-*rentier* economy requires debt writedowns, tax reform falling on economic rents, and public infrastructure investment to prevent monopoly-rent seeking. These changes in property relations are necessarily systemic and require complementary monetary and legal reforms to retain stability over time. Such systemic changes must be coordinated; they cannot be introduced piece by piece at different times. That is what makes real reform "revolutionary."

Mainstream economics throws up its hands at this point and says that structural problems are "exogenous," that is, outside the scope of marginalist models. Garbed in convoluted mathematics to deter the public from seeing their silliness, these models impose a tunnel vision to avoid describing the real world's debt and property dynamics. By not recognizing the polarizing forces at play, these models frustrate recognition of many necessary public policy reforms.

A nation's economic path is not predetermined but is subject to active policy decisions. That is why classical economists called their discipline *political* economy. The political context is shaped not only by reformers but also by their *rentier* adversaries, because structural reform does not occur without the vested interests fighting back. In the international sphere, where the U.S dollar is used as the major world currency under the Treasury-bill standard, the United States resists attempts by trade-dependent countries and dollar debtors to create a less exploitative and polarizing diplomacy. Threatening reformers with "color revolutions" and regime change, U.S. policy has been to install dictatorships and client oligarchies, praised as part of the "free world democracy" and "rules-based order" as long as they support the neoliberal Washington Consensus.

Rejecting the dollar standard and the finance-capitalist dynamic behind it requires an alternative economy organized to avoid privatization of economic rent and predatory finance. The starting point must be to recognize the distinction between earned income (wages and profits) and unearned overhead income (economic rent). It also must recognize how finance capitalism has gained power over industrial economies, above all in the United States, from which it seeks to project itself globally. Led by the financialized U.S. economy, today's New Cold War is a fight to impose *rentier*-based finance capitalism on the entire world. That requires blocking foreign economic reform.

Chapter 1 explains industrial capitalism's 19ᵗʰ-century aim to free economies from rent seeking, and how this reform program failed to be realized after World War I, leading to finance capitalism instead of socialism. Chapter 2 describes how finance capitalism has inverted the moral philosophy that underpinned classical economics and its concept of free markets, with mainstream economic ideology now defending *rentiers* instead of seeking to end their economic and political dominance. Chapter 3 traces how this counter-revolution has internationalized itself to create a cosmopolitan financial oligarchy whose business plan involves reducing most of the planet to debt and trade dependency.

To explain the dynamics at work, Chapter 4 reviews the classical concept of economic rent as unearned income and the result of privilege. Chapter 5 describes how the post-feudal landlord aristocracies that ruled Europe have metamorphized into today's financial oligarchies, whose income and wealth remain based on rent extraction from assets financed by interest-bearing debt. The effect is to transform rent into a flow of interest payments.

Chapter 6 places these dynamics in their international context. Free trade opposes government tariffs and actions to support industry and uplift the status and welfare of labor. Chapter 7 describes the most egregious attempts to block the authority of governments to protect their economies from social and environmental destruction. Reviewing how these destabilizing and polarizing economic dynamics have politicized themselves, Chapter 8 describes how the threat by democratic politics to legislate reforms has been countered by party politics to prevent moves to create economic democracy.

Chapter 9 elaborates how the *rentier* interests have consolidated their control of government despite nominal democratic politics, this having occurred most thoroughly in the United States with its oligarchic two-party duopoly. Chapter 10 describes the extent to which U.S. diplomacy has succeeded in making foreign countries keep their central-bank savings in the form of loans to the U.S. Treasury, thereby financing America's foreign military spending that remains the major cause of the U.S. balance-of-payments and domestic government budget deficits. Chapter 11 examines how U.S. neoliberal advice led the former Soviet Union to de-industrialize, and how the aim of neoliberal ideology is to turn public enterprises and utilities into rent-yielding financial vehicles.

The world does not have to follow this path. Chapter 12 reviews the classical concepts of value and rent that were intended to guide policy makers in creating a tax and regulatory system to minimize unearned income in the mixed economies toward which industrial capitalism seemed to be evolving in the 19th and early 20th centuries. The concluding Chapter 13 summarizes why a financialized and privatized economy is incompatible with economic growth and rising prosperity for most of the population. It contrasts the economic program of industrial capitalism and its seeming evolution toward socialism with the finance capitalism that has emerged and gained momentum since the 1980s to monopolize economic growth in the hands of the top One Percent of the population, with the remainder of the top five percent being given more modest opportunities for their role as cheerleaders and enablers.

Only a radical across-the-board reform can reverse the Western world's polarizing trends and dependency relationships. That is what makes today's New Cold War so critical in determining the future course of world evolution and avoiding a Roman-style economic and demographic collapse.

Part I

The Dynamics of Economic Polarization

1

Industrial Capitalism's Reform Program to Free Markets from the *Rentiers*

Any economic theory tends to express the vantage point of one class or nation relative to others. Economics therefore is inherently political. Its language and basic concepts are designed to shape how people think economies work, and therefore what policies they will support.

At issue for the past two centuries is whether the income that a landlord, banker or monopolist gets is called "earnings" for producing a good or service, or "economic rent," defined as unearned income, received without actually working or providing intrinsic value. The concept of "empty" prices without value was the essence of classical economics as it was developed in the 19th century. Its formulators sought to minimize the payment of economic rent to anyone but the tax collector.

But by the end of that century, defenders of landlords and monopolists claimed that there is no such thing as economic rent. This post-classical school has become the dominant economic ideology and won control of producing the national income and Gross Domestic Product (GDP) statistics that purport to measure an economy's growth or shrinkage. What is claimed to be an empirical scientific measure turns out to rest on the highly political issue of whether the wealthiest classes are helping the economy grow or acting parasitically. Are the *rentier* classes getting wealthy from financial, real estate and monopoly income that merely adds to the economy's price level – the cost of living and doing business – without actually producing real output?

Today's academic mainstream has been captured by the *rentier* classes. It is not immediately apparent that this modern school is a reaction diametrically opposed to the basic assumptions, logic, and above all the value, price and rent theory developed by classical economists in the 19th century. The classical aim was to promote industrial capitalism by limiting the intrusive power of the post-feudal *rentier* class. Adam Smith, David Ricardo, J. S. Mill and even Karl Marx are cited as founders of economics as a discipline, without acknowledgment that their basic concepts are rejected today, precisely because their common aim was to prevent the rent-seeking and financial problems that are plaguing today's financialized capitalism.

This opposition between the classical economists as critics of *rentiers* and today's celebration of them as the mainspring of economics helps explain why the history of economic thought has been dropped from the academic curriculum. "If the eye offends thee, pluck it out." And to the *rentier* classes receiving an economic free lunch, nothing is more offensive than the thought that they are not productive of real value, because that thought leads naturally to the classical policy of taxing away economic rent and keeping natural monopolies, basic infrastructure, and, above all, banking and money creation in the public domain.

That classical policy was supported not only by opponents of industrial capitalism, but by the industrial class itself, at least at a time before industry had become financialized. Surprising as it may seem today, classical political economy appeared to be leading toward what today would be called socialism, and indeed was widely called that, because the central elements of both it and socialism reflected the logic of early industrial capitalism. It advocated taxation of land rent to end the landlord class's privileges and lower the cost of doing business. Public infrastructure investment in natural monopolies promised to make industrial economies more competitive.

Industrial capitalism thus welcomed a strong state – one minimizing and also subsidizing the cost of doing business, including the cost of living that employers had to cover in paying their wage labor. By the late 19th century, this logic led most economic writers to expect that socialism would emerge in one form or another, especially in view of the rising role played by the democratic reforms that were ending the political domination of hereditary landlords and their associated real estate and financial interests. There was Christian socialism, Ricardian socialism (taxing land rent and other privileged income), Marxist socialism and even a libertarian anarchist socialism.

All successful economies are mixed economies, with checks on the financial sector

Britain achieved industrial dominance in the 18th century by mercantilism, protecting its own industry and restricting its colonies from producing their own manufactures, and establishing sterling as a key currency to control their monetary, credit and banking systems. Likewise, the United States introduced protective tariffs after its Civil War ended in 1865. That, along with a far-reaching public infrastructure system to subsidize its manufacturers, enabled American industry to overtake that of Britain by World War I.

The most important sector to keep in government hands is banking and credit, along with other basic services. China has kept banking and credit public and subsidized its industry by creating a vast economic infrastructure, headed by public education and health, transportation and communications. Yet when Chinese students take economics classes at American, British or other Western universities, they are taught that this road to success is not supposed to work; or at least, mainstream economic theory cannot explain *why* it works.

According to textbook theory, China should not have become a success story. The doctrine of comparative advantage teaches that it would have been better off remaining an agricultural country, because government planning to subsidize industrial and agricultural modernization is a "wasteful" and "intrusive" distortion of free markets.

A corollary of this neoliberal logic is that the United States should have become richer as a result of its financialization and privatization since 1980. However, this policy has sharply increased market prices for housing, stocks and bonds. These forms of property and financial securities are not actual means of production, but *rentier* claims on income and output. Typical American families are obliged to spend whatever rise in wages they receive on the cost of housing (rents or mortgage payments), as interest, financial fees and penalties on other borrowings, and on privatized health care and education. That is primarily why financialized wealth has been concentrated at the top of the economic pyramid, leaving the bottom 90 Percent more deeply in debt.

The "success story" of finance capitalism has been achieved by leaving the U.S. economy debt-ridden and its living standards stagnating over the past four decades. The shift to debt-financed education has left students and many of their parents burdened with debt, while rising housing prices have forced new buyers to go deeply into debt to obtain homes of their own to start their own families.

As a result of these *rentier* dynamics, Western economies are not in a "cyclical downturn" from which they are scheduled to emerge by some presumably regular periodicity shaped by the operation of self-correcting automatic stabilizers. The West's post-1945 prosperity has reached its financial limit. Diverting income to pay interest and rent is preventing economies from escaping from their current stagnation.

Neoliberal economics cannot explain why this financialization has de-industrialized the United States, made its economy less productive and turned it into a "post-industrial economy." Official statistics depict this as economic growth, not decadence. Lloyd Blankfein, head of the leading U.S. investment bank Goldman Sachs, has claimed that his firm's partners are the most productive individuals in the United States, as shown by the fact that they make the highest salaries and bonuses. And the National Income and Product Accounts (NIPA) count these as additions to Gross Domestic Product (GDP) for providing "financial services."

The working assumption is that productivity is measured simply by whatever income one receives, regardless of whether it is obtained by building a factory and employing labor to manufacture industrial goods, or by buying real estate and charging rent – not to mention engaging in financial fraud on a scale so vast that the above-mentioned Goldman Sachs has had to pay billions of dollars in fines for its misbehavior. The associated legal costs are of course added to GDP calculations as "legal services."

The U.S. economy is still limping along under the debt-ridden financialization that Mr. Blankfein bragged was making his firm's partners so remarkably productive and rich – as if the two measures automatically go together. The Forbes' 500 list of the richest men in America (and in the world) are not captains of industry but real-estate pyramiders and monopolists. There is a similar widespread disparagement about how they gained their money (parasitically, at the public's expense) to that which classical antiquity felt about usury (moneylending) and commercial inventions, and that pro-industrial economists in the 19th century felt about landlords, as the paradigmatic "idle rich." But the concepts of value, price and economic rent underlying those earlier critiques have become a lost world today.

Rentier income is burdensome, unearned and economically polarizing

What obviously is needed is an economic theory that can explain how China and other countries can avoid the problems that are plaguing the United States and Europe with polarization and austerity. Such a body of theory would involve explaining why China is growing so prosperous while most of the U.S. economy is suffering a chronic depression characterized by debt deflation for labor and industry. That is a key dynamic of finance capitalism, which is quite different from the industrial capitalism that Marx and other classical economists studied in the 19th century.

Every economy obviously needs a financial system. Modern populations need credit to finance home ownership. The problem is how best to avoid the U.S.-type financial disease in which private bank credit inflates housing prices and obliges new buyers to pay more and more in principal and interest, while corporate financial managers use their revenue for stock buybacks and dividend payouts to inflate stock prices to keep enriching mainly the One Percent instead of the overall economy and society.

The distinguishing feature of finance capitalism is not the "real" economy of production and consumption, industrial profits and wages, but the financialization of income and wealth. That is what is imposing austerity, as a result of payments to the Finance, Insurance and Real Estate (FIRE) sector "crowding out" personal and corporate income. This phenomenon is a composite of debt deflation and rent deflation.

Explaining this problem was what classical political economy was all about: How to prevent landlords from dominating society, and how to prevent banks and creditors from enriching themselves at the expense of the rest of the economy. To understand today's dysfunctional economic system, we need to look at how it has diverged from the logic of industrial capitalism that British political economy was developing, and ended up reversing that logic and replacing it by new financial laws of motion.

To explain why wealth and income are becoming more unequal while economies are stagnating, it is necessary to understand how wealth is obtained. How have today's nouveaux billionaires gotten rich, and why is their financial and real estate wealth rising so much faster than national income, especially that of the 90 Percent?

To put matters in perspective, the magnitude of wealth is much larger than that of current income and GDP, and is distributed much more unequally. Today's wealth is financialized, so that wealth and debt go together. Most wealth – and therefore the fortunes of the One Percent – finds its counterpart in debt on the liabilities side of the balance sheet, consisting largely of the debts owed to the One Percent by the 99 Percent. In other words, the One Percent have become so wealthy since about 1980 because they hold the 99 Percent in debt to themselves.

Debt and credit, property and land rents are institutional variables

What people think of as the "real" economy – factories producing goods and services, which their workers buy with the wages they earn – is wrapped in a complex legal net of property rights created "outside" the "real" economic core. These rights are headed by land ownership, monopoly patents (enabling prices to be charged far in excess of normal profits, without reference to the actual cost of production), and other official privileges, capped by that of banks to create credit and receive support from governments.

These rights create opportunities to charge economic rent, defined as income stemming simply from privilege, with no tangible cost of production in the form of labor or materials, and without playing an economically necessary or productive role. Clipping the coupons on bonds and collecting rents from one's property or interest-bearing loans is income paid by the labor of others, not that of the *rentier* recipient.

Most new adults in America today are obliged to start their working life as debtors. They enter the workforce loaded down with student debt – a precondition for finding employment – and must soon take on a lifetime of mortgage debt to obtain homes to start families of their own. A lucky few are free from this destiny of debt peonage. Most members of this fortunate minority (or "meritocracy," as they favorably depict their position) inherit trust funds and family homes as members of the *rentier* class. As creditors and landlords, this class is becoming an oligarchy holding much of the population in debt to itself, owning the vast majority of stocks and bonds and using their financial power to pry away ownership of natural monopolies providing society's basic needs, while ruling a political system that is financial and whose politicians and judges are in reality appointed by the Donor Class, not democratically elected.

A realistic body of national statistics and economic theory would explain why so many Western financialized economies are suffering austerity while there are so many new billionaires. Why is income being sucked up to the top of the economic pyramid instead of "trickling down"? By explaining what has gone wrong and why so much of the world is getting poorer instead of richer for most people, such a body of theory would show how this can be reversed.

What blocks an understanding of the need for such a reversal is that the most distinguishing features of our epoch find little place in the academic curriculum that calls itself "economics." Most notoriously excluded as "external" is the concept of economic rent – which, as discussed above, is unearned income stemming from political and legal privilege and from the dismantling of public regulation and taxation.

Today's mainstream economic models block such discussion by treating finance merely as a veil, a "set of counters," not as the economy's dominant planner by allocating credit, and hence resources. The economics of wealth, savings and debt – real estate, banking, stocks and bonds – is centered in the Finance, Insurance and Real Estate (FIRE) sector. That is the sector that dominates today's financialized economies.

The classical economics of Ricardo and his contemporaries focused on how to make industrial Britain more competitive so as to undersell its rivals and gain world power – indeed, a world industrial monopoly.

In the decade after 1815, the main variable determining wage levels was the price of food. Industrialists therefore sought to buy food in the cheapest markets – in agricultural countries such as the United States or Latin America, where land was more widely available at a lower price than in densely-populated Britain, with its powerful landlord class demanding Corn Laws to protect high prices for crops and hence its land rents. Under these conditions, industrial capitalism went hand in hand with free trade, against Britain's agricultural protectionism.

Industrial economists in the late 19th and early 20th centuries explained that services for natural monopolies such as land, public utilities and banking with its privilege of monetizing credit creation, and basic infrastructure such as schools, roads, health care and communications, should be provided freely or at subsidized prices by governments. They saw that landlordism and the rest of the FIRE sector, along with privatized ownership and extraction of monopoly rents, increases the cost of living and doing business. Industrial capitalism sought to minimize these costs so as to enable industrial producers to undersell rivals in more rent-ridden economies. Victory in world markets would be won by nations that best freed their economies from *rentier* income, landlordship, monopolies and predatory banking and finance.

Today's finance capitalism is not following a path leading to industrial dominance by lowering domestic price structures to bring them down to the actual necessary costs of production (that is, value). Just the opposite: private equity's strategy is to buy out companies on credit, and then sell their assets and load them down with pseudo-costs (including new borrowing) to pay themselves dividends. This process of asset stripping is being built into today's industrial economies as if it is a natural and necessary component, not an extraneous addition.

The U.S. economy is de-industrializing. A rising share of wages and industrial profits is being paid to the financial sector and its allied insurance and real estate sectors, in the form of interest, financial and insurance fees, and privatized property rents. The most basic public services have been turned into privatized monopolies since the great "raid on the commons" by rent seekers in the 1980s. Roads have been turned into toll roads, and public health care into privatized insurance. The Internet, cable, electric power, water and other natural public infrastructure monopolies have been turned over to buyers treating them as monopolies and charging as much as the market will bear, without regard for the cost of production for these services.

Value, price and rent – the key concepts of classical political economy

Classical economists developed value and price theory as a means of segregating economic rent, defined as the excess of price over and above the necessary cost of production (including normal profits). Isolating economic rent as unearned income provided a basis for avoiding land rent and monopoly rent, as well as financial rents. Yet most of the wealth in today's Western economies is concentrated in the sectors generating such rents, and most new billionaires are emerging in the *rentier* sectors – and making their wealth tax-exempt. The concepts of land rent, monopoly rent and financial rents provide a basis for analyzing how wage income, profits and tax revenues are being siphoned off to pay landlords, banks and other creditors, insurance companies and monopolists in the symbiotic FIRE sector.

The classical idea of a free market was one free *from* economic rent, not free for landlords, monopolists and creditors to charge whatever they wanted without reference to the cost of production. To repeat, the 19th century's classical economics was all about value, price and rent theory, defining rent as the excess of prices above the socially necessary costs of production. The idea was to minimize rent, not maximize it.

This classical approach to economics has been all but censored from the academic curriculum. The status quo has become so unfair that populations would demand change if economists and their national income accounting format revealed the extent to which wealth is gained in parasitic, predatory ways. What typically is celebrated as wealth today, as billionaires become public celebrities, is actually a form of economic overhead, not part of the production process. It is a cost that classical economics sought to eliminate, or at least minimize. But the study of economics is not what it used to be. The role of today's mainstream economics is to prevent any change in taxes, anti-monopoly regulation or de-privatization that might threaten *rentier* wealth. To achieve this anti-classical counter-revolution, the discipline of economics has been turned into an unrealistic and tunnel-visioned caricature of reality.

Clearing away feudalism's *rentier* legacy

From Roman times through the Middle Ages the "idle rich" had mobilized the government and the military to obtain income without playing a directly productive role. The *rentier* mentality of feudalism evolved out of the warlord bands that conquered medieval Europe and imposed rents as, effectively, taxes paid to themselves. Warlords were not idle, of course, but they were not productive either; they were destructive and predatory. It was their heirs' attempt to maintain their privileges won by force that threatened to hold back industrial capitalism.

The French Physiocrats, Adam Smith, John Stuart Mill, Karl Marx and their followers saw the historical role of industrial capitalism to be one of freeing society from feudalism's legacy of *rentier* privileges for hereditary landlords, creditors and monopolists to impose rents and charge prices that had no corresponding cost of production. Originating in the 18th and 19th centuries as a tax-reform movement led by advocates of industrial capitalism, the program of classical economics was revolutionary in aiming to end the special privileges of Europe's aristocracies living off inherited rights to receive land rent and avoiding paying taxes. The labor theory of value aimed to show that no real cost-value or productive enterprise was entailed in collecting land rent, monopoly prices, interest and other fees. Such charges therefore were deemed to be inefficient – and unfair.

By the end of the 19th century a second aim developed. In addition to ending the domination of landlords over law-making and politics, advocates of industrialization emphasized the need for more public infrastructure to provide low-cost health care and education, transportation, the post office and communications at subsidized prices instead of letting monopolists charge prices above normal profits. This public investment in infrastructure would ensure that natural monopolies and choke points would not become privatized as rent-seeking vehicles in the hands of a new aristocracy.

This fight for economic reform was led by the pro-industrial Conservative Party in Britain, and the Republicans in the United States. Both parties sought to make their nations the industrial workshop of the world. Britain's Conservative Prime Minister Benjamin Disraeli (1874-80) sponsored the Public Health Act of 1875. "The health of the people is really the foundation upon which all their happiness and all their powers as a state depend," he explained.[1]

Disraeli followed up with the Sale of Food and Drugs Act, and then his Education Act. The Conservative government would provide these basic public services, recognizing that if private employers or their employees had to pay for costly housing, health care and other basic needs, they would have less wages or profits remaining to spend on goods and services. That would have meant less profit for industrial producers.

---

[1] Speech of June 24, 1877. He used Latin and said "*Sanitas, Sanitatum*" and translated it as "Sanitation, all is sanitation." It was a pun on a more famous aphorism, "*Vanitas, vanitatum*," "Vanity, all is vanity."

This perception set industrial capitalism on the road toward social-ism, coupled with the fact that up until World War I, it seemed that industrial capitalism's most basic political step was to free economies from the costly overhead of special privileges and rent seeking. We can see the logic at work today by comparing European socialized medicine with America's privatized and financialized health-insurance system and its associated drug-company monopolies. At nearly 18 percent of U.S. GDP, the costs of U.S. medical care and pharmaceuticals – the high-est-priced yet also the least efficient in the modern West – helps price products made by U.S. industrial labor out of world markets. Other costs pushing up the break-even wages of U.S. employees include high housing costs (inflated by bank credit), private education fees and monopoly prices charged for privatized infrastructure services.

Privatization of public infrastructure has led financialized *rentier* econ-omies to be high-cost and increasingly de-industrialized in the United States and other privatized, Thatcherized and financialized economies. Greed is said to be good, and productive in proportion to how much money it makes, and therefore should be deregulated, as if the resulting economic polarization and concentration of wealth is progressive. It is considered progress from the vantage point of finance capitalism, in that health-insurance and pharmaceutical companies are among the stock market's leaders, and real estate is the largest market for bank credit in the United States.

Economic ideology thus has made an about-face over the last century. It now defends *rentier* privileges and advocates that planning be shifted to financial centers in Wall Street, the City of London, the Paris Bourse and Frankfurt. National treasuries have been taken out of the hands of democratically elected governments and replaced by central banks that serve the commercial banks and bondholders who have gained control of government spending. Bank headquarters now tower over the world's major capitals, dominating their skylines as the modern analogue to medieval churches, temples and mosques.

The result is a vast cultural change from the early Christian banning of usury. First the religious reforms against usury (surviving until quite recently in vestigial anti-usury laws) and then the classical pro-indus-trial reforms against hereditary landlordism and *rentiers* have all been rejected, along with the logic for rationalizing economies and making them more productive. In contrast to the classical economists who devel-oped the concept of economic rent to describe post-feudal exploitation as a burdensome overhead on society, today's economic mainstream no longer seeks to strip away such exploitation. Just the opposite: Its distinguishing feature for the past century has been to deny that any income is unearned, or that any exploitation occurs.

The successful error

So successful is this anti-classical reaction that the history of economic thought no longer is taught to economics students. The deceptive pretense is made that classical economists advocated a libertarian free market against socialism and governments strong enough to tax and regulate the *rentier* class. This neoliberal rewriting helps reinforce existing power relationships by implying that the inequality that is polarizing economies is a transitory anomaly, not an inherent and universal tendency of *rentier* economies to polarize.

The post-classical *rentier* counter-revolution denies the central value and price theory that classical political economists refined: Not all income is earned – that is, earned productively by contributing to the production and distribution process. Economic rent – land rent and related natural-resource rent (the center-point of Chapter 2 of David Ricardo's 1817 *Principles of Political Economy and Taxation*), monopoly rent, and financial rent in the form of interest and fees – is not a socially necessary cost of production, and thus is unearned income. But post-classical economics insists that all income is earned, and infers that all wealth also is earned, being the capitalized value of income that is earned productively.

The "product," such as it exists, takes the form of a transformation of society, a steeply rising economic pyramid sucking income and wealth up to the top in the form of rents and interest. City skylines are dominated by the tallest and brightest buildings, those of the major banks and insurance companies. The "laws of motion" become financial, property-based and monopoly-based. Real estate, stocks and bonds are concentrated. The result looks much like the feudal societies of old – systems of privilege and inherited wealth in the form of financial and property claims. Home ownership rates decline as financialized economies turn back into rental economies. Wealth is stratified along increasingly hereditary lines, similar to today's racial and ethnic layering of net worth throughout the American population. These are the dynamics that Chapter 2 will discuss.

Today's financialized and increasingly privatized economies are all about predatory rent seeking, despite the fact that (or, if you are a *rentier*, precisely because) rent seeking is polarizing economies and concentrating income and wealth at the top of the economic pyramid, without concern for enhancing productivity and prosperity for the population at large, and de-industrializing economies. In retrospect, therefore, the early philosophy of industrial capitalism was overly optimistic, even on the part of its critics such as Marx. A Gilded Age emerged that was the opposite of how industrial capitalism was expected to evolve. The interests of feudalist, private wealth fought back. The fight was political, ideological, military, and violent.

The backwash of the reaction to rid the economics discipline of classical rent theory, especially since the reaction's poisonous flowering in the 1980s at the hands of Margaret Thatcher and Ronald Reagan, has stopped wage growth but led to an explosion in the wealth of the One Percent. Neoliberal sponsorship of the vast increase in housing and infrastructure costs and debt has promoted the strongest bond rally and prolonged stock market boom in history. But that has occurred alongside a chronically weakened economy buckling under the debt burden and squeeze on household budgets to pay the rising *rentier* charges that have led to this concentration of wealth in the hands of the One Percent.

Opposition to taxing *rentier* income was elaborated into an across-the-board political attack on government regulation and fiscal power. Under the slogan of opposing central planning, resource allocation was shifted from elected officials to Wall Street. The effect was much like subordinating the power of Congress to a new aristocratic Upper House of financial lords. All *rentier* economies are oligarchies, and their political strategy is to prevent democracy from having any real legislative, taxing or regulatory power. This reverses the long 19th-century fight to strengthen Britain's House of Commons over the House of Lords, and the democratically elected lower houses of government throughout the world.

Denial that *rentier* income is unearned – insisting that it is earned in proportion to one's contribution to "GDP," producing a "service" of equal value – has led to a hopeless confusion of GDP accounting with regard to what is a "product" and what is merely a *transfer payment* with no *quid pro quo*, and hence an overhead charge. Defining productivity in terms of one's income, without regard for how it is obtained, has turned the rhetoric of today's mainstream economic discourse into a muddle of circular reasoning.

Opposition to the classical distinction between earned and unearned income has succeeded only by excluding the history of economic thought from the curriculum. That dumbing-down has led the economics discipline into a blind alley of special-interest pleading trying to convince voters that a stock-market boom for the One Percent is an economic boom despite leaving the debt-ridden 99 Percent with stagnant net worth.

In sum, the guiding policy thrust of industrial capitalism at its 19th-century take-off was that if basic economic services are essential, they should be subsidized or free, not left to become privatized rent-yielding monopolies. A corollary was that to the extent that banking was to be left in private hands, it was to be transformed so as to extend only productive credit for industrial capital formation and infrastructure investment. In effect, money and credit creation would function much as a public utility along with other basic services in a mixed economy.

That has not occurred, as Chapter 2 will describe.

[Chapter 1: Summary for Chinese Edition]

In many ways China today is following a similar path to that by which the United States industrialized in the late 19th century. It calls itself socialist, but so did many of the leading American protectionists. The common denominators include strong public investment in basic infrastructure to hold down the cost of living and hence the wage levels that industrial producers have to pay. Also, China has accepted the Economy of High Wages doctrine: that highly paid labor is more productive. Being better educated, better fed and with better health standards and public consumer protection, this labor is able to out-produce and hence undersell the labor of more pauperized economies.

China has been able to realize aims that U.S. protectionists and industrial strategists urged, above all keeping money and banking as a public utility instead of letting it be privatized. This helps explain the U.S. fury and animosity to China: China has achieved the industrial program that has failed in the United States, where *rentier* interests led an anti-classical counter-revolution that is de-industrializing America.

2

Finance Capitalism Promotes Rent Seeking and *Rentier* Tax Avoidance

Real estate, stocks and bonds constitute the bulk of wealth in today's economies, because most wealth is obtained by rent-seeking – land rent, monopoly rent and financial charges for special privileges – and even more by capitalizing *rentier* revenue into financialized assets, all supported by tax favoritism. In contrast to industrial capitalism's drive to minimize *rentier* charges to create a lower-cost economy with less overhead, finance capitalism increases this burden. Regardless of how financiers and billionaire *rentiers* make their fortunes, this rise in *rentier* wealth is counted as an addition to GDP, not subtracted as an exploitative transfer payment.[1]

Much as the land and England's Commons were privatized in the Enclosure movements from the 15th through 19th centuries by a combination of force, legal stealth and corruption, today's post-1980 privatization wave aims at appropriating basic public infrastructure to create opportunities for charging monopoly rent, along with bank lending to privatizers. Privatization and financialization tend to go together – at the economy's expense.

Rentiers have gained popular homeowner support for opposing land taxation as housing has been democratized – on credit. Banks support homeowners in lobbying to keep land taxes low, realizing that what is not paid to the tax collector is left available to be paid as interest to themselves. The land rent formerly paid to hereditary aristocracies is now paid to banks as mortgage interest. Land rent has merely changed its recipients, remaining a quasi-tributary charge.

Most bank loans are collateralized by pledges of rent-yielding assets, headed by housing and commercial real estate. Finance capitalism accordingly is centered on the FIRE sector, mainly mortgage lending, followed by natural-resource rent extraction. And as "the mother of

---

[1] I elaborate the rhetorical sleight-of-hand of modern economic orthodoxy in *J is for Junk Economics: The Vocabulary of Economic Deception and Reality* (Dresden: 2017).

trusts," investment banking organizes and finances corporate mergers and takeovers powerful enough to charge monopoly rents.

Marx's analysis of financial dynamics in Volume III of *Capital* (and the corresponding passages in his posthumous *Theories of Surplus Value*) emphasized that the aim of finance capital is to make gains from "outside" the production process, independently of the industrialist's employment of wage labor. This perception led his followers to become the major analysts of finance capitalism.[2]

Exploitation of labor under finance capitalism

Industrial capitalism and finance capitalism exploit wage labor in different ways. Industrial capital seeks to maximize profits by minimizing wages paid to its work force. Financial and other *rentier* capital seeks to maximize the obligation of labor to pay its wages for debt service and to buy basic needs that are monopolized to produce monopoly rents.

This contrast in the modes of exploitation explains why the aim of industrial capital in minimizing the cost of employing wage labor was long at odds with rent-seeking exploitation. Driving labor into mortgage debt, consumer debt, student and credit-card debt requires labor to pay interest – and penalties. The financial sector's political influence has succeeded in rolling back anti-usury laws, privatizing health care and other insurance (along with basic infrastructure services), and shifting taxes off real estate and the rest of the FIRE sector. As a result of this privatized extraction of interest and other rents, the financial sector has become a major exploiter of labor, directly by indebting it, especially by financing home ownership on credit, and indirectly by raising the cost of housing and of basic infrastructure services whose supply is increasingly privatized on credit and monopolized.

As industry itself has become financialized, a harmony of interest between industrial and *rentier* capital has been established by recognition of the fact that indebting wage labor also helps to spur corporate profits indirectly, by creating an employment "marketplace" in which losing one's job leaves workers in a precarious economic position. If they don't earn enough to make their monthly *rentier* payments, their credit-card charges will rise to penalty rates around 29 percent. And privatiz-

---

[2] Rudolf Hilferding's *Finance Capital: A Study of the latest Phase of Capitalist Development* (1910) and Lenin's more incisive *Imperialism: The Highest Stage of Capitalism* (1917) emphasized the financial character of the imperialism that had come to characterize the pre-World War I world and would become even stronger from the 1920s onward.

ing health care (and the need to pay for medical insurance) has become an increasingly important way of locking U.S. workers into their current jobs. Having to pay for their own medical insurance (averaging $11,000 per person in 2014) leaves them prone to bankruptcy if they become sick, unless they have an expensive elite policy.[3] And workers indebted with home mortgages run the risk of foreclosure and eviction if they are fired or lose their job.

The result is what Alan Greenspan called the "traumatized worker" syndrome: wage earners have become afraid to form unions and go on strike, or even complain about unsafe or abusive working conditions, for fear of losing their jobs.

To cap matters, financializing pension funding has made labor's retirement income dependent on the financial sector's success – even when financial gain-seeking is achieved at the expense of industrial investment and employment. Finance capitalism has left little prosperity for labor to share in recent decades. The *rentier* principle is, "Your money or your life." In the end, it is the entire economy's life.

Finance capital grows by compound interest, faster than the "real" economy

Any economy-wide volume of debt – along with the corresponding savings of bank depositors and other creditors – tends to grow by compound interest. And any rate of interest implies a doubling time.[4] This purely mathematical principle is independent of the economy's ability to pay. So it should not be surprising that debts have significantly increased since 1945 relative to personal and corporate income, government revenue and GDP.

Like a Ponzi scheme, this expansion path requires an exponential influx of new credit to carry the rising debt burden. Banks typically try to avert insolvency by lending debtors enough new credit to pay their interest charges. But this debt cycle cannot be sustained indefinitely. It typically culminates in a wave of foreclosures.

---

[3] "Private Health Insurance Spending Per Capita by State," for 2014, Kaiser Family Foundation. https://www.kff.org/private-insurance/state-indicator/private-health-insurance-spending-per-capita-by-state/?currentTimeframe=0&sortModel=%7B%22colId%22:%22Location%22,%22sort%22:%22asc%22%7D.

[4] I describe the "magic of compound interest" in Chapter 4 of *Killing the Host* (Dresden: 2015). See Chapter 5 for a more detailed discussion of the dynamics of compound interest and the exponential growth of debt.

Most creditors since the 1980s have been siphoning off income to themselves by various financial stratagems. Bill Black has described the business model of the S&L frauds of the 1980s as "bankruptcy for profit." Executives used customer deposits to pay themselves salaries, bonuses and dividend payouts. They made loans to their own captive entities, which passed the money on to safe havens, leaving bankrupt shells in their wake and S&Ls stuck with bad loans.[5] Their experience provided a model for banks to emulate in the vast junk-mortgage fraud leading up to the 2008 financial crash. Banks threatened with insolvency then asked for a bailout, holding the economy hostage if the government would not save them, along with their bondholders and large depositors.

Corporate financial managers have spent company earnings to support stock prices by stock buyback programs and dividend payouts to create capital gains for stockholders – and for themselves as bonuses – by cutting back investment. Long-term research and development programs, for example, are seen as leaving less revenue available for dividend payouts, stock buybacks and debt service. With the tax and other policy support of captured governments, financial management seeks to benefit owners of stocks, bonds and real estate, while central banks create enough credit to keep increasing the expansion of new credit and debt to prevent a financial collapse.

The financial time frame is short-term: Take the money and run

This is not a long-term strategy for prosperity, real wealth or even survival. De-industrialization, itself the result of financialization, has paid the financial sector at the expense of the overall economy. Instead of using industrial engineering to develop new products and set up marketing plans, financial managers give priority to enhancing stock prices. Over 90 percent of U.S. corporate revenue (ebitda: earnings before interest, taxes, depreciation and amortization) is used for share buybacks and dividend payouts to support company stock prices and hence the value of the stock options held by financial managers and speculators.

That helps explain why America is de-industrializing. The financial sector lives in the short run. A longer-term time frame would have led U.S. managers to reinvest their corporate revenue in expanding productive powers and cutting costs. But that traditional road to indus-

---

[5] William K. Black, *The Best Way to Rob a Bank is to Own One: How Corporate Executives and Politicians Looted the S&L Industry*, 2nd ed. (Austin: 2014 [2005]).

trial dominance would have left less revenue to flow into the financial markets, and therefore was not the aim of financial management.

To inflate asset-prices, the financial sector needs central-bank support

Asset prices traditionally were set by discounting earnings at the going rate of interest. An asset's price (P_A) was determined by dividing earnings (E) by the rate of interest (i), so that $P_A = E/i$. If the finance sector simply reflected the 2008-2021 industrial economy's earnings, stock and bond markets would have shrunk. But that did not happen. Recent decades have seen stock, bond and real estate prices rise much more rapidly, over and above the declining rate of interest that has increased the price/earnings capitalization rate.

A major reason for the rise in P/E ratios is that the volume of savings tends to grow at compound rates, as noted above. The exponential growth of interest and debt service is recycled into new purchases of stocks, bonds and real estate, and new lending. Most of this credit takes the form of loans to buy rent-yielding assets (real estate and companies) and financial securities already in place. The result is a rising focus on capital gains, which receive much more favorable tax treatment than wages and profits.

The main problem is that financial overhead and the rent extraction that it sponsors divert income from being spent in domestic markets for the products of industry. That shrinks these markets, and thus eats into corporate profits and their derivative stock prices. Financial managers then turn to central banks to help inflate prices for stocks, bonds and real estate (and hence, the viability of real estate mortgages) on credit. Since 1980, and especially since 2008, the central bank's Quantitative Easing – money creation to spend in the financial markets and *rentier*-oriented banking system, not into the "real" economy to increase employment or invest in means of production – has driven down interest rates to support prices for these assets.

Lowering interest rates and bidding up prices for real estate, stocks and bonds enables a given flow of revenue to be capitalized at higher prices. In theory, the near-zero interest rates such as recent years have seen should raise stock market prices approaching infinity, but investors are satisfied simply to make financial gains by arbitrage, borrowing at a low rate to buy stocks, real estate mortgages or bonds yielding a somewhat higher return.

Although real estate and financial markets collapsed in 2008, Quantitative Easing reinflated asset prices. Central banks preserved the monetary valuation of wealth for owners of stocks and bonds. And in March 2020 the $2 trillion sent out to American citizens by the Coronavirus Aid, Relief, and Economic Security Act (CARES) was overshadowed by a scheduled potential $8 trillion of credit to bid up stock and bond prices (inclusive of corporate bonds, including junk bonds) and to support bank mortgage loans. Statistical surveys showed that most of the CARES Act's $1,200 *per capita* checks were used to pay down the debts that recipients had been running up, not spent on goods and services. An indirect but main effect of the CARE's Act's support for wage earners thus was to save banks and landlords from losing money by their clients and renters defaulting. That was postponed – but hardly can be averted if the economy's heavy debt overhead remains in place.

Finance capitalism shifts economic planning away from governments

Finance capitalism has mounted a libertarian attack on government power to regulate and tax. Ever since the Federal Reserve was created at year-end 1913, the political strategy of finance capitalism has been to capture the public sector and shift monetary and banking power – and hence, economic planning – from Washington to Wall Street, the City of London, Frankfurt, the Paris Bourse and other financial centers.[6]

Regulatory capture has enabled the financial sector to translate its economic power into political power, above all by creating central banks to take economic policy away from public-sector treasuries. Today's main role of the U.S. Federal Reserve and the European Central Bank is to support prices for financial assets – stocks, bonds and real estate mortgage claims – while keeping down wages and commodity price inflation. Quantitative Easing by these institutions since 2008 has subsidized and inflated asset prices even in the face of the shrinking "real" economy.

The most blatant example of the *rentier* aim to bring government under control of the neoliberal agenda is the Trans-Pacific Partnership's proposal to create Investor-State Dispute Settlement (ISDS) courts. Corporate-appointed judges were to be empowered to rule on corporate lawsuits against governments that reduce profits by enacting laws to prevent environmental pollution or consumer or social injury. (See Chapter 7 for the details.) Companies would have been able to demand compensation for the profits that they might have made, had they been

---

[6] I give the background in "How the U.S. Treasury avoided Chronic Deflation by Relinquishing Monetary Control to Wall Street," *Economic & Political Weekly* (India), May 7, 2016.

permitted to keep polluting the environment and causing injury to consumers or society. This institution would have effectively blocked public law-making power in the national interest, reversing the 19th century's democratic political reforms.

Having failed to achieve the anti-*rentier* reforms advocated by classical economics, the hoped-for democratic destiny of industrial capitalism is now in an advanced stage of being replaced by a financial oligarchy. Economic planning is being centralized in the hands of the *rentier* classes ruling via the corporate state's financial centers and the central banks they have captured in every country.

While not anticipating the rise of a financial oligarchy specifically, George Orwell in his essay "Second Thoughts on James Burnham" (1946), summarizing the thesis of *The Managerial Revolution* (1941), described the emergence of an oligarchic society akin to the one that has arisen under finance capitalism: "Capitalism is disappearing, but Socialism is not replacing it. What is now arising is a new kind of planned, centralized society which will be neither capitalist nor, in any accepted sense of the word, democratic. The rulers of this new society will be the people who effectively control the means of production: that is, business executives, technicians, bureaucrats and soldiers, lumped together by Burnham under the name of 'managers.' These people will eliminate the old capitalist class, crush the working class, and so organize society that all power and economic privilege remain in their own hands."

This class was called the bourgeoisie a century ago. Today it is often called the Professional-Managerial Class (PMC), attaching itself (and aspiring to join) the *rentier* class. Instead of promoting wealth creation by employing labor to produce goods and services, this Professional-Managerial Class seeks wealth primarily in the form of what the 19th-century recognized as "fictitious capital" – financial gains achieved by inflating real estate and financial asset prices on credit, by debt leveraging, and by privatizing infrastructure monopolies from the public domain to extract monopoly rent under the guiding hand of the financial sector, which remains today what it was accused of being a century ago: "the mother of trusts."

Finance capital seeks to avoid taxes

America's first income tax was legislated in 1913, the year in which J. P. Morgan and his banking colleagues created the Federal Reserve. It fell mainly on the *rentiers*, with only about one percent of the population being obliged to pay. But wealth always has sought to avoid paying

taxes – and the financial sector seeks to protect other *rentier* interests
(and the wealthy in general). The oil, mining and real estate sectors soon
obtained tax "loopholes" that treated much of their cash flow (ebitda:
earnings before interest, taxes, depreciation and amortization) as an
un-taxed pseudo-expense, even though depreciation was not actually
paid, while interest was paid mainly to finance asset acquisitions, not
current production. The aim of corporate tax accountants is not to
report any taxable profits at all.

The countries with the twelve highest *per capita* GDP are not industrial
economies but tax havens. Corporate accountants set fictitious transfer
prices to give the illusion that all the worldwide income of their companies is made where taxes are lowest – or preferably, non-existent. U.S.
and British banks have created branches in the Caribbean and other
enclaves, as they first did in Panama and Liberia, two quasi-states that
use the U.S. dollar as their own currency so as to enable U.S. oil companies to avoid currency fluctuations when they assign their global profits
to trading offices in these offshore banking centers, which refrain from
having an income tax.

These enclaves are headed by Panama and Liberia for the oil
industry, Luxembourg and Monaco for European tax avoiders, Ireland,
where Apple's accountants pretend to make its worldwide profits,
Cyprus for the post-Soviet states, and the Cayman Islands, Bermuda
and Switzerland for kleptocrats and criminal gangs.[7] These tax havens
are not "investment hubs" in the sense of tangible capital investment in
means of production. Their nominal GDP consists mainly of financial
and legal services for the multinational companies that organize the
elaborate charade.

Taken together, the above-cited forms of special tax favoritism – fictitious depreciation, tax deductibility of interest, and transfer pricing via
tax havens – have reversed the 19th century's aim of taxing away land
rent, natural resource rent and financial rents. Fictitious depreciation –
sometimes called "over-depreciation" – permits absentee landlords to
pretend that their buildings are losing value as they wear out (despite
laws requiring them to keep their properties in good repair, which typically absorbs about 10 percent of rental revenue). This deduction – along
with the treatment of interest as a tax deductible "necessary expense"

---

[7] I discuss such centers in *Finance Capitalism and its Discontents* (Dresden: 2012),
Chapter 9.

– makes real estate investment income-tax free.[8] The ultimate beneficiaries are the banks and bondholders to whom industry and natural-resource exploitation have become increasingly indebted.

A corollary of Asset-Price Inflation is Debt Deflation

Most bank loans are to finance the purchase of real estate and other assets already in place. This means that the most important prices affected by bank money are asset prices for housing, stocks and bonds. Bank credit and savings on an economy-wide scale grow exponentially, simply by banks recycling their interest receipts into new loans. This compounding of interest on interest is supplemented by new credit creation. Prices for housing, stocks and bonds tend to follow suit – price gains that are increasingly debt-leveraged. So asset prices and debts rise together exponentially – but wages and output (GDP) grow more slowly than debt. And since 2008, asset prices have soared while production and consumption have stagnated for most of the non-FIRE-sector economy.

Rising asset prices normally go hand in hand with higher charges to carry the loans that have been bidding up these prices. The process becomes self-fueling for a while. More bank lending raises asset prices, enabling borrowers to take out even larger loans, which raise asset prices even further. What limits this expansion is the ability of labor and business to pay debt service on this lending after meeting the basic break-even expenses.

As banks increase the amount of debt that they are willing to create for their customers, prices are inflated on bank credit. Like prices for housing, those for education are set by the amount that banks will lend. This credit creation has obliged workers to go deeper into debt to pay for these basic needs in today's world. Businesses are similarly affected by rising commercial real estate prices, and the need to pay their employees enough to afford debt-inflated prices. Real estate assets and future earnings are pledged as collateral to creditors, from housing and commercial property to entire corporations pledged by corporate raiders issuing high-interest "junk" bonds.

Higher debt leverage leads in due course to many loans being defaulted. Prices crash (at least temporarily) and much of this collateral is transferred from debtors to creditors or new buyers, as occurred in the aftermath of the junk-mortgage collapse in 2008. Despite rising rates

---

[8] I discuss the technicalities in *The Bubble and Beyond* (Dresden: 2012), Chapter 8, pp. 215-46.

of insolvency and foreclosures, government insurance programs guarantee the banks against loss – the Federal Housing Authority (FHA) for home mortgages, and other agencies for student debt. So banks have little concern for losses resulting from the inability of their debt customers to pay, because the losses have been nationalized. Although neoliberal textbooks teach students that interest is compensation for risk, banks have been able to avoid risk through such guarantees against loss, and because they have, through regulatory capture, been able to avoid criminal prosecution for fraud after the 2008 junk-mortgage fiasco.

Rising asset prices and debt service for mortgages, student loans and credit-cards puts home ownership and other basic needs further and further out of reach of the population at large. As noted above, the central bank's Quantitative Easing supports commercial bank credit to support real estate and securities prices. The resulting debt service and related financial fees, penalties and overhead eat into the income available to be spent on the non-*rentier* economy as access prices for housing and other basic needs are pushed further out of reach of wage earners. The post-2008 decline, followed by the full-blown polarization that economists call a K-shaped "recovery" since the Covid-19 crisis of 2020-22, has seen the FIRE sector and financial markets prosper while the "real" economy limps along under the burden of debt and economic rents.

Rising credit and debt creation has obliged the working population, the corporate sector, and also state and local governments to pay interest and financial fees that have absorbed more and more personal income, corporate income and government tax revenue, leaving less to spend on non-financial goods and services. The result is debt deflation, imposing austerity by debt service absorbing a rising share of personal income, corporate income and public revenue. That has become the distinguishing feature of today's economic malaise from North America to Europe.

The phenomenon of debt deflation has transformed the once-popular formula linking money and credit creation (M) to wages and consumer prices (P) in the industrial economy. (P sometimes is calculated as the GDP inflator referring to current goods and "services.") The familiar formula $MV = PT$, means that more money (M) raises prices (P). Creating money to bid up real estate prices makes access to housing more expensive. The portion of disposable personal income payable as mortgage debt service insured by the U.S. Federal Housing Authority has risen from 25 percent in 1945 to 43 percent today. That leaves 18 percent less personal income available to spend on goods and services.

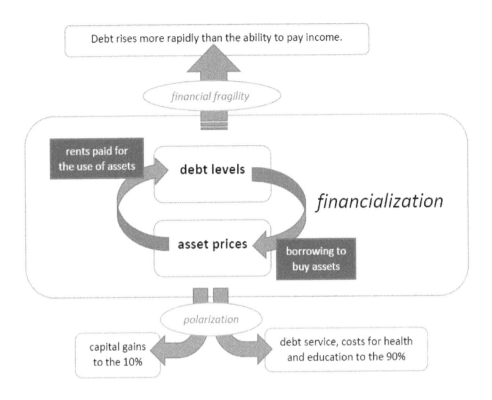

Inflating housing prices on credit thus leaves less income to spend on goods and services, and therefore tends to reduce consumer spending and prices.

Asset-price inflation also leads to debt deflation in other ways. Bank credit to buy stocks and bonds (including corporate raids and stock buyback programs) raises corporate stock prices – which means lowering their yields. Central banks contribute to this by lowering interest rates. This increases the amount that corporate and public-sector pension funds need to set aside in fixed-income securities to yield a given income. That leaves less to spend into the non-FIRE-sector economy.

Nonetheless, such asset-price inflation has become government policy to help the financial sector remain solvent and profitable, not to help the 99 Percent to become more prosperous. It was to sustain the solvency of indebted landlords and speculators (and hence their commercial bank creditors) that central banks flooded the asset markets with new credit after 2008 to help bank customers "borrow their way out of debt."

Central banks claim that rising credit is necessary to revive the industrial economy, as if the debt overhead should be financed, not written down. The inherent problem is that financialized economies can be kept solvent only by turning them into Ponzi schemes. An exponential increase in new credit to pay debt service is required to keep them from collapsing (as Chapter 5 will elaborate in more detail).

Rentiers sponsor statistics that celebrate them as being productive

The prime objective of saving banks and financial systems instead of the non-*rentier* economy has been supported in recent years by the financial sector's capture of GDP statistics, which depict the FIRE sector as being responsible for most growth, even though it doesn't actually produce anything except *rentier* claims *on* the economy. Today's seemingly empirical national income and GDP accounting formats depict the FIRE sector and its allied rent-seeking sectors as an addition to national income, not a subtrahend. The idea of "product" is (re-)defined to include economic rents as additions to GDP, and all forms of revenue are counted as "earnings."

This ideology rejecting the classical idea of rent as unearned income categorizes any and all income as being earned by making a necessary economic contribution to production. Interest, rents and monopoly prices are counted as "earnings" – as if all economic rents are earned as intrinsic parts of industrial capitalism, not as zero-sum transfer payments siphoned off *from* the production-and-consumption economy. *Rentier* asset growth thus appears as wealth that is earned.

The financial sector is said to produce a product, not to impose zero-sum transfer payments as formerly was the case.[9] Decades of lobbyists have fought to recast national income accounting to count banks' penalty fees and kindred FIRE-sector charges as contributing to GDP, not as a cost.[10] Not only is landlord rent revenue included, but also homeowners' estimates of how much the rising market rent of their home would be if they had to rent it to themselves (at what an absentee landlord would charge) instead of owning it. These latter estimates represent about 8 percent of current U.S. GDP.

---

[9] I review and chart the GDP imputations and "fictitious production" in "Rent-seeking and Asset-Price Inflation: A Total-Returns Profile of Economic Polarization in America," *Review of Keynesian Economics*, Vol. 9 (2021): pp 435-60.

[10] See Jacob Assa, *The Financialization of GDP* (London and New York: 2017), and Jacob Assa and Ingrid Harvold Kvangraven, "Imputing Away the Ladder: Implications of Changes in GDP Measurement for Convergence Debates and the Political Economy of Development," *New Political Economy*, January 11, 2021.

Also counted as a "product" are the financial penalties and fees that banks and credit-card companies charge when debtors fall behind on their debts. These fees typically push the annualized charge to 29 percent or more. They are reported as "financial services," as if such income transferred to the FIRE sector actually creates a product.

Along with finance and real estate, insurance companies round out the *rentier* FIRE-sector core of finance-capitalist economies. When people pay more premiums in the privatized U.S. health-insurance system, these rising medical costs are counted as an increase in "product." So is the cost of hiring lawyers to dispute insurance companies' fight to avoid paying their policy holders. And so are the enormous legal costs entailed in the financial sector's corporate raiding and political lobbying.

Chart 2.1 Imputed Financial Services and Imputed Owner-Occupier Rents as Percent of U.S. GDP

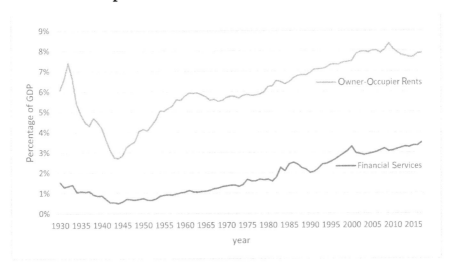

Source: National Income and Product Accounts (NIPA)

Because the NIPA depict interest and other financial charges, insurance and monopoly rents as an inherent part of the industrial economy, countries following this NIPA accounting format but which have a lower FIRE sector overhead report a correspondingly smaller GDP. Today's national income statistics thus provide seemingly empirical "proof" that *rentier* economies are doing better, precisely because they add to overhead – as if this is not *de-industrializing* the United States and other financialized economies.

Finance capitalism's focus on capital gains

The distinguishing feature of finance capitalism is to divide the private sector into two parts: The production-and-consumption economy is wrapped within the FIRE sector that is the core of finance capitalism (along with its allied monopolization and privatization of basic infrastructure and other economic needs).

Chart 2.2 The FIRE Sector's Role in the Domestic Economy

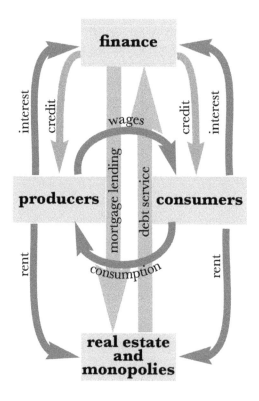

A realistic statistical profile would recognize that most fortunes in finance-capitalist economies are obtained by capital gains, not by earning profits by investing in means of production or even by receiving interest and other economic rents. I prefer the term "finance-capital gains," because they result from debt-leveraged asset-price inflation. The tendency is for the financial sector to absorb a rising share of the economy's flow of income while increasing the Q-ratio – the price of a company's stock relative to its book value. This is much more than a bubble phenomenon. It is a combination of compound interest, endog-enous bank-money creation, tax shifts and monopoly power, backed by old-fashioned corruption and fraud.[11]

Chart 2.3 Cumulative Total Returns: the Sum of U.S. GDP, Equities, Bonds, Land Values and Depreciation, 1950-2018 (Nominal, $bn)

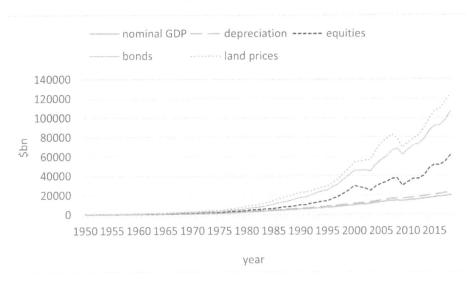

Source: Federal Reserve's Flow of Funds

Central banks provide liquidity to commercial banks by buying gov-ernment securities from them directly and in the open market. U.S. banks deposit the money they receive with the Federal Reserve. But after the Covid-19 virus hit in March 2020, the Fed went far beyond merely maintaining solvency. It pumped $3 trillion into the bond market, raising its bond holdings to $7.4 trillion by the end of 2020. That was much more than wage earners received with their $1,200 CARES checks. It did not revive employment, or make them whole for having lost their jobs, but it did save the wealthiest classes from losing market value for their stocks and bonds, whose prices soared.

---

[11] It often is difficult to characterize the financial sector's "super-profits" as rents. Hyman Minsky pointed out that "bubble"-type financial returns cannot be ex-plained either by "fundamentals" in the form of rising earnings or by monopoly privileges, but simply by a herdlike bubble mentality. That certainly was the case with the Internet bubble that burst in 2000, and the similar junk-bond boom in 2020-21.

For the first time in its history, the central bank started to buy corporate debt, even bonds that "sank to junk status during the pandemic." Prices for what had been "high-yield" junk bonds rose to yield less than 4% by early 2021, creating huge price gains for risk-taking investors. "Hence, debt-laden companies were rewarded for their past sins and large companies benefited from cheap credit,"[12] according to former FDIC head Sheila Bair and Treasury economist Lawrence Goodman.

Speculators and other holders of junk bonds were bailed out, making the riskiest speculators the greatest beneficiaries. Neither the Fed nor other regulators made any attempt to deter companies from borrowing simply to push up the price of their stock by paying out dividends to shareholders (and bonuses to their managers), "even though Congress considered such limits when it approved the facilities." As the economy entered the worst slump since the Great Depression with over 10 million unemployed, no attempt was made to oblige companies benefitting from central bank support to maintain employment. "A House committee report found that companies benefiting from the facilities laid off more than one million workers from March to September." And to make matters worse, Bair and Goodman concluded, the Fed's actions "created a further unfair opportunity for large corporations to get even bigger by purchasing competitors with government-subsidized credit."

Central banks create credit for the financial sector and its *rentier* clients, not for labor and industry, states and localities, or for capital or infrastructure investment and employment. While the stock and real estate markets soared to historic highs for asset holders, the economy plunged for people who had to work for a living. Many restaurants, neighborhood stores and other local middle-class businesses failed. What soared for the shrinking "real" economy were debt arrears.

"The serial market bailouts by monetary authorities – first the banking system in 2008, and now the entire business world amid the pandemic," noted Bair and Goodman, is transforming the economy's political shape in a way that has become "a greater threat [to destroy capitalism] than Bernie Sanders." Control of the economy is being concentrated in the hands of firms with the largest access to almost free bank credit. The Fed's "super-low interest rates have favored the equity of large companies over their smaller

---

[12] Sheila Bair and Lawrence Goodman, "Corporate Debt 'Relief' Is an Economic Dud," *Wall Street Journal*, January 7, 2021. Noting that the multinational food distributor Sysco used the money to pay dividends to its shareholders while laying off a third of its workforce, the authors concluded that "there's little evidence that the Fed's corporate debt buy-up benefited society."

counterparts," the very companies that are "the primary source of job creation and innovation."

Low-interest credit also saved debt-leveraged speculators and debt-pyramided companies from defaulting, and thus saved banks from having to write down their debts. It also gave large national companies a great opportunity to buy out smaller local competitors. By monopolizing the debt and bailout market, these giant companies are able to gobble up smaller companies, further concentrating financial and corporate wealth in the hands of the One Percent.

Radhika Desai calls this "creditocracy," rule by the institutions in control of credit.[13] It is associated with central banks taking over economic policy from elected political bodies and the Treasury, and using it to back giant corporate groups to take the lead in privatizing economy-wide control. As Nomi Prins sums up the decade-long arch since the 2009 Obama bank bailouts:

> The Dow Jones Industrial Average, aided by an ultra-loose monetary policy, steadily <u>rose</u> from a financial-crisis low of 6,926 on March 5, 2009 to 27,090 by March 4, 2020, which was when Covid-19 briefly trashed its rally. ... Rally 2.0 took the Dow to a new record of 30,606.48 as 2020 closed.
>
> Meanwhile, as 2020 ended, the richest 10% of Americans owned more than 88% of the outstanding shares of companies and mutual funds in the U.S. ... the combined net worth of the top 1% of Americans was $34.2 trillion (about one-third of all U.S. household wealth), while the total for the bottom half was $2.1 trillion (or 1.9% of that wealth).[14]

The result, Prins points out, has been that since 2010 "the top 1% of Americans possess more wealth than the whole of the middle class." This is above all a financial phenomenon in view of the fact that: "By 2018, about 75% of the $113 trillion in aggregate U.S. household assets were financial ones; that is, tied up in stocks, ETFs, 401Ks, IRAs, mutual funds, and similar investments. The majority of nonfinancial assets in that mix was in real estate."

---

[13] Desai, Radhika, "The Fate of Capitalism Hangs in the Balance of International Power," *Canadian Dimension*, October 12 2020. https://canadiandimension.com/articles/view/the-fate-of-capitalism-hangs-in-the-balance-of-international-power. See also Geoffrey Gardiner, *Towards True Monetarism* (Dulwich: 1993) and *The Evolution of Creditary Structure and Controls* (London: 2006). The post-Keynesian group Gang of 8 popularized the term "creditary economics" in the 1990s.

[14] Nomi Prins, "War of the (Financial) Worlds: Or Let the Markets Go Wild While the People Go Down," *TomDispatch*, January 10, 2021. https://tomdispatch.com/war-of-the-financial-worlds/.

Financialization engages in war against other economies and their governments

What is called "capitalism" is a conglomeration of different layers inter-acting with their own distinct laws of motion. Productivity and employ-ment tend to taper off in S-curves, but compound interest grows exponen-tially. Industrial capitalism's distinct characteristic is the employment of wage labor to sell products at a profit. Finance capital exploits industry and governments as well as labor, first by charging interest, and indi-rectly through monopoly rent and natural-resource rent, and raising the cost of real estate and privatized infrastructure, followed by transfer-ring real estate and other property from defaulting debtors to creditors, including from indebted governments to bondholders (often foreign).

Finance capitalism aims to avoid what Marx and indeed the majority of his contemporaries expected: that industrial capitalism would evolve toward socialism, peacefully or otherwise. By finding its main source of exploitation to be rent-seeking, not only from land and natural resources but increasingly from privatizing public investment in infrastructure and creating new monopolies, finance capitalism renders economies high cost. That prevents industrialists from underselling competitors in less rent- and debt-strapped economies. Mixed economies such as China's can out-compete nations that lack strongly democratic public sectors. Such economies can subsidize their industry and keep economic rent as the tax base so as to prevent landlords, bankers and monopolists from imposing *rentier* charges.

That is why it seemed a century ago that the destiny of industrial capi-talism was to evolve into socialism. Public education, health care, roads, and basic infrastructure and pensions were coming to be provided by government at subsidized administered prices or freely. Industrial capital backed this policy as a means of shifting as many "external" costs as possible onto the public sector.

But that is not the way matters have turned out. And today's victori-ous finance capitalism, centered in the United States, is trying to prevent its takeover of industrial economies from being rolled back. That means preventing such a rollback from occurring in other countries. It also requires overcoming other countries' resistance to finance capital's takeover of their economies.

That fight is the essence of today's Cold War 2.0. It is being led by the United States and by the unipolar international organizations it has created, headed by the International Monetary Fund and World Bank established as World War II was ending. The Washington Consensus is the political game plan of finance capital, to be imposed internationally, euphemized as democracy and free markets – and even as peace instead of warfare. But it is the kind of Roman-style peace that turns its victimized economies into a desert.

Table 2.1

Industrial Capitalism's Aims	Finance Capitalism's Aims
Make profits by producing products.	Extract economic rent and interest.
Minimize the cost of living and prices.	Add land and monopoly rent to prices.
Favor industry and labor.	Give special tax favoritism to the Finance, Insurance and Real Estate (FIRE) sectors.
Minimize land rent and housing costs by taxing land rent and other rent-yielding assets, not industry or labor.	Shift taxes off land-rent to leave it available to pay as interest to mortgage bankers.
Provide public infrastructure at low cost.	Privatize infrastructure into monopolies to extract monopoly rent.
Reform parliaments to block rent-seeking.	Block democratic reform, by shifting control to non-elected officials.
Avoid military spending and wars that require running into foreign debt.	Use international organizations (such as the IMF or NATO) to force neoliberal policy.
Concentrate economic and social planning in the political capital.	Shift planning and resource allocation to the financial centers.
Concentrate monetary policy in the national treasury.	Shift monetary policy to central banks, representing private commercial banking interests.
Bring prices in line with cost-value.	Maximize opportunities for rent seeking via land ownership, credit and monopoly privileges.
Banking should be industrialized to finance tangible capital investment.	Banks lend against collateral, bidding up asset prices, especially for rent-yielding assets.
Recycle corporate revenue into capital investment in new means of production.	Pay out revenue as dividends or use it for stock buybacks to increase stock price gains.
The time frame is long-term to develop products and marketing plans: M-C-M'.	The time frame is short-term, hit-and-run by financial speculation: M-M'.
Industrial engineering to raise productivity by research and development and new capital investment.	Financial engineering to raise asset prices – by stock buybacks and higher dividend payouts.

Focuses on long-term development of industrial capitalism as a broad economic system.	Short-term hit-and-run objectives, mainly by buying and selling assets.
Economy of High Wages, recognizing that well fed, well-educated labor with leisure is more productive than low-priced "pauper" labor. Long-term employment security is encouraged.	A race to the bottom, burning out employees and replacing them with new hires. Mechanization of labor treats workers as easily replaceable and hence disposable.
M-C-M' Profits are made by investing in means of production and hiring labor to produce commodities to sell at a higher price than what it costs to employ labor.	M-M' "Capital" gains made directly by asset-price inflation.
Banking is industrialized, to provide credit mainly to invest in new capital formation. This increased credit tends to bid up commodity prices and hence the living wage.	Increased bank credit to finance the bidding up of housing, stocks and bonds raises the cost of housing and of buying pension income, leaving *less* to spend on goods and services.
Supports democracy to the extent that the lower house will back industrial capital in its fight against the landlord class and other *rentiers*, whose revenue adds to prices without adding value.	Finance capital joins with "late" industrial capitalism to oppose pro-labor policies. It seeks to take over government, and especially central banks, to support prices for stocks, bonds, real estate and packaged bank loans gone bad and threatening banks with insolvency.
Industrial capitalism is inherently nationalistic, requiring government protection and subsidy of industry.	Finance capital is cosmopolitan, seeking to prevent capital controls and impose free trade and libertarian anti-government policy.
Supports a mixed economy, with government paying for infrastructure to subsidize private industry. Government works with industry and banking to create a long-term growth plan for prosperity.	Seeks to abolish government authority in all areas, so as to shift the center of planning to Wall Street and other financial centers. The aim is to dismantle protection of labor and industry together.
Banking and credit are industrialized.	Industry is financialized, with profits used mainly to increase stock prices via stock buyback programs and dividend payouts, not new R&D or tangible investment.
Keep banking and credit as a public utility, and establish strong financial regulations.	Privatize banking and credit, and take control of the central bank and financial regulators.

3

The Democratic Imperialism of Finance Capital

Emerging from a Group of Seven video meeting to address the Munich Security Conference on February 19, 2021, President Joe Biden described the world as having reached "an inflection point" forcing a choice between American leadership and "those who argue that ... autocracy is the best way forward." Promising to "prepare together for long-term strategic competition with China," he acknowledged that the challenge was to "demonstrate that democracies can still deliver for our people."[1]

But America's financialized K-shaped economy – up for financial markets creating wealth for the One Percent, but down for labor markets and the 99 Percent – is antithetical to real democracy. The human resources firm Zenefits placed the United States at the bottom of its 2021 list of national policies for health care, unemployment, retirement, parental leave, paid vacation and sick days.[2] Life expectancy is declining for Americans, especially for racial and ethnic minorities, in contrast to China and East Asia, whose economies and living standards have been rising much faster than those in the West.

China's policy of keeping banking as a public utility, along with basic infrastructure instead of privatizing it, is what the U.S. president calls "autocracy." That invective typically is applied to government power not sponsored by the United States and controlled by pro-U.S. private-sector financial planners. For instance, it refers to democratically elected leaders seeking to improve their nations' prosperity independent of U.S. control, prompting their overthrow by the United States, as occurred in

---

[1] William Mauldin, "Biden Defends Democracy at Summits with European Allies, Seeing China as 'Stiff' Competition," *Wall Street Journal*, February 19, 2021.

[2] Cinnamon Janzer, "Data Reveals United States Ranks Last in Labor Benefits," *Workest by Zeneca*, February 1, 2021. https://www.zenefits.com/workest/data-reveals-united-states-ranks-last-in-worker-benefits/.

Iran and Guatemala in 1953-54 down through today's Latin American coups and "color revolutions" in the post-Soviet sphere.

The word "socialism" finds rising approval over "capitalism" among younger Americans facing an economy that is locking them out of the path to prosperity that existed back in 1945. Most Americans want federal support for schooling and upgrading of infrastructure, and for it to be financed largely by more progressive taxation. Opinion polls in the United States report that the majority of Americans want the public health care ("socialized medicine") advocated by Vermont Senator Bernie Sanders. But President Biden supports the Obamacare program sponsored by the pharmaceuticals and health-insurance monopolies. And there is little opportunity in America's two-party duopoly to vote for leaders advocating the policies favored by most Americans. The Supreme Court's ruling in the Citizens United case has entrenched privatized oligarchic politics and law-making, placing electoral power in the hands of the Donor Class led by Wall Street and the corporate monopolists largely responsible for the selection of major political candidates.

At the abovementioned G7 Munich meeting, President Biden criticized the Europeans for not paying enough for America's military confrontation with Russia and China. Chancellor Angela Merkel replied that Germany's interest was to trade more with China, with which Europe had just signed a new trade and investment pact. And German business was still fighting against U.S. sanctions aimed at blocking imports of Russian gas via the Nord Stream 2 pipeline. French President Emmanuel Macron called for "a dialogue with Russia," and urged "strategic autonomy" from the United States, not only with regard to trade and investment with China but also militarily. He also said that NATO was "brain dead," having no function that really benefited Europe since the Warsaw Pact was dissolved.[3]

China's foreign ministry spokesperson Hua Chunying summed up the growing attitude: "We oppose the imposition of rules made by several countries on the international community under the pretext of multilateralism. We also oppose the practice of ideologizing multilateralism to form values-based allies targeting specific countries."

The strategy of U.S. military and financial imperialism is to install client oligarchies and dictatorships, and arm-twist allies to join the fight against designated adversaries by subsidizing not only the empire's costs of war-making ("defense") but even the imperial nation's domestic

---

[3] David E. Sanger, Steven Erlanger and Roger Cohen, "Biden Reaffirms Alliances' Value for U.S. Policies," *The New York Times*, February 20, 2021.

spending programs. America's dollarized Free World tributary system transfers affluence to itself, creating rising tensions with its NATO and other allies. Hardly by surprise, historians have found some parallels with classical Athens and Rome, whose empires were prone to similar strategic aims and internal strains.

Some valid and false parallels with ancient Greece

It has become faddish to characterize U.S. opposition to China and other countries that resist Dollar Diplomacy as a "Thucydides problem," as if war is inevitable between a rising power and an established one.[4] But what actually was at stake between Sparta and Athens in the 5th century BC was whether the Greek-speaking world would have an oligarchic or democratic political and economic system.

The Peloponnesian War lasted on and off from 431 to 404 BC, and engulfed all the Greek states, not just the main contenders. But it was only one episode in the long conflict extending from the 7th to 3rd centuries BC that saw repeated popular revolts demanding debt relief and land redistribution throughout the Greek-speaking world. Sparta backed oligarchies, while Athens backed democracies.

There are indeed similarities between the conflict between Sparta and Athens, oligarchy and democracy, and today's New Cold War. The latter is basically being waged by U.S.-centered finance capitalism backing *rentier* oligarchies against nations seeking to build up more widespread self-reliance and domestic prosperity.

Oligarchic Sparta's militarized, non-commercial (and barely monetized) citizenry of "equals" did not own land in central Sparta itself, but lived austerely, having turned neighboring Messenia's population into serflike helots forced to produce a crop surplus. That freed Spartans from agricultural labor so that they could spend their time practicing military exercises. Wealthy Spartan landowners were a distinct class and controlled the city-state's politics. The parallels with America are apparent, as it now relies on foreign industrial labor to produce what no longer is made in the United States. And it too has a wealthy *rentier* oligarchy controlling its political system, while ordinary Americans face increasing austerity, debt peonage (serfdom) and declining home (land) ownership.

What Sparta opposed was not Athenian prosperity (which it itself shunned), but Athens' democratic reforms, fearing that they might be

---

[4] Graham Allison, *Destined for War: Can America and China Escape Thucydides's Trap?* (Boston: 2017).

contagious to neighboring lands. Under Solon in 594 BC, Athens had been one of the last Greek city-states to end debt bondage. Soon thereafter, Peisistratus and his sons developed a thriving public sector, and the economy was further democratized in the 5th century BC under Pericles and Ephialtes.

The "Thucydides problem" and "clash of civilizations" theories also neglect the strains caused by Athenian moves to create an empire via the Delian League, based on the sacred island of Delos, to rival Sparta's oligarchic Achaean League alliances with Macedonia and Delphi, and with Persia. "The whole Hellenic world was convulsed," wrote Thucydides, for there were "struggles being everywhere made by the popular chiefs to bring in the Athenians, and by the oligarchs to introduce the Lacedaemonians [Spartans]."[5]

A striking characteristic of U.S. policy since World War I has been its ability to exploit its allies as well as the enemies it has defeated. Likewise in antiquity, all the Delian League's treasurers were Athenian. They collected annual tribute from League members, originally about 400 talents, financing as much as two-thirds of the Athenian budget.[6] The money was paid in Athenian four-drachma "owls" – the "dollars" of their day, the most prevalent silver coins, minted out of ore from Athens' own mines at Laurion.

Just as the United States creates its own dollars to spend as the "money of the world" to pay the military costs of its empire, Athens used its silver to build its fleet of trireme ships, buy military support and hire mercenaries, and pay its own soldiers to dominate other Greek cities and islands. The tribute it received from its allies for these efforts enabled Athens to avoid imposing new taxes on its own citizens, and indeed to build the Parthenon largely with Delian League tribute during 447-432 BC. Athens tripled the Delian League's annual tribute to over 1,200 talents by 425, an inflow that continued until Sparta finally defeated it in 404.[7]

---

[5] Thucydides, *History of the Peloponnesian War*, 3.82.1.

[6] Andreas Andreades, *A History of Greek Public Finance* (Cambridge, Mass.: 1933), p. 268. Rome's exploitation of its provinces (not allies, because they were not independent) was even more extreme. Andreades calculates that over 90 percent of Rome's budget in the 1st century BC came from tribute levied on its provinces. By the time Egypt paid tribute under Augustus, Italian taxes represented less than 5 percent of the Roman budget.

[7] Thucydides 1.96-99 and 2.9, and Pausanias, *Description of Greece* 8.52.

Athenian "democratic imperialism" to fund this war effort created modern-style financial strains as less prosperous cities experienced a debt crisis. In Corcyra in 427, Thucydides (3.81.4) reports:

> During seven days that Eurymedon [an Athenian general backing the "democratic" faction against the oligarchs] stayed with his sixty ships, the Corcyraeans were engaged in butchering those of their fellow citizens whom they regarded as their enemies: and although the crime imputed was that of attempting to put down the democracy, some were slain also for private hatred, others by their debtors because of the monies owed to them.

The Delian League became an exploitative system of "democratic imperialism" in which Athens demanded support from its allied city-states. It was doing what the United States does today when it taps its allies for military support via NATO and "the Coalition of the Willing" to destroy Iraq and Libya. But the main ancient Greek analogy with today's U.S. opposition to China, Russia, Iran, Venezuela and other countries that resist the American neoliberal drive to privatize their natural resources and public infrastructure was the Greek opposition between oligarchy and democracy. Much as U.S. diplomacy installed Pinochet in Chile and similar dictatorships throughout Latin America, oligarchic Sparta backed the notorious Thirty Tyrants in Athens after its victory in 404.

Aristotle noted that democracies tend to evolve into oligarchies. This might happen so smoothly that many constitutions that appeared to be democratic were in fact oligarchic, he said. As used in the language of today's international diplomacy, the word "democracy" has become disconnected from its classical meaning of "rule [kratos] by the people [demos]." It has come to mean rule by U.S. proxies, regardless of political forms, and is applied freely to client oligarchies.

Athenian democracy had in fact been turning into an oligarchy already in 411 after Athens lost in Sicily and its Delian League allies withdrew support. Wealthy Athenians staged a coup, installed a council of the Four Hundred, and restricted the popular Ecclesia assembly to 5000 large landowners. Protesting against the tax burden that fell mainly on themselves, these leading families stopped social spending that benefited the lower classes (*Athēnaion Politeia* 19). That has been a constant among wealthy elites throughout history.

The modern analogy with ancient Greece actually has the United States on both sides: On the one hand it resembles Athens as leader of pro-American nominal democracies (any country is called a democracy if it supports U.S. diplomacy), tapping its NATO allies much as Athens

did when it built up its civic architecture largely with foreign contributions supposedly for military protection. In another way the United
States is like Sparta, backing dictators and client oligarchies against
democratic land reformers and pro-labor leaders as it itself becomes
more oligarchic.

But demanding financial domination over foreign economies and
installing political oligarchies is not rivalry, nor is it jealousy. It is subjugation, and today's mode of subjugation is more financial than military.
The Soviet Union did not understand this in 1991 when Russia and
other countries let U.S. advisors impose neoliberal "shock therapy,"
voucher privatization giveaways to kleptocrats appropriating and selling
post-Soviet resources to Western financiers.

Sparta's victory over Athens led to an influx of silver into Sparta,
taken by its elite landowning families. They used it to buy out the land
of smaller holders. By the 3rd century BC so many Spartans had lost
their economic status that kings Agis IV and Cleomenes III moved to
cancel debts and redistribute the land so as to rebuild Sparta's military
power. The neighboring oligarchies called in Rome, which destroyed
Sparta – and then devastated Athens and all of Greece, stripping its
wealth and ending its independence.

Neither China nor Russia fit into this parallel history between ancient
Greece and today's New Cold War. Neither nation is interfering with
other countries or their politics, either democratic or oligarchic, and
they are not demanding tribute or military allegiance.

Roman imperialism as a dress rehearsal for American empire

What does indeed provide a parallel is the response of conquered
provinces and territories to Roman conquest. The final century of the
Roman Republic saw its oligarchy accumulate fortunes not by increas-
ing productivity and prosperity at home, but by stripping other regions.
The historian Sallust (who lived from 86 to 35 BC) quoted a letter from
Mithridates, king of Pontus, to Arsaces, king of the Parthians:

> The Romans have one inveterate motive for making war upon
> all nations, peoples and kings: namely, a deep-seated desire for
> dominion and for riches. ... Do you not know that the Romans
> ... have possessed nothing since the beginning of their existence
> except what they have stolen – their home, their wives, their
> lands, their empire? ... no laws, human or divine, prevent them
> from seizing and destroying allies and friends, those near them
> and those afar off, weak or powerful, and from considering every

government which does not serve them, especially monarchies, as their enemies. ... it is by audacity, by deceit, and by joining war to war that they have grown great. Following their usual custom, they will destroy everything or perish in the attempt.[8]

Rome claimed to bring order to its empire – having become such already in Republican times prior to the crowning of Augustus in 27 BC. The depredations of its financial class – the publicani "knights" with sufficient land and wealth to qualify for the cavalry as a military-economic class just below senatorial rank – prompted the historian Livy to write that "where there was a publicanus, there was no effective public law and no freedom for the subjects." This class imposed austerity on Roman provinces much as the International Monetary Fund does today on behalf of the U.S. financial sector and its allies. Summarizing their behavior, Ernst Badian notes that Cicero described them "as ruthless exploiters who nevertheless have to be appeased because of their economic resources and political power." [9]

A century later the historian Tacitus quoted the words of Calgalus, a Scottish opponent of Rome, c. 87 AD, to describe Rome's oligarchy: "If their enemy have wealth, they have greed; if he be poor, they are ambitious. ... To plunder, butcher, steal – these things they misname empire. They make a desolation and call it peace." [10]

What is ironic is that it was the reformers Tiberius and Gaius Gracchus (133-121 BC) who empowered the publican "knights" to act as the jury class in hope of controlling corrupt governors. Their assumption was that financial managers would work honestly in the public interest, but that always has been erroneous. It is in the nature of the financial class (as Aristotle would say) to use its power against society at large. The financial class historically has been the major beneficiary of empires by acting as collection agents. The *publicani* contracted to collect taxes and tribute on behalf of Rome, and they and fellow creditors lent Roman provinces the money to make these payments, seizing public property and enterprises illegally to cover the interest charges. (Brutus, who stabbed Julius Caesar, charged 42 percent.) They manipulated the courts to prevent themselves from being prosecuted for theft, most noto-

---

[8] Sallust, Historiae 4.69, transl. J.C. Rolfe (Cambridge: 1960), pp. 435-41, quoted in Aldo Schavione, *Ancient Rome and the Modern West* (Cambridge, MA: 2000), p. 84.

[9] Ernst Badian, *Publicans and Sinners* (Ithaca: 1972), p. 12, citing Livy, *History of Rome* 45.18.4 and Cicero.

[10] Tacitus, *Agricola* 30.

riously managing to get the governor Q. Mucius Scaevola and his aide P. Rutilius Rufus removed when they tried to stop the publican misbehavior in 92 BC.

In a vocabulary of invective much like U.S. accusations calling Non-Aligned leaders "Communist" or socialist, Rome accused its own reformers of "seeking kingship," meaning "big government" strong enough to restrain the creditor elite from monopolizing the land and reducing much of the population to debt dependency. While the narrow ruling class benefited financially from Rome's empire, the domestic debt burden led to constant civil warfare and helped concentrate landholdings into vast *latifundia*, which Pliny blamed for being "the ruin of Rome."

Rome's collapse into a Dark Age of subsistence production is the most relevant lesson to be drawn from ancient empire-building. Rome, with its imperial center's domestic debt burden, polarization of wealth and bleeding of its allies, can be viewed as a precursor of today's American empire. Rome's resulting collapse into serfdom stands as a warning to civilization to avoid the dangers inherent in today's similar financial and oligarchic polarization.

Creating the U.S. imperial system in the wake of World War II

As Chapter 10 will describe, the first aim of American diplomats structuring the post-World War II world in 1944-45 was to absorb Britain's colonial empire and Sterling Area into the dollar sphere. That was achieved by lending a desperate Britain $3.75 billion, conditional on it opening up its Sterling Area to free trade and investment. That obliged the Sterling Area countries to open their economies, mainly to U.S. exporters and investors. Britain had to agree not to seek to regain markets by devaluing its currency until 1949 – too late to save its export markets from being lost to U.S. producers.

Britain also capitulated to U.S. demands to create the International Monetary Fund and World Bank as vehicles to open up trade and financial markets to U.S. exporters, and to enable U.S. investors to buy control of foreign natural resources and industry. Britain's capitulation set the rules for Europe and other regions to subsequently join these two institutions, leaving no practical alternative means of organizing world trade and investment. The World Bank's policies include opposing land reform, and it organizes loans mainly to create infrastructure linked largely to exports, not to create domestic self-sufficiency. The aim is to lock in foreign dependency on U.S. farm exports and other essentials.

The major leverage over foreign economies is financial. The IMF finances U.S. allies and withholds credit from recalcitrant countries. Dollar credit is used as a lever to indebt foreign countries and force them to adopt "free market" deregulation and tax policies that serve U.S. interests. IMF "currency stabilization" loans typically are made to countries facing imminent devaluation stemming from foreign debt pressures.

The broadest step in this "strategy of underdevelopment" is to use IMF pressure to turn public infrastructure into privatized monopolies by forcing their selloff to raise money to settle trade and balance-of-payments deficits. And aiming to reverse the 20th century's pro-labor reforms, the IMF's notorious "conditionalities" for its loans oppose labor unions and pro-consumer policies as threatening to impair the profits of U.S. and other foreign investors. The pretense is that low labor costs will enable debtor countries to produce exports less expensively and thus "earn their way out of debt." The reality is that austerity shrinks the economy and drives it even deeper into foreign dependency.

The IMF then steps in to subsidize capital flight by client oligarchies, lending foreign central banks the money to support their exchange rate long enough for companies to move their money into dollars or other hard currencies. Then, when the local currency is allowed to collapse, the debtor country is told to impose further austerity and anti-labor policies to "restore competition," and to sell off more land, natural resources and public enterprises to repay the IMF for its capital-flight loans.

Some 750 U.S. military bases protect this financial underdevelopment policy. NATO and SEATO were created as military arms against nations seeking to manage their own economies independently of U.S. financial and military control. Among the U.S. Defense Department officials appointed to head the World Bank are Assistant Secretary of War John McCloy (1947-49), Secretary of Defense John McNamara (1968-81), and Deputy Secretary of Defense Paul Wolfowitz (2005-07).

As Under-Secretary of Defense under George H. W. Bush in April 1992, Wolfowitz and Lewis "Scooter" Libby presented a memorandum on "Defense Planning Guidance: 1994-99," asserting that: "We must maintain the mechanism for deterring potential competitors from even aspiring to a larger regional or global role." U.S. officials announced that they felt American security to be threatened if they could not control the political and economic policy of other countries. Michael Ledeen, a neoconservative at the American Enterprise Institute, spelled out the U.S. tactic of intimidation: "Every ten years or so, the United States needs to pick up some small crappy little country and throw it against the wall, just to show the world we mean business."[11]

Backing client oligarchies to control the oil trade

U.S. policy initially was anti-colonialist in order to absorb the Sterling and Franc areas into the dollar sphere. But foreign military and political intervention escalated in 1953 under the Eisenhower Administration (1953-60), administered by Secretary of State John Foster Dulles and his brother Alan Dulles as head of the CIA.

There was a reason why the first major move to block foreign self-determination occurred in Iran. After World War I the U.S. Government "encouraged the petroleum industry to extend its operations to foreign areas in both hemispheres and lent its active support when necessary. Since then, more than half of the huge petroleum reserves outside the United States have been found by American-owned companies."[12] Mohammad Mosaddegh had been elected Prime Minister in 1951, promising land reform and a land tax, and to gain control of the nation's oil resources from Anglo-Persian Oil. The company paid royalties of less than 20 percent on "profits" that its tax accountants minimized by selling its oil at an artificially low price to its offshore trading affiliates. Iran's parliament voted to nationalize the company, noting that it had made no attempt to fulfil its 1933 commitment to raise wages and build schools and hospitals.

Winston Churchill and Clement Attlee urged Truman to oust Mossadegh, but the American president and State Department viewed him as a nationalist bulwark against the Communist Tudeh party. The incoming Eisenhower Administration, however, viewed nationalists as virtual communists inasmuch as they shared a common advocacy of domestic control of natural resources. Control of oil and foreign mineral resources was (and remains) a basic element of U.S. foreign policy (and also that of Britain and Holland). So in 1953 the CIA and Britain's MI6

---

[11] Jonah Goldberg, "Baghdad Delenda Est, Part Two," *National Review*, April 23, 2002, citing a speech by Ledeen in the early 1990s. The sources are discussed in https://historynewsnetwork.org/blog/6772, and by Simon Mars's interview with Noam Chomsky, April 2, 2005, at https://chomsky.info/20040402/.

[12] Statistics that I compiled in *The Balance of Payments of the Petroleum Industry* (Chase Manhattan Bank, 1966) show that "By 1964, total free world gross petroleum investment amounted to over $136 billion, with the U.S. petroleum industry accounting for $71 billion at home and $23 billion abroad."

organized a coup (led by Kermit Roosevelt on the U.S. side) to impose the Shah as dictator.[13]

Mosaddegh was imprisoned in his own home, where he was buried when he eventually died so as to prevent a public funeral from reviving Iranian resistance to foreign control. This was heralded as bringing democracy to Iran – with "democracy" meaning "anti-Communism" in the U.S. rhetoric applied in international diplomacy, as if real democracy was compatible with foreign ownership of Iran's natural resources and their rents, and U.S. rights to install heads of state as neo-colonial satraps.

Imposing a U.S.-backed dictatorship in Iran was part of a common policy toward Venezuela, Iraq, Libya and similar nations suffering from the "curse of oil" attracting foreign resource grabbers. But America refrains from overthrowing governments in oil-rich royal despotisms like Saudi Arabia and Kuwait, as long as they remain pro-U.S. and recycle their oil revenue to the U.S. economy.

For many decades the United States imported oil only from its own transnational firms – just eight companies in 1947, expanding to 32 by 1964. These firms organized their foreign oil production legally as part of the U.S. economy – not as corporately distinct affiliates operating as part of their host-country economies, but as branches whose operations are consolidated into the parent company's balance sheet. Only a small fraction of the nominal price of the oil imported by these companies actually is paid in foreign exchange, so most of the nominal price never leaves the U.S. economy.

Purchase of U.S. capital goods and equipment accounted for about 45% of the oil industry's average annual new investment outflow, so "little over half of the industry's new investment 'outflow' actually left the U.S. shores in a financial form. ... When such receipts are added to capital goods exports ... [t]his raises the balance-of-payments return to over 34% per year, indicating a payback period in balance-of-payments terms of under three years." Most of the rest of the investment outflow was absorbed by parent company profits (laundered through offshore tax-avoidance centers), interest to U.S. banks, and payments to U.S. employees and for U.S. management services. And indeed, "the payback period is seen to be even shorter when the indirect effects of new foreign

---

[13] Ervand Abrahamian, *The Coup, the CIA, and the Roots of Modern U.S.-Iranian Relations* (New York: 2013), James Risen, *State of War: The Secret History of the CIA and the Bush Administration* (New York: 2006), and Stephen Kinzer, *All the Shah's Men: An American Coup and the Roots of Middle East Terror* (New York: 2003). Anglo-Persian Oil was renamed British Petroleum in 1954.

investment are properly taken into account. Host countries tend to spend a substantial portion of U.S. investment funds to purchase U.S. exports and to build up dollar deposits in the U.S."[14]

Foreign resource extraction has gone hand in hand with the creation of an array of offshore banking centers and tax havens. U.S. parent-company branches in oil-producing countries sell their oil at low prices to trading affiliates incorporated in Liberia or Panama, whose "flags of convenience" are an accounting deception to avoid having to pay U.S. income taxes. Neither Liberia nor Panama have an income tax or even a currency of their own, but use dollars so that companies using these tax-avoidance centers will not run a risk of currency devaluation.[15]

Having bought their oil at low prices from the producers, the trading affiliates sell it to their refiners and distributors in North America and Europe at prices so high that these downstream affiliates have no profits to declare and be taxed. This tactic is now used by companies across the economic spectrum, not only by mining conglomerates but by multinationals such as Apple, which pretends to make its worldwide profits in low-tax Ireland.

Guatemala and U.S. agricultural imperialism

After Iran, the next notorious coup to prevent a foreign democracy from gaining control of its own destiny occurred in Guatemala in 1954. Ten years earlier a revolution had replaced its dictator with a democratic regime. When President Jacobo Arbenz introduced land reform to give peasants land, Eisenhower and the Dulles brothers were convinced that this was inherently anti-American and therefore likely to be Communist.

Guatemala's aim of achieving self-sufficiency in food produced by locally owned farms threatened the plantation holdings of the United Fruit Company. American diplomacy has long sought to maintain Latin American countries as plantations for U.S. companies, which are to keep

---

[14] The above-cited *The Balance of Payments of the Petroleum Industry*, which I believe remains the only detailed statistical analysis of this phenomenon. The contribution of oil to the U.S. balance of payments was deemed so high that copies of this report were put on the desks of every U.S. Senator and Representative, and led the oil industry to be declared exempt from President Lyndon Johnson's "voluntary" balance-of-payments controls, on the ground that every dollar of U.S. oil investment abroad was returned to the U.S. economy in just 18 months.

[15] I trace the evolution of such centers in my introduction to R. T. Naylor, *Hot Money and the Politics of Debt*, 3rd ed. (Montreal: 2004), pp. ix-xxxiii, reprinted in my *Finance Capitalism and its Discontents: Interviews and Speeches, 2003-2012* (Dresden: 2012).

for themselves the income from exporting their plantation crops. This exploitation required a fight against indigenous populations such as the Maya, who attempted to use the land to produce their own food. The U.S. response was to support a landowning military dictatorship under Carlos Castillo Armas.

Land reform to produce a country's own food is contrary to U.S. promotion of foreign dependency on U.S. grain exports. After the European Economic Community was formed in 1957, American diplomats opposed its Common Agricultural Policy of U.S.-style price supports and subsidies for many years before finally giving up when Europe stood its ground. Food dependency facilitates U.S. economic control of a country and can be used as a weapon, as when the U.S. Government imposed grain sanctions against China in the 1950s in an attempt to starve out Mao's revolution.

"Democratic imperialism" via client oligarchies to suppress democratic independence

The Non-Aligned Movement became a threat to U.S. global strategy in 1961. Founded in Belgrade, it was headed by five leaders, each of whom was his country's first president: Sukarno in Indonesia, Josip Broz Tito in Yugoslavia, Gamal Abdel Nassar in Egypt, Kwame Nkrumah in Ghana, and Jawaharlal Nehru in India. The United States had no "jealousy" of such countries, any more than it was jealous of oil-rich Iran and other Near Eastern producers, or agricultural Guatemala. Non-Aligned meant creating a trade and finance diplomacy, independent of control by the United States, which simply wanted to subordinate foreign economies to serve U.S. corporate and financial prosperity.

U.S. diplomacy accordingly sought to isolate and overthrow these Non-Aligned leaders, typically using ethnic divisions to create ethnic or race wars and what CIA jargon calls "color revolutions." In Indonesia, for instance, Sukarno had led the resistance to the Dutch Empire in 1945. Recognizing that his country's large Chinese population was especially active in the commercial and finance sectors, he strengthened ties with China in the mid-1950s, and convened the Bandung Conference of leaders of 29 Asian and African states in April 1955. Under his leadership Indonesia also became the largest recipient of Soviet military aid. So in 1965 the CIA sponsored a widespread anti-Chinese massacre and assassination of progressive leaders, turning the country over to brutal military rule by General Suharto.[16]

A similar coup was organized in Chile in 1973 to overthrow its elected president Salvador Allende. As Henry Kissinger quipped, "I don't see why we need to stand by and watch a country go communist due to the irresponsibility of its people. The issues are much too important for the Chilean voters to be left to decide for themselves."

The copper mines had been "Chileanized" at the suggestion of Anaconda and Kennecott copper companies, on the condition that all copper be sold via these companies so as to secure supplies of the metal (at low "producer's prices") for their long-term customers. But President Allende rejected this commitment, asserting that Chile could sell its copper to whomever it chose.

That was neither the kind of free market nor the kind of "democracy" that American diplomacy supported. The U.S. antidote was University of Chicago "free market" principles. Every economics department in every Chilean university except for the Catholic University was closed down under General Augusto Pinochet. Companies and their pension plans were privatized and financialized. Chilean companies created *grupo* conglomerates run by banks to siphon off corporate revenue and empty out pension funds in financially engineered looting, leaving bankrupt shells in their wake. This tactic reduced pension rights to a trickle. (In 2020-21, Chilean voters rebelled and sought to restore a democratic constitution and protest its president Pinera's neoliberal "Chicago" leadership, including destruction of labor's pension rights by schemes that Pinera himself had designed.)

Chile's privatization and financialization at gunpoint inaugurated a wave of terror that spread throughout Latin America. The U.S. State Department organized Operation Condor to assassinate more than 60,000 labor leaders, progressive academics, land reformers and Liberation Theology Catholics, installing a new legacy of Latin American dictatorships. In 2009, Secretary of State Hillary Clinton sponsored the overthrow of Honduras's president Manuel Zelaya, who was promoting

---

[16] See for instance Vincent Bevins, *The Jakarta Method: Washington's Anticommunist Crusade and the Mass Murder Program that Shaped Our World* (New York: 2020), reporting that CIA operatives "provided the killers with lists of real and imagined Communists. U.S. officials conditioned U.S. military support on protection of U.S. oil installations and elimination of the PKI," the Communist Party of Indonesia. Estimates of the numbers killed range from 500,000 up to 2 to 3 million.

a modest land reform. (An earlier Honduran coup had occurred in 1963 to prevent the election of a democratic regime.)

Aiming to appropriate ownership of Latin American and other continents' land, natural resources and infrastructure, U.S. policy seeks to block land reform and oppose agricultural self-sufficiency, as well as local attempts to retain basic infrastructure in the public domain instead of privatizing it. To the United States, power means the privilege of intervening in the politics of other nations to prevent them from deviating from financial, trade and military dependency on the United States. The result is a form of globalization that seeks to subjugate any country that might act independently of U.S. control by protecting its industrial and agricultural self-sufficiency and growth.

Creating a neoliberal post-Soviet oligarchy after 1991

America's victory in the Cold War was capped by the dissolution of the USSR in 1991. That cataclysmic event was mapped out in a Houston meeting on December 19, 1990, where World Bank and IMF planners laid out a blueprint for Russia's leaders to impose austerity and give away its assets – it didn't matter to whom – in a wave of "shock therapy" to let the alleged magic of free enterprise create a neoliberal free-for-all.[17] The result was to endow kleptocrats by registering public assets in their own names or companies, and for them to obtain value for these takings by selling shares to foreign buyers.

For U.S. investors, this was a financial success story. Russia became the world's best-performing stock market even while – indeed, precisely because – industry was dismantled throughout the former Soviet republics, whose economies suffered depression and demographic loss as bad as that caused by the military destruction of World War II. The population plunge was especially serious in the neoliberalized Baltics, where it is still continuing, having fallen by over 20 percent since independence in 1991.

Americans were furious when President Putin sought to stop Russia's collapse and financial conquest by foreign investors. U.S. denunciations of Russian autocracy are aimed at post-Yeltsin attempts to stop Mikhail Khodorkovsky and other kleptocrats from appropriating and selling off Russia's Yukos and other oil resources and companies to U.S. buyers, and evading Russian taxes. The fact that Mr. Putin was demo-

---

[17] See *The Economy of the USSR. A study undertaken to a request by the Houston Summit* (Washington: 1990), by the IMF and World Bank, the Organization for Economic Cooperation and Development (OECD) and the European Bank for Reconstruction and Development (EBRD). For details, see Chapter 11.

cratically elected does not matter. As long as a "democracy" is defined as being pro-American and "autocracy" means blocking U.S. attempts at takeover, these words have little to do with the political system or popular voting preferences.

Ending the Cold War with the former Soviet Union did nothing to curtail U.S. military spending. Just the opposite. NATO expanded, despite the Warsaw Pact's dissolution and the promise by James Baker in the George H. W. Bush Administration not to move it eastward. U.S. officials continue to assert the right to first use of nuclear weapons, along with the right to use military force unilaterally. As the Clinton Administration's May 1997 *Quadrennial Defense Review* (whose principal author was the hawkish Assistant Secretary of Defense for Strategy, Michele Flournoy) explained, the United States no longer felt itself bound by the UN Charter prohibiting the threat or use of military force. The report framed the unilateral use of military force all over the world as justified in "defending vital interests," which it defined to include "preventing the emergence of a hostile regional coalition" anywhere, and "ensuring uninhibited access to key markets, energy supplies and strategic resources." The report added that "when the interests at stake are vital ... we should do whatever it takes to defend them, including, when necessary, the unilateral use of military power."[18] International law defines this as aggression, the "supreme international crime" according to the judges at Nuremberg.

The New Cold War waged by U.S.-centered finance capitalism

The Cold War was not won by military conflict. Force ideally is not necessary for the most successful empires, except for local police actions. The key mode of control is financial and trade dependency. Like overtly military occupation, America's Dollar Diplomacy aims to control the commanding heights of foreign economies – their finance and banking, land and natural resources, transportation and power utilities, and information and Internet monopolies. Countries that resist such economic takeover become America's enemies, its designated adversaries.

The result today is a New Cold War waged by the United States and its NATO satellites not only against China and Russia, but against any countries resisting privatization and financialization under U.S. sponsorship. "The most distinctive feature of our time," Russia's foreign minister Sergei Lavrov observed in October 2020, "is this: everyone

---

[18] Quoted in Media Benjamin and Nicolas J. S. Davies, "Will Michele Flournoy Be the Angel of Death for the American Empire," *Counterpunch*, September 24, 2020.

understands that a redistribution of power is taking place, and this is exactly what our Western colleagues are fighting so adamantly, clinging to their centuries of dominance."[19]

U.S. military and financial diplomacy has become so exploitative that it is driving its allies as well as victims to break away, along with those countries successfully resisting economic takeover, most notably nuclear armed China and Russia. No country with atomic weapons is likely to be militarily attacked by the United States, let alone occupied. If it does not let itself be neoliberalized (and is not susceptible to "color revolution"), realistically the most the United States can do is seek to isolate it.

At issue in this New Cold War is whether the world economy will be one of finance capitalism and rent extraction, or industrial capitalism evolving into socialism. As Rosa Luxemburg put matters a century ago, the choice is whether the world will have socialism or barbarism. American finance capitalism threatens to create an economic Dark Age. Its basic dynamic is to concentrate wealth in the hands of the *rentier* One or Ten Percent at the top of each country's economy, impoverishing the rest of society by using financial and allied *rentier* property "rights" as choke points to secure control.

Wealth is addictive and incites greed, which is rapacious and victimizing. Finance capitalism knows no limit as it compulsively seeks every drop of income for itself. Privatizers of natural resources and infrastructure monopolies claim that their rent seeking is productive rather than socially destructive. But it siphons off the income of labor and also the profits of industry. That ultimately is as destructive as when Rome stripped its provinces and enserfed its own population, leaving an economic Dark Age. Today's populations from Greece to Latvia, and indeed from America's Rust Belt to Texas, are told they themselves are responsible for the hunger, illness and financial anxiety leading to early death among the indebted poor, not that they have been victimized by the privatized and financialized system sponsored by the Washington Consensus.

---

[19] Speech to the Valdai Club on the causes of turbulence in modern international politics, October 13, 2020. Lavrov added that "the substance of the modern epoch is an objective process of formation of a more democratic, multipolar international order. It is a difficult and long process. It will probably take an entire epoch," and "if the EU is arrogant enough to declare, with this sense of unconditional superiority, that Russia must understand there will be no 'business as usual,' well, Russia wants to understand whether there could be any business at all with the European Union under these conditions. ... So we should probably stop communicating with them for a while."

Creating a multipolar world

Countering the dynamic of U.S.-centered finance capitalism is looming as the great economic struggle of the remainder of the 21st century. Decoupling from Dollar Diplomacy requires mobilizing a broad enough membership of nations to become self-sufficient in essentials so that national economies cannot be untracked by U.S. moves to isolate them. Such a critical mass was lacking in 1945 when U.S. financial diplomacy used its monetary power to gain control of Britain, France and the rest of Europe. When the Bandung Conference met in Indonesia in 1955, and again when the Non-Aligned Movement was attempted in 1961, their members also lacked the economic range – and military defense – needed to break from the U.S. moves to isolate them. But the Shanghai Cooperation Organization (of China, Russia and other Eurasian countries, including soon Iran) and the Belt and Road Initiative promise to be more successful.

As will be described in later chapters, a viable alternative to Dollar Diplomacy requires creation of a multipolar monetary system independent of the dollar, along with a tax system that discourages wealth extraction through monopoly privileges and debt leveraging. A guiding legal principle should be that no country should be obliged to pay foreign debt by forfeiting its own natural resources and capital investment, or by cutting back labor's living standards. That demand is at the root of U.S. financial domination.

Avoiding financial and trade dependency requires a cancellation of debts that are unpayable except by reducing living standards and privatizing public infrastructure. This is hardly a new perception. A common demand of democracy for the past 2500 years, from classical Greece and Rome down to modern debtor revolts, has been for debt cancellation and land redistribution.

Chapter 13 will describe why democracies are more prone to evolve into oligarchies than were Near Eastern monarchies. From Sumer in the 3rd millennium BC and Hammurabi's Babylonia in the 2nd millennium BC down to the Neo-Assyrian, Neo-Babylonian and Persian Empires in the 1st millennium BC, rulers held the support of their local populations by proclaiming Clean Slates that annulled debts, liberated bondservants and restored self-support lands to debtors who had lost them to creditors.

Debt cancellations were proclaimed in Greek city-states by reformer "tyrants" – and according to some reports, by early Roman kings. Greek oligarchs denounced as "tyrants" leaders who advocated cancelling debts and redistributing rental lands to their cultivators, as reformer-"tyrants" had done in the 7th and 6th centuries BC to open the path for the

Greek takeoff in Corinth and other leading city-states that overthrew their mafiosi-style autocrats monopolizing local land and credit. Oligarchic Rome feared the very idea of kingship, on the ground that such power might be used to annul creditor claims. Strong popular leaders down through Julius Caesar were assassinated for "seeking kingship," being suspected above all of planning to consolidate support by cancelling debts and redistributing the land that oligarchs had appropriated. That spirit of limiting "big government's" role survives in today's world.

The Washington Consensus depicts dependence on a financialized U.S.-centered world economy as being so natural that it appears to be part of a free market, even having a patina of democratic choice as long as the choice is limited to political leaders who accept the logic of neoliberal finance capitalism. National self-reliance and policies to sustain resilience are depicted as economically wasteful, and hence doomed to failure by violating "free market" principles, losing out in a Darwinian struggle for economic efficiency, imagined to consist of cutting the cost of labor and of government social programs.

This slashing of long-term social and economic investment to sustain economic resilience is not the classical idea of cutting costs. The classical economists' 19th-century political fight was to cut *rentier* costs. But today's neoliberalism seeks to maximize them, by removing society's ability to protect itself from them. A precondition for breaking away from this anti-government tunnel vision is to recognize that "the market" is controlled by high finance in alliance with predatory rent seekers.

Central to America's financial imperialism is its promotion of an economic ideology (libertarian neoliberalism) controlling how its victims perceive the world, and hence their self-interest. An alternative political economy is required to counteract the neoliberal economic doctrine now taught in schools and propagandized by mass media throughout the world – both part of what former CIA analyst Ray McGovern calls the MICIMATT (Military-Industrial-Congressional-Intelligence-Media-Academia-Think Tank) complex.

The starting point for such an alternative economic and political program obviously should be what to avoid and where the path of financialization and privatization leads. That is what classical political economy was all about. It was based on the distinction between earned and unearned income, defining the latter as economic rent. The following chapters outline the logic that was developed over the past two centuries to counter oligarchic tendencies to polarize and impoverish societies along the lines that today's "free market" Washington Consensus would have the world follow.

4

Economic Rent: Price without Value

A major reason why China has been able to grow so prosperous so
rapidly over the past generation is because it has treated banking
and money creation, education, health care and other basic needs as
public services. That has kept down its cost of living, giving its labor and
industry a cost advantage over economies dominated by a more privatized FIRE sector.

But one great problem exists for any economy: How to keep housing
and commercial real estate affordable so as not to raise the cost of
living and doing business. How can China avoid catching the American
disease of rising house prices, forcing home buyers to go so deeply into
debt that, after paying their mortgage debt service, they have insufficient income remaining to buy enough goods and services to keep the
economy growing and living standards rising?

America's privatized health care absorbs 18 percent of U.S. Gross
Domestic Product (GDP). Many students also need to borrow as much
as $40,000 each year to get a university degree. And topping these U.S.
expenses are rent or mortgage debt charges for housing, which often
absorb over 40 percent of a family's income. Taken together, these
Finance, Insurance and Real Estate (FIRE) sector costs dominate U.S.
GDP growth.

GDP statistics do not depict the rise in housing and debt charges,
interest and even monopoly rents as overhead. Absurd as it may seem,
these overhead charges are held to be the drivers of GDP growth, as
if these payments to the *rentier* sectors reflect a correspondingly rising
product. That illusion has helped deter steps to reverse the U.S. de-industrialization and deepening debt deflation.

The mainstream economic theory taught in Western universities
cannot explain America's industrial failure, any more than it can
explain China's success. A broader approach is needed to avoid the
blind spots of Western neoliberal economics, which depicts the privatization of land rent, bank credit and money creation, health care, education and other basic needs as the way for an economy to get rich. Yet the
result of such privatization is to create a loan market to buy out public

enterprises – which, upon being privatized, impose monopoly rents that require their customers to go into debt to obtain access to these basic services. Inflating housing prices and the cost of obtaining an education on credit requires more income to be spent on servicing rising mortgage debt and student debt, and repayment of automobile loans and credit cards absorbs further income. That forces a rising proportion of personal income to be paid to creditors and their allied *rentier* sectors.

Throughout the West these charges have grown much faster than wages and industrial capital investment. Depicting these *rentier* charges as adding to GDP gives the impression that rent- and debt-ridden economies are growing faster than rent-free and less heavily indebted economies and those whose basic needs are provided publicly. Yet real growth is fastest where the *rentier* element of GDP is lowest and least privatized.

This perception was the essence of 19th-century political economy. No classical economist describing industrial capitalism imagined that the way for an emerging middle class to get rich would be to borrow to buy real estate, whose price would be inflated by bank credit. Adam Smith, John Stuart Mill and his "Ricardian socialist" followers advocated that land rent should become the tax base.

Britain, France and other Western nations spent most of the 19th century fighting to break the power of the hereditary landlord class. Britain's House of Lords and other upper houses of government survived from the Viking-Frankish warlords who conquered Britain and other European lands. By World War I this *rentier* class's stranglehold on political power in national parliaments was ended, and with it their hereditary land rents. Housing and land ownership began to be democratized – but on credit, with governments leaving most of the land's rental value to be paid to the banks as interest.

That has enabled bank profits to soar, because about 80 percent of bank loans in the United States and Britain are for real estate mortgages. The financial and real estate sectors have risen together as larger and more debt-leveraged mortgage loans have bid up real-estate prices. Rental value still exists, but it has been paid to bankers whose mortgage loans enabled the land, housing and commercial real estate to be democratized.

At first, this seemed to be a good thing. After World War II ended in 1945, buying a home became the criterion for being a member of the middle class in the United States and other Western nations. Homes became by far the major asset for most families. Prices rose as general prosperity increased and urban amenities were enhanced, and increasingly by banks increasing the loan-to-value ratio of their credit lines. Easy access to credit enabled absentee landlords to borrow to buy rent-yielding properties with little of their own money, getting rich "in their sleep," as John Stuart Mill expressed it. And the net worth of households soared as real estate was increasingly debt-leveraged.

Home ownership rates rose to over two-thirds of the U.S. population and over 80 percent in much of Europe by the early 2000s. Nearly everyone in the 1940s and 1950s could borrow to buy a home with a 30-year self-amortizing mortgage. Bank lending was limited to sums that would not absorb more than 25 percent of the debtor's income. By the end of 30 years the mortgage would be paid off, leaving the owner's home free and clear of debt.

In the United States the beneficiaries were mainly a white middle class, to be sure. Black neighborhoods were red-lined and denied the civic services and good schools that were raising land and housing prices in the rest of America. Banks would not write mortgages for black buyers even in "good" neighborhoods, and the U.S. Federal Housing Authority (FHA) would not guarantee loans to them. Inner cities were gutted and "white flight" to the suburbs left New York City near bankruptcy in 1974. But beginning in the 1980s, inner cities and slum neighborhoods were torn down and gentrified, creating a new wave of house-price inflation – and the mortgage debt that went with it.

It took less than thirty years for what seemed to be a middle-class dream to turn into a financial nightmare. What inflated housing prices from 1980 onward was bank lending. A property is worth whatever banks are willing to lend against it, and the U.S. FHA and its mortgage financing agencies (headed by the Federal National Mortgage Association, FNMA, popularly called Fannie Mae) helped banks inflate "home-owner wealth" by guaranteeing mortgages, with the permissible level of debt service now having risen to absorb up to 43 percent of the borrower's income. Real estate prices were bid up as banks lent on terms that drove families deeper into debt – but thinking that this was worth it, if housing prices rose even faster than the rate of interest.

Banks became wealthy by financing the purchase of almost every asset, from homes and office buildings to entire corporate buyouts, and also the increasingly privatized public domain. The one part of the economy that did not share in this rising wealth was state and local finance. Untaxing land squeezed U.S. state and city budgets, leading most conspicuously to New York City's near bankruptcy in 1974. Something like a new Enclosure Movement resulted as New York and other cities and states paid their bondholders and other creditors by raising prices for hitherto subsidized public services and selling off public property to private buyers.

The private sector was being turned into a vast Ponzi scheme, needing new buyers and new credit to keep bidding up prices by enough to pay the interest charges. The new buyers borrowed in anticipation of land-price gains being inflated. And for nearly two decades their faith paid off.

But having to pay rising housing costs – along with housing insurance (so that the banks' collateral would not be lost in an accident), other debts, pension and Social Security contributions, health insurance and Medicare – leaves less remaining income to spend on the industrial sector's goods and services. The economy shrinks, except for the One Percent whose wealth comes from owning banks, bonds, stocks and other financial assets that extract debt service and other *rentier* income from the economy's 99 Percent.

This polarization of wealth is an inherent dynamic of finance capitalism – which in turn is characterized by a symbiosis of the Finance, Insurance and Real Estate sectors. Having to pay this FIRE sector for basic needs (not only for housing but also for education and health care) prices labor and industry in financialized *rentier* economies out of world markets. That is what has led to America's de-industrialization. Yet mainstream trade theory treats international prices as reflecting labor costs without distinguishing between *rentier* overhead and more necessary basic costs of living.

This chapter and the next will explain how today's polarization and de-industrialization threat is largely a result of financializing *rentier* income instead of collecting it publicly as the tax base.

How can China best avoid the American problem of becoming "house-poor"?

Rental values and hence housing prices in China will tend to rise as it grows more prosperous. That is natural as income becomes more widely distributed and cities build more transportation and related infrastructure, parks, schools and other urban amenities. But real estate prices ideally should only reflect the intrinsic cost-value embodied in buildings and other capital improvements. Letting these prices be bid up simply by central bank manipulation of interest rates or credit would be to the detriment of the economy's real producers and consumers.

U.S.-style rent and debt deflation (and its associated de-industrialization) may serve as a warning about the dangers of having rising housing prices and rents enrich a class of absentee landlords and their bankers at the expense of the population at large and its spending power. What has happened to the United States, Britain and much of continental Europe is not a natural result of population growth pushing up real estate prices. Housing price inflation is a product of financializing real estate while governments refrain from taxing the land's rent, enabling it to be capitalized into bank credit and turned into a flow of interest payments. Instead of reflecting prosperity, it is *preventing* widespread prosperity.

Taxing the rising rental value of land saves it from being pledged to banks for loans and paid out as interest. Having homeowners pay higher land taxes will have two great benefits: It will prevent debt-driven house-price inflation, and the land tax will be more than offset by freeing homeowners from having to pay income and sales taxes.

Classical economists sought to prevent a *rentier* class appropriating the land's site value for itself. Their solution was to make this rental valuation the natural tax base, because it was better to tax it for the public than to leave it in the hands of a landlord and mortgage-banking class. The best tax system would avoid burdening labor and industry with income taxes and sales and excise taxes on goods and services. Such taxes increase the basic cost of living and hence force up the wages that industrial employers need to pay. Taxes on land, natural-resource rents and monopoly rights are sufficient to defray the costs of government. They do not raise the cost of living or doing business, because the rents that are taxed are not a cost of production. Landlords do not provide any productive service, but merely own the economy's major choke point. The land is simply "there," regardless of how much is (or is not) paid for it.

Avoiding debt-driven housing-price inflation is a precondition for China to remain a low-cost economy – without a predatory landlord class and the financial class that stands behind it. The great virtue of a land tax is that it does not leave the rental value of good sites available to be paid to bankers as mortgage-debt service. That keeps the market price of housing down. The after-tax rent-of-location should leave only enough rent to pay lenders for the cost-value of the building. This way, real estate prices will not be inflated on debt-leveraged credit.

Creating land tenure in proportion to its tax-paying ability – its fiscal rent

The great problem is the political power of vested interests. Absentee landlords and private creditors have always tried to pry the land's rent away from public authorities. Civilization has experienced a struggle for five thousand years over whether government or private individuals will get the land's "free" rent. To show how this struggle has shaped the evolution of land tenure over time, I will start by explaining how land tenure came into being in the first place.

By the 4th millennium BC, Mesopotamia and Egypt had begun to schedule their public corvée labor needs for basic infrastructure – building city walls, temple and palace buildings, and digging irrigation systems – as well as service in the military. To organize and support this labor, standardized land lots were assigned to community members, on the basis of their obligations to perform corvée and military duties.[1] Land was valued in terms of the labor or crop usufruct that a given plot would support.

These archaic corvée labor and military duties were taxes-in-kind. They determined the land tenure assigned to community members, to feed and support labor in performing these duties. Building public works with such labor was the great socializing process of archaic times, with participants being fed large amounts of beer, and also meat at the festivals held during the work periods.

At some point, cultivators were able to commute their labor obligations by paying in crops or other commodities whose monetary value was set by royal fiat or custom as being equivalent to that of the labor or crops that were owed. Similar commutations occurred in medieval Europe.

Labor was the scarce resource in all early societies, including for military duty in a world under almost constant threat of attack. But by the third millennium BC, personal liberty began to be disrupted as interest-bearing debt came to be owed to members of the palace bureaucracy and merchants. Their loans or credit provided the sums owed to the palace that cultivators needed to cover basic expenses during the agricultural year, or for rites of passage or other personal reasons. Creditors typically took interest in the form of labor to work off the debts. In time, they foreclosed on the self-support land debtors pledged as collateral.

The past five thousand years have seen an ongoing conflict between creditors and the governing institutions over who should have priority in receiving the land's rent. In the early Near East from the third to first millennium BC, civic authority had priority, not creditor claims. New

---

[1] For more details see my article, "How the Organization of Labor Shaped Civilization's Takeoff," in Piotr Steinkeller and Michael Hudson (eds.), *Labor in the Ancient World* (Dresden: 2015), pp. 649-64. The land was not simply taken by individuals who monopolized it and made its cultivators pay rent to use it. Palaces would have lost labor and crop rent. Any archaic community permitting this would have quickly lost its members. Money was first developed as a means of denominating payment to palaces and temples for the obligations associated with land tenure. Austrian and other individualistic speculations leave these large institutions out of account, and thus fail to see how land and its rent originally were a public utility.

rulers taking the throne normally annulled the personal debts of cultivators, liberated bondservants and returned to the debtor's family the slaves or land that had been pledged to creditors.[2]

These royal acts re-asserted the ruler's power to claim corvée labor, military service and crop taxes. By restoring the "normal" distribution of land and personal liberty, that made the debtor's loss and forfeiture only temporary. But despite numerous early revolts in classical Greece and many popular demands for debt cancellation in Rome, antiquity did not inherit from the Near East this practice of more or less regular Clean Slates. Down through the modern world, the land's rent has been shifting away from paying taxes to paying interest to private creditors.

Where kings survived, as in early Rome, they were overthrown by landowning warlord oligarchies that accumulated the land of smallholders by lending and foreclosing, or simply grabbing it by force. Rome's leading Senate families wrote pro-creditor laws to entrench their power, and this spirit of the law survived the collapse of Rome's Empire to serve as a fundamental element of Western legal philosophy ever since.

The main legacy surviving from European feudalism was a hereditary landlord class. After the Norman invasion of England in 1066, William the Conqueror ordered compilation of the Domesday Book to calculate how much rent could be extracted from English land, and appointed his companions as local warlords to administer it. A century later, when King John (1199-1216) abused his power, the land barons who were the heirs of William's conquerors led a revolt and forced the king to sign the Magna Carta in 1215. That went a long way toward privatizing the land's rent for the warlord aristocracy. Similar privatizations occurred throughout Europe, endowing a hereditary *rentier* class with tribute that absorbed most of the economy's surplus for themselves and the kings – with many members of the nobility being in hock to creditors such as the Templars and Italian bankers.

Kings spent most of their taxes on tribute to the papacy and payments to these bankers for credit, especially to wage wars to conquer foreign rent-yielding land. That left less revenue for investing in industrial capital formation. The silver and booty seized from the New World by Spain and Portugal, for example, flowed right through them to other

---

[2] Such royal amnesties are documented down through the early 1st millennium BC. I document these royal proclamations in "*... and forgive them their debts*": *Credit and Redemption From Bronze Age Finance to the Jubilee Year* (Dresden: 2018). See also Michael Hudson and Marc Van De Mieroop (eds.), *Debt and Economic Renewal in the Ancient Near East* (Bethesda: 2002).

countries from which they purchased luxuries and war materials, instead of being used for productive investment opportunities at home.

The "Adam Smith Tax" on land rent as the focal point of classical value and price theory

Rents and taxes in 18th-century France were so high that its domestic industry could not compete with that of Britain and other European countries. A group of reformers clustered around the royal surgeon, Dr. Francois Quesnay, who created the first major statistical accounting format, the *Tableau Économique* (1758), to trace the circulation of revenue within the French economy. Calling themselves the Physiocrats or *Les Économistes*, they traced how the landlord class and royal estate appropriated almost all of France's economic surplus – the *produit net* (net product) – as land rent. In order for France to industrialize and become more affluent, the Physiocrats argued, it had to break free from its *rentier* overhead.

Among the visitors to France was Adam Smith. Upon returning to Scotland, he adopted the major Physiocratic reform proposal: Taxes should fall on the land, not on labor or industrial capital. Private ownership of the land was a chokepoint to extract the value of its crop surplus over and above the cultivator's living costs and the expenses necessary to produce crops. "Landlords love to reap where they have not sown," Smith wrote in *The Wealth of Nations* (1776), "and demand a rent even for its [the land's] natural produce." Driving the point home, he added: "The dearness of house-rent in London arises ... above all the dearness of groundrent, every landlord acting the part of a monopolist."[3]

Ricardo's theory of differential land rent

Taxing land rent was politically difficult, because the landlord class controlled the upper houses of parliaments throughout Europe. But various vested interests, including bankers and other advocates of industrialization, began to criticize landlord demands for higher rents in the wake of the 1789 French Revolution, which led to Napoleon's wars to spread liberal reforms.

---

[3] Adam Smith, *Wealth of Nations*, Book I, Ch. 6 §8, and Ch. 10 §55. Smith added that landownership privileges "are founded on the most absurd of all suppositions, the supposition that every successive generation of men has not an equal right to the earth ... but that the property of the present generation should be ... regulated according to the fancy of those who died ... five hundred years ago," that is, the Norman conquerors (Book III, Ch. 2 §6).

His war with Britain started in 1798 and continued until 1815, imposing a Continental barrier that disrupted Britain's seaborne commerce.

Unable to import as much food as usual, Britain was forced to fall back on its domestic farming sector. Crop prices rose to reflect the more limited and high-cost supply. Upon the return to peace in 1815, British landlords sought to maintain the high agricultural rents that they had enjoyed during the years of wartime isolation, by persuading Parliament to impose tariffs on food imports – the Corn Laws. The effect was to artificially maintain high domestic crop prices.

The ensuing three-decade fight over the Corn Laws (which finally were repealed in 1846) became the occasion for a landmark debate between Thomas Robert Malthus arguing on behalf of Britain's land-lords, and David Ricardo, the parliamentary spokesman for the nation's banking class. Although industry was not yet a major bank client, the major bank market lay in financing foreign trade. Bankers therefore had an interest in promoting industry to promote an international division of labor in which Britain would be the "workshop of the world," exporting manufactures in exchange for foreign raw materials and handicrafts.[4]

At the center of the trade debate was the concept of economic rent that Ricardo refined as part of his argument against protective tariffs, doing so in the process of explaining how Britain might achieve an industrial cost advantage by freeing its economy from high crop prices and land rents supported by protective agricultural tariffs. A cost advantage for British manufacturers required minimizing the wages they had to pay – the basic wage, determined by the cost of living, headed by the price of food.

Minimizing the cost of feeding wage earners required obtaining low-priced food from abroad. That required repealing the protectionist Corn Laws so as to buy much less expensive grain from the United States, Latin America and other less industrialized countries. And repeal of these laws meant lower land rents. This logic of foreign trade advantage set the needs and political dynamic of industrial capitalism against Britain's *rentier* aristocracy.

---

[4] When Western economies began to recover in the 12th century (thanks largely to the monetary loot grabbed by the Crusaders when they sacked Constantinople), Christian law had banned usury, but permitted a loophole for banks to charge foreign-exchange agio fees for the service of transferring payments from one country or currency to another. The banking class's interest therefore was to increase international trade and its specialization of production between industrial Britain and countries providing its industrialists with raw materials.

The resulting controversy prompted Ricardo to write in 1815, soon after the Treaty of Ghent restored peace to Europe: "The interest of the landlords is always opposed to the interest of every other class in the community."[5] For Ricardo, "the community" meant mainly his own banking class and the industrialists that he hoped would produce exports. As for the wage-earning class, Ricardo assumed that wages would tend to remain at the subsistence level in any event.

Ricardo spent the next two years writing *On the Principles of Political Economy and Taxation* (1817). Chapter 2 defined economic rent in terms of classical value and price theory. His discussion (and Malthus's response) helped shape classical value and rent theory for the remainder of the century. Value was defined in terms of necessary costs of production, ultimately reducible to the cost of the labor.[6] But many products sold for higher prices, especially the products of agriculture. Ricardo believed that crop prices would rise as a result of diminishing fertility on marginal soils, which would need to be brought into cultivation to feed the growing population. Diminishing returns would lead crop prices to be set by the highest-cost producers. That would leave more rent in the hands of owners of more fertile land with lower costs of production. The excess of market price over and above the costs to these low-cost producers was called differential economic rent.

Ignoring the role of agricultural chemistry, Ricardo thought that the land's fertility differentials were permanent, persisting even after land was improved.[7] Each plot of land was held to receive a distinct rental income in accordance with its inherent fertility differential, with the poorest and most marginal land not yielding any rent at all. For him,

---

[5] Ricardo, *Essay on the Influence of a Low Price of Corn on the Profits of Stock* (London: 1815), p. 21. To be sure, city merchants typically looked forward to investing their wealth in landed estates (as Roman merchants had done), and Ricardo himself had bought Gatcombe Park as the family seat in 1814.

[6] Numerous writers already had described the basic elements of this theory. Their writings are reviewed in Marx's *Theories of Surplus Value*, Vol. II (Moscow: 1968), compiled posthumously by Karl Kautsky from Marx's notes. The three volumes of that work reveal how Marx came to refine his labor theory of value as an outgrowth of classical rent and exploitation theory, and thus are complementary to the corresponding three volumes of Marx's *Capital*.

[7] Ricardo, *Principles of Political Economy and Taxation*, 3rd ed. (London: 1821), p. 67. He added (pp. 412-13): "Improvements in agriculture ... increase the quantity of raw produce obtained from each [plot], but probably do not disturb the relative proportions which before existed between the original and indestructible powers of the soil."

there was only differential rent, not absolute monopoly rent. By contrast, James Andersen and David Buchanan described "absolute" monopoly rent as existing over and above the differential rent that Ricardo described, although Buchanan believed that the major cost differences stemmed from capital productivity and transport costs.[8]

Heinrich von Thünen emphasized the latter, replacing Ricardo's idea of fertility differentials with the rent of location. In *The Isolated State with Respect to Agriculture and Political Economy* (1826), he created the formula $R = Y(p - c) - Yfm$. Land rent (R) was the market price (p) of its yield per land unit (Y), less the cost of production (c), and less the transport costs, which were determined by the freight rate for the crop per mile (f), multiplied by the distance over which the crop had to be transported to market (m).

Adam Smith had recognized the rent of location: "The corn which grows within a mile of the town, sells for the same price with that which comes from twenty miles distant," but the latter must bear the costs of shipping the crop to the urban market.[9] Rent of location thus was supplied by geography, and increased as the economy's overall prosperity increased. If crops had to be brought from further away, their supply price rose, with the "rentless land" being the most distant.

By the end of the 19th century the rent of location was recognized as resulting not only from transport costs but also from public amenities (parks, schools and museums), urban improvements and the special desirability or prestige of certain neighborhoods. But the major rent of location indeed results from convenient transportation. And that rental value of land is often sufficient to cover public expenses for basic needs. When London, for example, spent £3.4 billion to extend the Jubilee tube line to the Canary Wharf financial district, the capital improvement raised the valuation of land along the route by over £10 billion. The entire cost of this public construction could have been defrayed by taxing the land's increased rent-of-location – an unearned free lunch. Instead, London taxed wage earnings and profits. Taxpayers bore the

---

[8] Ricardo, *Principles*, 3rd ed., p. 71. Adam Smith (above) had referred to land as a monopoly, as had David Buchanan, *Observations on the Subjects Treated of in Dr. Smith's Wealth of Nations* (Edinburgh: 1817), pp. 34 and 37. Joan Robinson, *The Accumulation of Capital* (London: 1956), pp. 289-93, emphasized rent as a monopoly "good," reflecting the fact that all land is scarce. That point was made also by Thomas Perronet Thompson, *The True Theory of Rent, in Opposition to Mr. Ricardo* (London: 1826), p. 6.

[9] Smith, *Wealth of Nations*, Book III, Ch. 1.

cost, while "land owners contributed nothing towards the increased value that accrued to their assets."[10]

A similar rent-of-location giveaway occurred when New York City built its Second Avenue subway for about $3 billion. Rents and property prices rose along the new route by a reported $6 billion, because people no longer had to walk a mile to the overcrowded Lexington subway. That increase in rental valuation was much more than enough to cover what it cost the city to build the system. That cost could have been met by imposing a "rent recapture" tax on the land sites whose market prices rose. Instead, the city borrowed and paid interest to bondholders, and increased income taxes on labor and business. That made the city's cost of living and doing business higher – while landlords received a windfall without effort or new investment of their own.

Seeing that bus and subway lines, streets and other public infrastructure enhance real estate's site value, Thorstein Veblen described American urban politics as being concerned mainly with civic improvement projects to promote real estate for the benefit of land speculators. His 1923 book *Absentee Ownership and Business Enterprise in Recent Times* pointed out that most cities should be viewed as real estate development projects by property owners seeking to increase prices for their holdings, looking to sell at a gain.[11] The aim of public infrastructure spending in the United States is indeed to increase land prices. Real estate developers try to keep all the land-price gains for themselves, making the public pay for the cost of enhancing their rent of location.

Joseph Stiglitz has caused some confusion by coining what he called the Henry George Theorem in 1977: Under certain conditions, beneficial investments in public services, most notably transportation, parks and other improvements, will increase aggregate land rents by at least as much as the investments cost.[12] But George had no classical value and price theory. He emphasized rural land, above all absentee English

---

[10] Fred Harrison, *Ricardo's Law* (London: 2006), p. 83, and Don Riley, *Taken for a Ride: Trains, Taxpayers and the Treasury* (London: 2001).

[11] *Absentee Ownership and Business Enterprise in Recent Times* (New York: 1923), pp. 142ff. I discuss this in "Veblen's Institutionalist Elaboration of Rent Theory," in Michael Hudson and Ahmet Öncü (eds), *Absentee Ownership and its Discontents: Critical essays on the Legacy of Thorstein Veblen* (Dresden: 2016). Veblen's point was that the cost of these improvements is made at public expense, to benefit the real estate developers who dominate local politics in most cities and states.

[12] Joseph E. Stiglitz, "The Theory of Local Public Goods," in Martin S. Feldstein and R. P. Inman (eds.), *The Economics of Public Services* (London: 1977), pp. 274–333.

landlordship in Ireland, not urban land. The rent-and-improvement "theorem" really was developed by Veblen, who also focused on the role of politics and fiscal financing.

Most land-price gains attributable to rent-of-location stem from public infrastructure investment that makes neighborhoods more desirable. Who should get the benefit of such improvements? How should cities and municipalities pay for the cost of improving the means of transportation and other neighborhood amenities? What seems most fair is to finance such improvements by taxing back the increased rental value of the land sites. Otherwise, landlords will receive free rental value at public expense. The result of *not* taxing this rise in rents is to channel an increasing proportion of national income to landlords, and ultimately to the finance sector at the expense of wages and profits, as Ricardo proceeded to explain in his analysis.

Rent deflation as industrial capitalism's Armageddon

Ricardo warned that rising land rent was the great threat to industrial capitalism's survival. It would raise the cost of living and hence employment of industrial labor by crowding out profits. That result may be called rent deflation. "The natural tendency of profits then is to fall; for, in the progress of society and wealth, the additional quantity of food required is obtained by the sacrifice of more and more labor,"[13] assuming (erroneously) diminishing returns from new land brought into cultivation. As Marx summarized Ricardo's theory, the limit on "the capital that can be applied with a profit would be reached at the point where food prices (and the associated wage levels) were so high that the employment of industrial labor no longer could provide the industrialist with a profit. The economy and its population at that point would reach its upper limit, and new capital investment and employment would stop."

That process could be postponed temporarily, Ricardo acknowledged,

> by the improvements in machinery, connected with the production of necessaries, as well as by discoveries in the science of agriculture which enable us to relinquish a portion of labour before required, and therefore to lower the price of the prime necessary of the labourer. The rise in the price of necessaries and in the wages of labour is however limited; for as soon as wages should be equal ... to ... the whole receipts of the farmer, there must be an end of accumulation; for no capital can then yield any profit whatever, and no additional labour can be demanded, and con-

---

[13] Ricardo, *Principles*, 3rd ed., Ch. 6: "On Profits," pp. 120f., cited in Marx, *Theories of Surplus Value*, Vol. II, p. 544.

sequently population will have reached its highest point. Long indeed before this period the very low rate of profits will have arrested all accumulation, and almost the whole produce of the country, after paying the labourers, will be the property of the owners of land and the receivers of tithes and taxes.[14]

"This, as Ricardo sees it," summarized Marx, "is the bourgeois 'Twilight of the Gods' – the Day of Judgement." Despite the increase in technological productivity and wealth, real estate and other natural resources (and implicitly, natural monopolies) would concentrate a rising proportion of income in the hands of *rentiers*, whose rent (R) was unearned. That is the central message of classical value and rent theory.

Rent (R) is the excess of Price (P) over Value (V), so R = P – V. As the excess of market price (P) over intrinsic cost-value (V), rent has no counterpart in necessary costs of production. Rent recipients have no out-of-pocket costs for supplying landlordship or monopoly "services" for what basically are transfer payments, that is, income with no socially necessary *quid pro quo*. All economic rent thus is by definition unearned, since it is not based on necessary costs of production. Land has no cost of production, any more than air or mineral wealth in the ground yielding natural-resource rents, or marketing privileges yielding monopoly rents.

Farming in today's world has become so industrialized and treated with fertilizers that Ricardo's theory of differential agricultural rent has become one of the least significant areas of rent seeking. There is, to be sure, substantial monopoly rent in the case of the great grain-trading monopolies such as Cargill and Archer-Daniels, and seed bioengineering from Monsanto-Bayer. But the rent of location is now minimal for agriculture. Canning companies and stockyards have moved closer to production sites and transport charges have been lowered. By far most land rent is urban, much of it reflecting public infrastructure investment and amenities. What remains, however, is the concept of economic rent generalized beyond land to the FIRE sector, natural resources and monop-

---

[14] *Principles*, 3rd ed., p. 123. Ricardo adds: "Long before this state of prices was becoming permanent, there would be no motive for accumulation; for no one accumulates but with a view to make his accumulation productive, and ... consequently such a state of prices never could take place. The farmer and manufacturer can no more live without profit, than the laborer without wages. Their motive for accumulation will diminish with every diminution of profit, and will cease altogether when their profits are so low as not to afford them an adequate compensation for their trouble, and the risk which they must necessarily encounter in employing their capital productively."

olies in communications and the broadcasting spectrum, transportation and other infrastructure, and in patented pharmaceuticals, biotech and information technology.

The political fight to tax land, from John Stuart Mill to subsequent land taxers

Ricardo argued that the way for a nation's manufacturers to win the competition for foreign markets was to cut costs, starting with what employers had to pay to cover the necessities of life, headed by food. The way to minimize this labor cost was to minimize land rent. To Ricardo that meant free trade. His theory of differential land rent did not aim to tax away the landlord's rental income or the rise in land prices as later 19th-century economists would advocate. But after the trade issue had been settled by repeal of the Corn Laws in 1846, British reformers sought to free economies from private land rent and, by logical extension, to prevent predatory monopoly pricing by other rent-seekers.

This drive to cut *rentier* income was inherent in industrial capitalism in countries where landlords and monopolists enjoyed special privileges, as they did in Britain, whose House of Lords blocked reforms proposed by the House of Commons. This division of government into two chambers appears already in history's earliest written records in the third millennium BC. The Sumerian epic of Gilgamesh describes the men of military age (in Greek the *demos*, the root of *democracy*) voting on whether to go to war. Drafting laws seems to have been made by councils of elders (Rome's Senate, as in *seniors*). That kind of bicameral congress has survived down to the modern world, with the population at large struggling against the upper chamber's *rentier* interests since classical antiquity.

Most populations in ancient societies had one ultimate recourse: to refuse to fight for regimes that they considered oppressive; or, what was the same thing, to walk out, as in Rome's repeated Secessions of the Plebs seeking debt cancellation and land redistribution. But oligarchic *rentier* power was not checked in the Roman Empire, nor after the Middle Ages as wealthy hereditary landowners continued to dominate the upper houses of European governments. The landlord class, along with the bankers, used their wealth to control governments and shift the tax burden off themselves onto labor and industry. As Richard Cobden summarized in 1842:

> It certainly was only when the power of the state had fallen into the hands of a landed oligarchy that the people were taxed in order to

exempt the landowners. At the time of the conquest, and for the succeed-
ing 150 years, the proportion of tax contributed by the land amounted
to nineteen-twentieths of the whole revenue of the kingdom. From that
period down to the reign of Richard the 3rd, the proportion contributed
by the land was nine-tenths; thence, to the time of Mary, it was three-
fourths; to the end of the Commonwealth it was one-half; to the time of
Anne one-fourth; in the time of George 1st one-fifth; of George 2nd one-
sixth; for the first thirty years of George 3rd one-seventh; from 1793 to
1816 one-ninth; and from that time to the present only one-twenty-fifth.

The land-tax was a fraudulent evasion, for it was in reality a substitution for feudal tenure. The land was formerly held by right of feudal
services. The honourable gentleman quoted a passage from Blackstone,
describing the commutation of feudal services into a land-tax of 4 shil-
lings in the pound on the real rental. Now could anyone suppose that
land would always remain at the valuation of 1692? And yet it was upon
that valuation that the land-tax was charged.[15]

Throughout Europe the aristocratic upper houses of government
protected landlords against democratic reformers. Challenging the
landlord class therefore required democratic political reform to free
the Commons from veto by the upper house. In Britain this fight cul-
minated in the 1909-10 constitutional crisis when the House of Lords
rejected a land-tax bill that the Commons had passed. Matters were
resolved by a ruling that the Lords never again could veto a revenue act
passed by the Commons.

It is a reflection of how global the campaign for land-tax reform
became that in Qingdao, in Shandong province, the German colonial
administrator and land reformer Wilhelm Schrameier adopted a 6
percent land tax in 1897. Sun Yat Sen visited the town in 1912 and
called its land tax a model for China's future. His *Three Principles of the
People* opposed letting land rent be paid to landlords, and extended this
same principle to public infrastructure: "The railroads, public utilities,
canals, and forests should be nationalized, and all income from the land
and mines should be in the hands of the State. With this money in hand,
the State can therefore finance the social welfare programs."[16]

Taxing the land was less revolutionary than nationalizing or socializing it outright, as John Stuart Mill and other "Ricardian socialists"
sought to do after the Corn Laws were repealed in 1846. The theory of

---

[15] Richard Cobden: Corn Bill, Burdens on Land (House of Commons Debate, 14
March 1842, Vol 61 cc519-81).

[16] Cited in Karl Williams, "Sun Yat Sen and Georgism," at https://www.prosper.
org.au/geoists-in-history/sun-yat-sen-and-georgism/, and Simei Qing, *From Allies to*

land rent was elaborated beyond what Ricardo had advocated, to justify taxing land-price gains and to make rent the national tax base. Socialists aimed to restore land to the public domain, just as mines and other natural resources and basic infrastructure had long belonged to the public sector. An argument percolated over whether governments should buy out the landlords' holdings. Just as Americans opposed paying Southern slave owners for having freed the slaves and erased their value as chattels, it was argued that rights to land originally granted for the public benefit should simply be treated as non-compensable property if taken back for public use. Buying out the landlord class would simply convert it into a dominant financial class. And as estates came to be taxed, many landlords did sell their land to invest in financial markets.

Rent theory extended to monopoly rents in industry

By the end of the 19th century the concept of land rent as unearned income – the excess of price over necessary costs of production (value) – was extended to monopoly rent as well, especially to keep basic infrastructure in the public domain instead of being privatized, *e.g.*, roads and railroads, health care, the post office and communications. In industry, Alfred Marshall's *Principles of Economics* (1890) described quasi-rents as accruing as "super-profit" to low-cost producers, under market conditions where prices were set by the older higher-cost producers. This technically is what Ricardo called "differential rent," but in addition, there is monopoly pricing – control of a product to charge what the market will bear, regardless of production costs.

Marx elaborated the idea of monopoly rent as an exploitative charge into a critique of industrial profits made by employing wage labor. However, to the extent that the industrial capitalist played a productive role in organizing enterprise, profit was a productive category of revenue, because it created surplus value.[17] Rent and interest payments,

---

Enemies: Visions of Modernity, Identity and U.S.-China Diplomacy, 1945-1960 (Cambridge, MA: 2007), p. 19. See also Michael Silagi, "Land Reform in Kiaochow, China: From 1898 to 1914 the Menace of Disastrous Land Speculation was Averted by Taxation," *American Journal of Economics and Sociology* 43 (1984), pp. 167-77. (Qingdao is now known for its German beer-making practice introduced at the Tsingtao Brewery.)

[17] Marx placed that analysis in Volume I of *Capital*, leaving Volumes II and III to discuss the concepts of economic rent and compound interest that his predecessors already had reviewed and analyzed. His focus was on how these pre-industrial institutions survived under industrial capitalism and were to become subordinate to capitalism's guiding logic of cost cutting and economic rationalization.

along with monopoly rents, played no such productive role, and were economically unnecessary for production to take place. Such *rentier* income was to be explained politically and historically, as carry-overs from earlier modes of production. Likewise in the United States, the Institutionalist school described rent as a social and legal phenomenon carving out special privileges.[18]

A "factor of production" creates value, reflecting a cost of production ultimately reducible to that of labor. But nature provides land and sunlight freely. There may be a legal cost to appropriate and monopolize them, but no initial cost of production for labor or other payments. Their economic rent, being a charge without cost, is unearned, an element of price without underlying value. Such rents are transfer payments to privileged recipients, without a *quid pro quo*, not earned by contributing to economic growth and prosperity.

Rent-extracting privileges require a state-created title. That is why rent seekers aim at controlling governments to obtain such title, and to prevent it from being taken away. Land rent is a tollbooth charge for such a privilege. Land can be fenced off and access charges imposed. The "rights" to do so are created by legal and political privileges. But these privileges are distinct from the technologically necessary costs of production.

There isn't a charge for air – so far – because nobody has been able to monopolize it. The radio spectrum is like land in the sense that radio-wave frequencies are simply there, provided by nature. But the fact that radio production and broadcasting cannot take place without them enables rent-seeking opportunities to be created by levying an access charge or licensing fee. Water can be appropriated and sold instead of being left freely available, just as land can be cordoned off, legally as well as physically. Landlords, bankers and others are empowered to put up barriers or tollbooths to block entry by users of an otherwise free resource (a tollbooth on a road, a legal property title over land, a patent on an invention, or the privilege to create bank credit and charge interest on it).

De-privatizing rent as the classical free market reform

Today's anti-classical reaction has erased the concept of rent as unearned income and market price without cost-value. All income is said to be earned. Not only is land a "factor of production" deserving of

---

[18] I describe this in "Simon Patten on Public Infrastructure and Economic Rent Capture," *American Journal of Economics and Sociology* 70 (October 2011), pp. 873-903.

rent, but credit creation also is counted as a factor of production. That is the logic for including financial fees (including late fees and penalties) as part of GDP. The logic is that this buildup of debt (credit) is needed to finance production and also the distribution and sale of products and the assets that produce them.

The implication is that providing more bank credit to bid up housing prices on rising debt-to-value ratios makes the economy wealthier. Certainly most of the net worth of the American middle class consists of its housing. In that respect the rise in U.S. housing prices has endowed a middle class with household wealth. But in time – and that time has now been reached – it becomes economically self-destructive for society to try and get rich by buying housing whose market price is constantly being bid up by debt. Banks are winning the fight with the tax collector over whether land rent should be the tax base or be left to be paid out as mortgage interest.

Turning land rent into mortgage interest paid to banks instead of to the tax collector has raised the cost of housing and increased the debt overhead. The way to prevent debt-leveraged increases in housing prices is to tax land rent so as to prevent it from being capitalized into bank loans. Taxing land rent and minimizing other forms of rent would free wages and profits from taxes that raise the cost of living and doing business.

China today has become the workshop of the world, largely by restraining (so far) the *rentier* class responsible for de-industrializing the U.S. and other Western economies. The government is the nominal owner of the land. But if it does not tax the full site value, the rising rent-of-location will end up being paid to the banks as interest, as has occurred in the United States.

Chapter 5 will describe how banks are replacing landlords as the ultimate recipients of land rent throughout today's world. Ricardo had seen only an allegedly natural material cause, diminishing soil fertility, as increasing food costs and agricultural land rents. He did not acknowledge interest and financial fees as increasing the cost of living at the expense of industrial competitiveness, profits and investment. Whereas he envisioned landlords as monopolizing society's income, today's *rentier* oligarchy, centered in the FIRE sector, has replaced the post-feudal landlord aristocracy, and the rise in land rents that increases the cost of living for wage-earners is now largely a result of the debt-financed rise in housing prices. The effect is debt deflation, which plays the role that rent deflation played in Ricardo's analysis.

5

Financializing Rent and Imposing Debt Deflation

The 19th century's fight to tax away land rents nearly succeeded, but lost momentum after World War I. The most obvious reason is political: Land ownership has been democratized, no longer monopolized by the heirs of warlord aristocracies living off their hereditary land rents. Yet the beneficiaries have not been governments, which are collecting only a fraction of the rent that classical economists hoped to make the tax base. Nor has the private sector been freed from having to pay land rent. It still is being paid, but mainly to bankers as mortgage interest.

Democratizing home ownership and other real estate has made mortgage credit the major market for banks, accounting for about 80 percent of bank loans in the United States and Britain. Real estate lending has become banking's most profitable arm, leading bankers to lobby against property taxes, knowing that whatever rent is not taxed will be available to be paid to themselves as interest on loans to the new buyers of property.

Interest and other financial fees are much like the rents taken by the old landed aristocracy. Both forms of *rentier* income are unearned, and indeed have merged, with finance dominant and taking the lead in the symbiotic FIRE sector, which includes insurance, as Chapter 4 has described. Borrowers are required to take out insurance to protect the banks against loss of the collateral they take for their loans, and within the FIRE sector, banks and speculators gamble on taking out credit-default insurance. (That is what brought A.I.G. down in 2008.) This merger of the leading forms of rent and *rentier* interests has enabled today's financial oligarchy to usurp the dominant role that the landed aristocracy occupied in the past. Bankers now are the ultimate recipients of land rents, which are converted into interest charges by the creation of mortgage credit.

Interest as the paradigmatic form of economic rent

The idea of financial returns as "sterile" goes back to Aristotle asking how a barren metal (silver money) could be said to yield interest. Debtors did the work to pay, not the moneylenders. Classical economists echoed this logic in questioning how hereditary rights to demand land rent could be considered "earnings." These rights were a privilege (the Latin roots of which mean "private law"), that of owning a choke point able to block others from using the land without paying groundrent, just as a monopolist owning a toll road can deny users access unless they pay a fee.

All forms of *rentier* income – land rent, monopoly rent and interest – derive from state-granted legal privileges, sanctimoniously called "rights," ranging from rights to land and subsoil mineral resources to "intellectual property rights" and other monopolies, headed by banking and money-creating privileges. Such privileges are obtained from governments, and thus they and the rents resulting from them are political rather than technologically necessary costs of production.

Economically, rents deriving from these privileges are transfer payments, in the sense that they do not create a product but merely appropriate revenue in a zero-sum relationship. Yet post-classical national income accounting defines all such rents as "earnings." This usage reflects how little advocacy survives for ending *rentier* exploitation.

The term "rent" is derived from French *rente*, a government bond yielding a fixed income at regular intervals. An obvious parallel exists with landlords collecting agricultural rent at harvest time, or monthly rents for townhouses. The common denominator is a legal privilege to receive income through a property claim, not by one's labor or as a result of direct business costs of production. As Chapter 4 has described, such rent is defined as the excess of price over cost-value. Land has no inherent cost of production, but is appropriated or bought by landlords to charge groundrent to tenants or by homebuyers to enjoy for themselves. Bankers create credit on which they charge interest, with only a nominal marginal cost of creating this credit.

Already in the 13th century the Schoolmen discussed what should be a fair return to bankers for money-changing and whether charging interest itself was fair. To prevent exploitative unearned income, they focused on bringing prices in line with the necessary costs of production. That approach ultimately evolved into value theory at the hands of French and British political economists in the 18th and 19th centuries.

It hardly is surprising that Ricardo turned rent theory away from this early focus on interest. As a bond broker and the most renowned spokesman in Parliament for Britain's banking sector, he was not about to depict finance in a bad light. Nowhere in his labor and rent theory of value and price do interest or debt charges appear, nor do they enter into his trade theory of international cost structures and comparative advantage in Chapter 7 of his *Principles*.

By the 20th century, Frank Knight and his Chicago School adopted the medieval rationale for interest as reflecting the banker's risk of not being repaid. But today's banks avoid risk by lending only against collateral and making debtors pay the cost of insurance against loss. The financial sector also has obtained government guarantees for mortgage loans (via the FHA in the United States) and, ultimately, bailouts.

When excessive bank lending and debt extraction threatens to create a crash, bankers turn to government to save them from having to take a major loss. To avoid a widespread wave of bankruptcies and bank losses, the U.S. and European governments pursued a policy of Quantitative Easing from 2009 onward, and provided a new surge of support for real estate, stock and bond prices in 2020-21 to cope with the Covid-19 crisis. The financial sector's takeover of government's regulatory, law-making and enforcement power and central-bank policy leaves interest charges as almost pure economic rent.

Land rent is for paying mortgage interest

Nearly two-thirds of Americans own their own homes, and over four-fifths of Scandinavians. Unlike the case in antiquity, when running into debt was the first step toward losing the homestead, the 20th century enabled most families in the West to buy homes of their own – by taking on debt. Most families require credit to buy their homes. They can borrow the purchase price from the bank by signing a mortgage contract. Successful bidders pledge the rent that used to be paid to absentee landlords to mortgage bankers, who end up with this rent as interest.

Chart 5.1 Composition of U.S. Real Estate EBITDA, 1930-2015

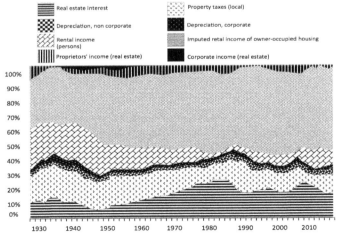

The financial sector has absorbed the real-estate sector, creating the FIRE sector

The aim of banks is not to take formal ownership of real estate. What they want is the land's rent. To end up with most of it, they lobby to block the government's tax take. They are happy to leave homeowners with formal ownership title and, as such, liable for all taxes, and also for buying casualty insurance to protect the collateral that they have to pledge to their banks in exchange for mortgage loans.

Fannie Mae and Freddie Mac pushed the U.S. home ownership rate to 69 percent during 1995-2008 by insuring borrowers. Easier credit terms obliged prospective buyers to bid against each other to see who would pay bankers the highest amount. Families found themselves obliged to take on a lifetime of debt before prices for homes rose even further. The result is that nearly two-thirds of the market value of U.S. residential real estate is now held by creditors, while homeowners' equity has declined from 85 percent when World War II ended to just over one-third today.[1] Homeowners' equity becomes much lower as one moves down the income, wealth, racial and age scales.

The insurance sector is the third component of the symbiosis between finance and real estate. Banks oblige new home buyers to buy insurance as a condition of signing their mortgage contract. Insurance companies also serve as financial intermediaries for personal savings in the form of life insurance policies and annuities, and most recently as issuers of collateralized debt obligations (CDOs) and credit-default swaps to shift the risk of debt default. The core of modern finance capitalism is thus the Finance, Insurance and Real Estate (FIRE) sector. It siphons off land rent and monopoly rents in the form of interest, financial and insurance charges at the expense of wages, profits and tax revenue.

Financializing monopoly rent

From antiquity until quite recently, Europeans kept natural monopolies and essential infrastructure in the public domain. Public institutions subsidized user fees so as to minimize the economy's cost structure. But

---

[1] Annual Chart, Federal Reserve Board, Balance Sheet of U.S. Households, Line 50: Homeowners equity. After the junk-mortgage bubble peaked in 2007, the debt/equity ratio rose over 50% for the first time. The U.S. home ownership rate reached 69 percent by 2008, but the rate fell to 63.4 percent by 2016 after the wave of Obama foreclosures on victims of junk mortgage loans. Meanwhile, the remaining homeowners have "owned" less and less of their homes, with mortgage lenders owed most of the property valuation.

Margaret Thatcher's privatizations of British Telecom, bus lines and other sectors in the 1980s enabled the new buyers to raise consumer prices, generating enormous stock-market gains in the ensuing race to the bottom with the usual deterioration of services. The gates were thrown open to the financial sector, long known as "the mother of monopolies," seeing and promoting privatization of key infrastructure as an opportunity to extract monopoly rents, just as it has defended and lobbied for monopoly rent extraction in oil and gas, heavy industry and information technology.

It is an old story. When the United States left railroads and other key infrastructure in private hands, it produced so great a disaster that it led to anti-trust regulation by the end of the 19th century, headed by the Interstate Commerce Commission's regulation of railway fares and the Sherman Antitrust Act of 1890. The aim of anti-trust regulation was to limit prices to the necessary costs of producing the goods or services of natural monopolies. Local and federal agencies regulated public utilities for electric power and gas, canals, and toll roads such as the Pennsylvania Turnpike, as well as for telephone systems and other communications. Payment of interest and dividends was limited to specific rates of return, while blocking privatized companies from increasing their prices by "watered costs" such as stock options or bonds issued to insiders, and other charges deemed unnecessary for production to take place.

But the past half-century's economic deregulation has all but stopped anti-monopoly legislation globally. Economies and politics are still dominated by the One Percent, mainly creditors who see monopolies and other rent-seekers as their most lucrative customers. Shifting economic planning away from elected governments to Wall Street, the City of London, Frankfurt, the Paris Bourse and other financial centers has re-created the power that the One Percent formerly wielded via the House of Lords and other upper houses of government. Financial control and rent extraction are thus achieved peacefully and even democratically, supported by mass media while business schools indoctrinate students to believe that this is all for the best.

Long active in organizing industrial trusts to control prices and markets, the banking sector has largely ignored credit to finance productive capital investment. In his draft notes on "Interest-Bearing Capital and Commercial Capital in Relation to Industrial Capital" for what became Volume III of *Capital* and Part III of *Theories of Surplus Value*, Marx wrote optimistically about how the historical task of industrial capitalism was to modernize banking and financial systems, rescuing society from usurious money lending and asset stripping, replacing the age-old parasitic tendencies of banking:

> The commercial and interest-bearing forms of capital are older than industrial capital, but ... [i]n the course of its evolution, industrial capital must therefore subjugate these forms and transform them into derived or special functions of itself. It encounters these older forms in the epoch of its formation and development. It encounters them as antecedents ... not as forms of its own life-process. ... Where capitalist production has developed all its manifold forms and has become the dominant mode of production, interest-bearing capital is dominated by industrial capital, and commercial capital becomes merely a form of industrial capital, derived from the circulation process.[2]

But that is not what occurred in the English-speaking world. Contrary to what Marx and other observers expected, bank lending did not find its major market in financing industry.[3] Bank lending played almost no role in Britain's early industrial takeoff, and most industrial investment today continues to be self-financed. James Watt and other inventors raised money mainly by mortgaging real estate. That also is how many 20th century producers raised money for their enterprises, from industrial inventors to movie makers. Banks rarely lend to create new means of production.

Financializing industry: The objective is to make capital gains

There are a number of reasons why banking failed to become a helpful part of the industrial economy. Banks lend mainly against collateral already in place. The effect is for bank credit to bid up prices for real estate and other assets bought by their customers. And as the volume of savings and credit grows, this lending becomes larger, accelerating the debt-inflated rise in housing and other prices. That raises the economy's cost of living and doing business while leaving less income to be spent on goods and services. Slower growth in markets erodes industrial profit opportunities.

New industrial capital investment is supposed to be financed by the stock market, through Initial Public Offerings (IPOs). But at the end of the first trading day financial underwriters and insiders often end up

---

[2] Marx, *Theories of Surplus Value* (Moscow: 1971), p. 468.

[3] I contrast the success of German and Central European industrial banking in the 19th century with the short-termism of Anglo-American commercial banking in Chapter 7 of *Killing the Host* (Dresden: 2015). Germany's defeat in World War I left the Anglo-American form unchallenged in its global spread.

with as much as the industrial entrepreneur.[4] And once on the stock market, financial managers engineer capital gains by using earnings to support stock prices. In recent years over 90 percent of the earnings of S&P 500 companies have been paid out as dividends or used for stock buybacks.[5] So instead of the financial sector being industrialized as Marx expected, industry has been financialized. Using corporate earnings for stock buybacks and dividend payouts is not a path to long-term industrial capital formation. Neither is financializing and privatizing public infrastructure. Raising prices for basic services is the antithesis of industrial capitalism's drive to undersell competitors.

Compound interest accrues independently of the economy's ability to pay

Every economy needs credit to finance housing, education (in the United States) and large consumer durables from automobiles to refrigerators. The problem is that the economy-wide volume of debt grows exponentially by compound interest. This financial expansion of debt (and of "savings" on the creditors' side of the economy's balance sheet) is extractive, deflating the industrial economy's circulation of production and consumption spending.

Any interest rate should be thought of as implying a doubling time.[6] Unlike the real economy, interest and debt service grow exponentially without limit at the economy-wide level – and usually beyond the ability of many debtors to pay. The existing volume of interest-bearing debt is subject to the growth formula for savings/debt of Capital $(1 + \text{interest rate})^n$, with n representing the number of years money is left to accrue interest.

Ricardo ignored the exponential growth of interest-bearing debt. It was left to Marx to elaborate (in Volumes II and III of *Capital*) that the financial system of credit and debt is external to industrial capitalism. It grows by purely mathematical laws, and these are independent of the economy's ability to produce and pay off the debts. As the rising debt overhead diverts income away from the industrial economy, creditors receiving this

---

[4] See *Killing the Host*, Chapter 9.

[5] See *Killing the Host*, Chapter 8, and William Lazonick, "Profits Without Prosperity," *Harvard Business Review*, September 2014.

[6] The Rule of 72 is a quick way to calculate the doubling time of any interest rate. Dividing 72 by the annual rate shows the number of years it takes for an investment or debt to double – that is, to accumulate a sum as large as the original principal. See *Killing the Host*, Chapter 4: The All-Devouring "Magic of Compound Interest."

exponential growth recycle their interest receipts into yet more lending, diverting more and more income to banks and bondholders, away from the industrial economy. What doubles is not real growth but the financial burden, leaving less income to be spent on goods and services.

The resulting exponential all-devouring path "assimilates all the surplus value with the exception of the share claimed by the state," wrote Marx.[7] The financial class seeks to capitalize and appropriate the economy's entire surplus as interest, absorbing the whole of the surplus over the necessary bare means of subsistence.

This inexorable growth means that in the end, debts cannot be paid. That is why financial cycles typically end in crashes. The crash may be the kind that occurs in the business cycle (typically eleven or so years), or long and drawn out as a chronic insolvency and debt deflation, as modern Greece is now suffering, as Germany suffered after World War I, and as the United States is just entering.

The problem is that the expansion path of debt (which finds its counterpart in the wealth of banks and bondholders to whom it is owed) does not reflect profit rates. Financial dynamics have different laws of motion from those of industrial capitalism. Hardly ever has an economy's growth rate been as high as the interest rate that determines the rate at which debts and financial savings grow.

Banks have the privilege of creating new credit at will. As their credit expands, the great bulk of credit is lent to real estate and other asset markets. A larger and larger proportion of the purchase price is lent to home buyers or commercial property investors. To make it easier for them to carry larger mortgage debts, banks reduce the down payment that is needed, and also the amortization rate – to the point of making loans where only the interest needs to be paid, not any principal.

Looking for new markets beyond real estate by the 1980s, banks and bondholders expanded into junk-bond lending for corporate takeovers, and other increasingly high-risk areas, including lending to foreign governments needing to cover their balance-of-payments deficits so as to stabilize their exchange rates. The process reaches its final stage when banks avoid default simply by lending clients the interest that is owed – but which keeps the debt overhead snowballing.

---

[7] Marx, *Capital*, Vol. III (Chicago: 1909), p. 699. I survey Marx's discussion in "'Creating Wealth' through Debt: The West's Finance-Capitalist Road," *World Review of Political Economy*, Vol. 10, No. 2 (Summer 2019).

Fictitious Capital

Bankers and other creditors produce interest-bearing debt. That is their product as it "appear[s] in the eyes of the banker," Marx wrote. Little labor (and less and less care about the debtor's ability to pay) is involved in loan making. Referring to money lent out at interest as an "imaginary" or "void form of capital,"[8] Marx characterized high finance as based on "fictitious" claims for payment. It consists not of actual means of production, but of bonds, mortgages, bank loans and other liabilities – that is, claims on the means of production on the asset side of the balance sheet.

Bank loans, bonds and other financial securities appear on the liabilities side of the balance sheet, as does "the capital of the national debt [, which] appears as a minus, and interest-bearing capital generally is the mother of all crazy forms."[9] Credit to buy or transfer ownership of land and other assets is not a directly productive form of investment in the sense that new industrial capital formation is productive. Instead of creating value by financing the creation of new productive assets in the industrial economy, bank credit absorbs value and income produced by the non-*rentier* sectors, ultimately driving a rising proportion of these sectors into insolvency.

Finance capital is fictitious because its nominal valuation cannot be realized in practice. Its claims for payment cannot be met, because the volume of debts mounts up exponentially, faster than the "real" economy can afford to carry it. Banks and investors hold "certificates of indebtedness (bills of exchange), government securities (which represent spent capital), and stocks (claims on future yields of production)" whose face value is "purely fictitious."[10] The interest that savers hope to receive cannot be paid when the indebted economy is basically insolvent in the face of the exponentially growing volume of debts. So the nominal value of financial collateral is based on the illusion that all debts can be paid and that mortgages and bonds actually are worth their face value.

Despite the inevitability of a crash, the returns to finance capital are higher than industrial profit rates. Fortunes are made most readily by indebting industry, real estate, wage earners and governments, siphoning off the economic surplus in interest, other financial fees and bonuses, and by "financializing" management of industrial companies to inflate prices for their stocks and bonds. Voters are led to believe that

---

[8] Marx, *Capital*, Vol. III, p. 461.

[9] Marx, *Capital*, Vol. III, p. 547.

[10] Marx, *Capital*, Vol. III, p. 551.

the way to get rich is to go into debt and seek "capital" gains, which can be made most easily by buying real estate and other assets on credit – as long as asset prices rise at a pace higher than the rate of interest.

The problem is that this process leads in due course to a "Ponzi" phase of the financial cycle.

From Ponzi finance to financial crash

The vocabulary describing how credit expansions proceed headlong into the Ponzi stage was coined by Hyman Minsky, who described a three-stage progression. The decades immediately following the end of World War II were the happy first stage. Borrowers are able to pay the interest while also paying down their debts out of their current earnings. In the second stage they can only pay the interest, not amortization, so their debts are not paid down. Indeed, banks and credit-card companies prefer that loans never are paid off, because their business is to maximize their loan volume.

The "bubble" or Ponzi phase of the financial cycle is an attempt to create a perpetual motion monetary machine. Such schemes (more recently called Madoff schemes, after Bernie Madoff, who "made off" with the money that investors entrusted to his management) promise high returns to investors, typically by claiming to have a sophisticated financial strategy. But in reality the high returns are achieved by attracting new investors, whose savings are not really invested but simply paid out to early entrants into the scheme. These schemes need an ever-expanding volume of new entrants to provide enough money to pay interest to the early players. The only way for this confidence game to postpone the inevitable collapse is to keep attracting new savings, while convincing its players to leave their savings in, hoping to keep accruing supposedly sound gains.

The debt expansion is threatened when debt-leveraged homeowners, companies, or even governments cannot even afford to pay the interest falling due. That is the point at which creditors must decide whether to foreclose on their loans (and possibly absorb a loss), or save appearances by lending debtors the interest falling due.

On an economy-wide level, the rise in debt on the liabilities side of the balance sheet finds no counterpart in new tangible capital investment on the asset side. This means lower profits and wages, and therefore slower growth in non-financial asset prices. That leaves the economy able to sustain its exponential debt growth – and the volume of creditor savings – only by "borrowing its way out of debt." This is now being done by inflating asset prices by enough to cover the interest charges falling due. Banks create enough new credit to keep inflating real estate, stock and bond prices at a rate that (for a while) enables debtors to stave off the financial collapse by covering the interest falling due by refinancing their mortgages. In effect, the interest is simply added on to the debt, which continues to grow exponentially. In reality the creditor claims are unpayable, making the illusion of viable savings growth merely a legal fiction.

That is the faith-based dynamic of real estate and stock market bubbles. They need the proverbial "greater fools" to enter the picture and buy out earlier investors, hoping that asset-price gains have become a fact of economic nature. America's junk-mortgage bubble that peaked in 2007, for instance, needed banks to attract new buyers to buy more real estate on credit – often 100% loans with no amortization, no down payment, and NINJA borrowers with No Income, No Job and no Assets. Mortgage credit finally was made available to black and Hispanic minority borrowers, who wound up as the main victims, left holding over-mortgaged homes at "high-risk" interest rates as housing prices plunged in 2008. After the wave of Obama foreclosures on victims of junk mortgage loans, the home ownership rate fell to 63.4 percent by 2016.

The banks themselves played the role of the "greater fool," providing an exponential wave of new mortgage loans, supported by the central bank creating credit to lower interest rates to help make it easier for borrowers to take out larger loans. There was logic in this "foolishness," to be sure. The aim was to provide a wave of new money to keep the scheme from collapsing as the wild credit creation enabled over-indebted property owners nearing default to sell out and pay the bank the accumulated debt falling due. And bankers managed to avoid risk by buying credit-default insurance and appointing financial regulators who proved willing to bail them out instead of taking over their banks and throwing them in jail. In contrast to what had occurred with the Savings and Loan Association (S&L) bankers in the 1980s, President Obama's Administration (2009-16) not only refused to prosecute for outright financial fraud the major perpetrators of bad loans based on falsified income statements and property appraisals, but bailed them out and, by guaranteeing the biggest banks (the worst offenders), greatly enhanced the concentration of finance by giving them advantages over smaller competitors.

How debt deflation leads to chronic depression

Ricardo described economic Armageddon as resulting from population growth leading to higher food prices as recourse supposedly was made to soils with declining fertility. Higher crop and food prices would force up the subsistence wage, eating into the profits of industrial employers, who would stop investing. Ricardo's agricultural assumptions were unrealistic, and as matters have turned out, the actual threat to industrial capitalism is the exponential growth of debt. Interest and financial charges threaten to bring industrial expansion to an end, by leaving less personal income, business profits and government revenue available for domestic spending on consumer goods and new business investment. The resulting debt deflation diverts wages, profits and tax income to pay creditors – banks and bondholders.[11]

Debt deflation is the financial equivalent of what Ricardo warned would result from permitting Britain's landlord class to extract more and more rent. He would have been the last to acknowledge that his own banking class would lead industrial economies into a financial Armageddon. But the hope that finance capitalism can continue its expansionary path is illusory. The self-expanding growth of financial claims, Marx wrote, consists of "imaginary" and "fictitious" capital whose nominal valuation cannot be realized over time. Insolvency leads to breaks in the chain of payments, causing crises when banks and bondholders recognize that no society's productive powers can long support the growth of interest-bearing debt at compound rates, because the real economy does not grow exponentially forever. The scheduled debt service implicit in the exponentially growing debt claims necessarily exceeds the ability to pay, ultimately making it impossible to pay such debt claims. "The greater portion of the banking capital is, therefore, purely fictitious."[12]

No economy can long keep pace with the exponential rise in debt. The financial sector's claims for payment become increasingly uncollectible in practice. The nominal increase in financial savings and investment has little chance of actually being realized. Seeing that the pretense must end, creditors call in their loans and foreclose on the property of debtors, forcing the sale of property under distress conditions. The financial system collapses in a convulsion of bankruptcy.

---

[11] Irving Fisher ("The Debt-Deflation Theory of the Great Depression," *Econometrica*, 1933) explained how bankruptcies and debt defaults wipe out bank credit and the ability of economies to invest and hire new workers.

[12] Marx *Capital*, Vol. III, p. 552.

Quantitative Easing to keep the Ponzi economy afloat in the face of Debt Deflation

In the absence of enough income to pay the debts growing exponentially by the mathematics of compound interest, the financial system may try to survive by carrying the dynamic forward, by creating enough new bank credit to keep inflating capital gains by yet more debt leveraging. To keep the Ponzi scheme from collapsing, interest rate levels under the post-2008 Quantitative Easing are in inverse proportion to risk. Low-interest and indeed almost free new credit is needed to enable the stipulated already-scheduled interest and fees to be paid, in the absence of the industrial economy's ability to grow in the face of rising debt service extracting more and more income.

It is at this point that the financial sector wields its political power to demand public bailouts in a vain attempt to preserve the financial system's ability to keep on expanding at compound interest. The banking sector tries to force governments to support its fictitious capital expansion by threatening to crash the economy if the central bank and national treasury do not print enough money to keep funding the illusion of solvency. "Fictitious capital" claims in the form of financial securities soared as a result of the asset-price inflation fueled by the Federal Reserve Bank, while the industrial economy was subjected to debt deflation. Much as environmental polluters seek to shift the cleanup costs onto the public sector, so the financial sector demands cleanup of its debt pollution at taxpayer expense.

Just as Ricardo claimed that technological improvements (capital productivity) could delay the profit squeeze resulting from higher food costs, so government policy may become the *deus ex machina* to delay the financial crash of over-indebted economies. New public money can be poured into the financial markets to sustain the expansion path of debt. Since 2008 the flood of Quantitative Easing by the central bank has lowered interest rates to near zero for stock and bond speculators. And the lower the interest rate, the higher a given flow of rent or other income can be capitalized, producing higher financial valuations.

Any flow of income can be capitalized by calculating it at the going rate of interest. The basic formula is Y/i, that is, income (Y) discounted at the going rate of interest (i). If a borrower earns 50 pounds a year and the interest rate is 5%, this earning power is deemed to be worth 1000 pounds. A lower interest rate will increase the capitalization rate – the amount of debt that a given flow of income can carry. Thus, Marx concluded: "If the rate of interest falls [from 5%] to 2.5%, the same securities

will represent a capital of £2000. Their value is always merely capitalized income, that is, the income calculated on the basis of a fictitious
capital at the prevailing rate of interest."[13]

So the lower the interest rate, the more a given flow of rents or other
income is worth. After the 2008 crash the U.S. Federal Reserve started
to buy packaged bank loans, corporate bonds and even stocks. Lowering
interest rates to only 0.1 percent for the financial sector provided arbitrage
opportunities for new buyers of financial securities and real estate on
credit. That attracted enough money into the stock and bond markets to
keep pushing up asset prices, even though the resulting bubble had ceased
to reflect real wealth and prosperity. The financially based One Percent
got richer, while the indebted 99 Percent faced deepening austerity.

Interest rates could not be permitted to rise without crashing asset prices.
That prospect locked the central bank into keeping interest rates low to
support the bond and stock markets, as well as real estate prices. Sustaining
financial fortunes and "fictitious capital" became a parasitic overhead on the
industrial economy. The financial sector was devouring its industrial host.[14]

In contrast to industrial capital and related tangible means of production, bank loans, stocks and bonds are legal claims *on* wealth. These
financial claims do not produce income; they *extract* it. Financial claims
are like sponges absorbing the income and property of debtors – and
creditors expropriate this property when debtors (including governments) cannot pay. "Usury centralises money wealth," Marx concluded.

> It does not alter the mode of production, but attaches itself to it as a
> parasite and makes it miserable. It sucks its blood, kills its nerve, and
> compels reproduction to proceed under even more disheartening con-
> ditions ... usurer's capital does not confront the laborer as industrial
> capital. ... [It] impoverishes this mode of production, paralyzes the pro-
> ductive forces instead of developing them.[15]

---

[13] Marx, *Capital*, Vol. III, p. 551. In the United States the term fictitious capital
passed into general circulation as meaning the capitalized value of unearned
income without cost value, mainly groundrent and monopoly rent. Henry George
picked it up in *The Condition of Labor* (1891), referring to the "fictitious capital that
is really capitalized monopoly."

[14] "Both usury and commerce exploit the various modes of production," Marx wrote
(*Capital*, Vol. III, p. 716). "They do not create it, but attack it from the outside."

[15] Marx, *Capital*, Vol. III, p. 699.

America's post-2008 Obama Administration financial austerity

Unlike medieval serfs, modern wage earners and other people can live anywhere they want. But wherever they live, they rarely have the choice to avoid running into debt and thus having to pay much of their wages to creditors and other *rentiers* for access to basic needs, from housing to education. Only those fortunate enough to have inherited trust funds or homes of their own and whose parents paid in full for their education are exempt from debt peonage to the *rentier* class. That class's affluence is based on interest and rent extraction from the industrial economy. We can see the results most obviously in debt-strapped Greece since 2012, or in Russia after 1991 during the Yeltsin years. Austerity and unemployment lead to poorer health, shorter lifespans, and rising suicide and crime rates. The main escape is to emigrate.

But few Americans had an option to emigrate when their unpaid debts after the 2008 financial crash left them subject to foreclosure on their real estate and other collateral pledged for the debts. Ever since antiquity, creditors have used usury as a lever to pry land away from smallholders. Millions of U.S. families lost their homes from 2007 to 2009, and the home ownership rate fell as large "private equity" real estate companies bought foreclosed properties at distressed prices and turned them into high-rent housing. The rate of return (profits plus capital gains) was enormous, as typically occurs following a crash. "The rate of profit is always highest in countries going fastest to ruin," Adam Smith said.[16]

An industrial economy's decline typically provides a grab-bag of opportunities for financial predators and vulture funds. National or local bankruptcy crises become new opportunities for financial managers and bondholder councils to gain control of policy-making. New York City's near bankruptcy in 1975 transferred control over spending and taxes to the euphemistically titled Municipal Assistance Corporation (MAC) under financier Felix Rohatyn. Wages were frozen, public transportation fares raised, hospitals closed, and the hitherto free City College imposed tuition. The Dow Jones Industrial Average plunged as a result of New York's financial predicament, and gold prices rose, reflecting the financial insecurity over how matters would be resolved.

But the collapse in property prices was a godsend for real estate developers who seized the opportunity to gentrify low-income neighborhoods

---

[16] Smith, *Wealth of Nations*, Book I, Chapter 11.

and de-industrialize lower Manhattan, turning commercial buildings into luxury living lofts for the expanding financial sector's managers.

Following the 2008 financial crash, American homeowners were not permitted to have their mortgages written down to the low distress prices that banks received in foreclosure sales. This pro-bank move by the Obama Administration was highly rewarding to Obama's Wall Street campaign contributors. Demonstrating the hypocrisy of American identity politics, it was a class war with a strong racial and ethnic bias against the black and Hispanic mortgage debtors who had been major supporters of Obama's electoral victory.

The ensuing Obama Depression squeezed public-sector budgets as the economy shrunk and taxes declined. That forced government at the local, state and federal level to scale back pension commitments to public employees, cut back social spending, and start selling off public land and natural resources, basic infrastructure and monopoly rights in order to obtain the revenue to pay bondholders while trying to sustain basic public services. Workers were squeezed by their rising debt burden, afraid to lose their jobs or be fired. That would have forced them to fall behind in their payments to the credit-card companies or banks and be charged high penalty interest rates (typically 29 percent), even as interest rates fell for the financial One Percent.

All this is being repeated in the 2020-22 Covid-19 crisis with its mass unemployment and collapsing state and local budgets. "Solutions" along similar lines to those following the 2008 crash are being imposed internationally as entire nations are subjected to IMF austerity programs. That institution's economic philosophy for the past half-century has been to squeeze international debt service out of local labor forces, mainly by currency depreciation. What is devalued most of all is the price of labor and its living standards.

First, finance crushes the economy; and then takes planning power into its own hands to make sure that creditors get paid. When neo-liberal "development" policy fails, the IMF subjects labor to austerity programs to squeeze out enough tax revenue to carry the debt overhead while ostensibly "making labor more competitive." But low-paid labor is less productive, and the austerity programs prevent governments from providing basic infrastructure services. That becomes an excuse for privatizing them to raise the cash to pay bondholders – pretending that private management will be more efficient.

That smash and grab financial planning is the ideology that U.S. advisors gave to Russia after 1991. It was the same policy that ancient Roman creditors followed in expropriating smallholders and creating the *latifundia* that evolved into feudalism. The debt-strapped economy is subjected to the equivalent of foreclosure by the financial sector.

The fact that this is now being done in the context of ostensibly democratic politics throws a leading assumption of political economy into doubt. If economies and populations tend naturally to act in their self-interest, how did the financial sector gain such extractive power to raid and dismantle industry and shed its tax burden? Why did the 19th century's logic of taxing *rentier* income and socializing credit and other natural public utilities *not* win out? How was this great fight by classical political economy subverted? To place economic planning in the hands of financial managers is like letting the House of Lords or other upper houses of government allocate resources and set policy, excluding the Commons or popular assembly.

Western society's reluctance to annul its unpayably high debt burden remains the great ideological tragedy of today's world. Its legal philosophy remains that of the pro-creditor principles inherited from oligarchic Rome (via feudal Europe). There is no acknowledgement that keeping the existing debt dynamic in place will block economies from progressing toward prosperity. Refusal to write down debts will polarize society between an increasingly wealthy creditor class at the top, and indebted families, businesses and governments falling into debt dependency. And within the international economy, neoliberal financial diplomacy imposes austerity on entire debtor countries by insisting that all debts must be paid, regardless of the social consequences. Originating as a U.S.-driven post-colonial form of monetary imperialism, this philosophy is now being applied at home by the U.S. and European governments on their own economies.

There ARE alternatives

Classical economic reformers spent the 19th century defining a free market as one free *from* economic rent, and hence from a *rentier* class, and advocating an alternative: taxing away the rent that was the taproot of the exploitation and free lunch enjoyed by the One Percent of their epoch. They were political economists in seeing that their tax reform required democratic political reform. The landlord aristocracy's economic and political control was dislodged, only to see it taken over by the emerging financial oligarchy.

Tax reform focusing on economic rent remains the most effective lever to reverse the ascendency of finance capital, because most of today's *rentier* fortunes take the form of creditor claims against the same land rent and other economic rent that was the source of wealth for the 19th century's ruling elite – the rents that the classical economists advocated taxing away. In view of the fact that these rents are now collateralized to pay the financial sector, the most important result of taxing them away would be to stop them being paid out as interest. They would be paid as taxes, replacing income and sales taxes.

The only way to achieve a lasting check on today's creditor and other financial claims is a debt cancellation to free society from the debt overhead that has been built up since 1945, and especially since 1980 and 2008. To leave the legacy of "savings" (claims on debtors) in place is to leave the existing One Percent with the purchasing power to impoverish society.

What is blocking this workable alternative is the persistent illusion that most debts can be paid, and the bank-sponsored ideology that they *should* be paid, even at the cost of imposing chronic economic austerity on society at large. This misguided optimism about ability to pay can best be dispelled by public awareness of the basic financial dynamic at work: The volume of debt in an economy grows exponentially by the magic of compound interest, but the real economy does not. This means that the volume of debt must necessarily grow to exceed the real economy's ability to pay.

The bank-sponsored ideology that all debts *should* be paid can similarly be dispelled by public understanding of the ethics as well as the financial dynamics involved. When debts cannot be paid, either debtors forfeit their property to foreclosing creditors (as is now occurring in the United States), or else creditors lose their financial claims for payment. Saving the creditors means sacrificing the indebted economy at large, consigning its labor and industry to financial austerity, potentially permanently.

Beyond freeing society from today's impoverishing debt overhead, banking and credit creation should be made a public utility. Creditors naturally resist public awareness of the fact that restoring resilience to debt-ridden economies requires turning banking and credit creation into a public utility free from *rentier* control. That is called socialism, but it in fact was the implicit dynamic of industrial capitalism in the 19th century. Failure to nationalize or socialize banking thus represents the failure of industrial capitalism to free itself from the pre-capitalist legacy of feudalism and thus fulfill its seeming historic destiny.

Financialization has hijacked industrial capitalism. The inherent dynamic of finance capitalism is to lead economies to polarize and collapse under the weight of their self-multiplying debt burden. The deepening financial crisis becomes an opportunity to impose emergency rule and push democratic lawmaking aside. These are the reasons why banking and finance should be de-privatized.

China has resisted this privatization of banking and money creation. So far, the government's strategy has been to use bank credit mainly to serve its industrial and overall economic development. But keeping banking and finance in their proper place will remain a rising political challenge as domestic wealth increases. To sustain China's remarkable economic growth requires preventing its economy from being taken over by an emerging financial billionaire class. That in turn requires resisting neoliberal Western ideological pressure to persuade China to financialize its economy by adopting the economics indoctrinated in Western schools.

To the extent that China sends its students to study economics in U.S. and European schools, they are taught the tactics of asset stripping, not tangible capital formation. They are taught that the easiest and best tax policy is to tax labor or sales via a value-added tax (VAT). They also are taught that privatization is more desirable than public ownership, and that financialization creates wealth, not that it creates a debt burden growing faster than the economy can keep pace with.

The most obvious way to expand the domestic market while, at the same time, minimizing the cost of living and doing business, is to cut back income taxes and sales taxes, which leave less wage income for spending. Taxes are best levied on unearned *rentier* income, above all on land rent, so as to prevent banks from inflating housing and real estate prices on credit.

As Chapter 9 will describe, in contrast to Frederick Hayek's 1944 anti-government *The Road to Serfdom* warning that any form of regulation is a slippery slope toward totalitarianism, the real road to serfdom – at least, debt peonage – is to leave the *rentier* class free to extract economic rent and interest. Hayek's road leads to a Pinochet-type Chicago School dystopia – totalitarian oligarchic control by stripping away government checks and balances and failing to check *rentier* extraction of income. That is what happens when society fails to check *rentier* interests. That kind of "free market" future would establish a hereditary autocracy whose privatization and financialization of rent-seeking would impoverish the economy at large, threatening a Dark Age like that following Rome's collapse. That makes it crucial for society to look to the alternatives just described.

It always should be borne in mind that solving the problem of finance capitalism and the *rentier* legacy of feudalism would still leave the class conflict of industrial capitalism in place. Freeing the economy from *rentier* overhead charges would not solve the problem of exploitation of labor by its employers. But taking the intermediate step of creating a classical economy free of *rentier* claims is a precondition before the labor/capital conflict can become the focal point of political reform, having finally freed capitalism from the *rentier* legacy of feudalism.

Creating a statistical format to measure rent-seeking vs. tangible economic growth

The current GDP format for national income statistics treats all income, including economic rent, as being earned productively as part of the "real" economy, not as overhead. If China's social objective is to increase real output to raise living standards and prosperity for its population, it must develop its own accounting format to measure how income and wealth is obtained.

Distinguishing the FIRE sector from the rest of the economy would enable China to compare its economic costs and overhead relative to those of other nations. The distinction between earned income and economic rent was the aim of classical political economy, but this distinction is not made in today's Western-style national income statistics. FIRE-sector lobbyists have brought political pressure to count interest and financial fees, economic rent and higher prices for residential real estate as adding to GDP, not as subtrahends eroding the disposable personal income available to be spent on industrial-economy production and consumption. Applying an accounting structure that measures rent-seeking and distinguishes the FIRE sector would show how Western economies are polarizing as a result of rent and interest payments crowding out spending on goods and services.

Such an accounting format would revive the classical distinction between earned and unearned income, and would add a measurement of capital gains to current income so as to trace how personal fortunes are being made purely financially, as distinct from tangibly. It would show the extent to which economic gains are made more on the liabilities (finance-capital) side than on the tangible industrial-capital side. This would show how much wealth is a result of tangible prosperity as distinct from higher rents, interest and financial charges and engineering of stock-market and other asset-price gains. That "total returns" approach would provide a guide to creating policies to minimize the kind of predatory wealth that leads to *rentier* oligarchies.

By treating interest, related financial charges and other economic rents as overhead, such national accounts would isolate fortunes obtained by zero-sum transfer payments for the rising rental valuation of land sites, natural resources and basic infrastructure monopolies. That would enable China to measure the economic effects of the banking privileges and other property rights that compel payments by labor and industry to the FIRE sector.

Most important, these statistics would explain the remarkable economic advantage that China has obtained in its progress toward socialism.

6

Free-Trade Imperialism and its Financialized Class War against Labor

When I began to teach international trade theory in 1969, my first task was to compile a reading list for my students. I was dismayed to find an academic wasteland of mathematical models depicting a hypothetical parallel universe in which foreign debts can be paid by cutting back living standards and social spending, and free trade and investment make countries more equal instead of locking in their inequality. There was no explanation of how the leading nations actually had obtained their lead, or why the international economy has polarized between creditor and debtor countries. Tariffs and subsidies are claimed to be counter-productive by "distorting markets," as if protectionism has not been the policy by which the leading industrial nations have developed.

I had worked for nearly a decade on Wall Street as a balance-of-payments economist analyzing how the international economy was polarizing between industrial creditor nations and the increasingly indebted Global South (at that time called the Third World). I had written my doctoral dissertation on the 19th-century American School of protectionists, whose policy turned the United States into the world's leading industrial power by tariff protection and subsidy, and by what were called internal improvements to raise productivity by public infrastructure investment to support industry and upgrade the labor force by investing in education, health and related services.

None of this appears in mainstream trade theory. Having achieved industrial dominance, Britain and the United States sought to convince other countries not to become more self-reliant but to concentrate on "what they are good at," using their "natural endowments" to specialize in plantation crops, raw-materials exports and low-wage handicrafts. The basic message was – and remains – "Do as we say, not as we have done to grow rich."

Race to the Bottom, or to the Top? The Choice between Free Trade and Protectionism

Free trade theory looks at the short run. The status quo is assumed to reflect the most efficient specialization of world production, debt and other economic relations. Existing productivity and cost structures are accepted as natural, not to be "interfered" with by government subsidy or tariffs. In fact, the wider the cost differences between nations, the greater the so-called "gains from trade" are calculated to be – these "gains" reflecting the price difference between the lowest and highest-cost producers.

Passive acquiescence in free trade leaves productivity and wealth disparities to continue widening. The resulting trade dependency drives low-income countries into foreign debt. They then are told to "tighten their belts" and cut back social investment even more.

The essence of British mercantilist policy in the 18th century, classical political economy and American protectionist policy in the late 19th century was to raise the productivity of labor by public investment in education, diet and living standards, while minimizing monopoly exploitation. This policy might be called state capitalism or even industrial socialism, and it has worked.[1] But that is not what students are taught in the United States and Britain. Mainstream trade theory does not explain how Britain and the United States became so successful, or how China has succeeded over the past four decades in overtaking so much Western industry. Textbook models teach that it would be a mistake to "distort markets" by subsidizing public investment and services, even when the aim is to increase productivity and living standards.

From British mercantilism to free-trade imperialism

A leading aim of trade theory should be to explain why the international economy is polarizing instead of helping "less developed countries" catch up. Why are they falling deeper into foreign debt? Why does China succeed, but not Latin America or Africa?

The explanation has long historical roots. European colonial powers in the 17th and 18th centuries forbid their colonies from developing their own manufactures. To make Britain's colonies dependent on their parent nation, Parliament in 1719 declared it "unlawful to set up in any

---

[1] I describe the American School in *America's Protectionist Takeoff, 1815-1914: The Neglected American School of Political Economy* (Dresden: 2010). See also my *Trade, Development and Foreign Debt* (new ed., Dresden: 2010; Chinese translation, Beijing: 2012).

colony furnaces for the production of cast-iron or for the manufacture of iron because 'the establishment of manufactories in the colonies tends to make them more independent of Great Britain.' ... [A]s new occasions arose, or as the enterprise of the colonists manifested itself in new directions, the laws became more strict, the limitations upon colonial activities became more numerous, and the execution of all restrictive regulations increased in severity."[2]

A similar enactment in 1732 "forbade the making of hats for the market. ... An incidental method of discouraging manufacturing in the colonies was by passing laws to keep industrial skill at home. The exportation of specified kinds of tools and machines to the colonies or elsewhere was prohibited, and skilled artisans were forbidden to leave the country."[3]

Describing how England's Navigation Acts and associated mercantile regulations had fostered its foreign trade, Marx wrote: "The system of protection was an artificial means of manufacturing manufacturers ... indirectly through protective duties, directly through export premiums. ... The European states ... forcibly rooted out, in their dependent countries, all industry, as, *e.g.*, England did with the Irish woolen manufacture."[4]

But nations rarely are able to monopolize technology, as the United States is learning today when it tries to impose sanctions on China. The most effective way to prevent less developed countries from catching up is to convince them that they are better off living in the short run and remaining dependent on low-priced imports. Since Ricardo's day a rhetoric has been popularized depicting trade as providing mutual gains that are shared in proportion to what seemingly natural "market forces" dictate.

Ricardo "cooked" his free-trade calculation of how the gains of trade were distributed, by describing Portugal as gaining the most when it exchanged wine (and by extension, other agricultural produce) for British woolens. His logic depicted the non-industrialized country as "winning," not losing out over time. Refusal by mainstream textbooks to alert readers to this false logic claiming to demonstrate the virtues

---

[2] Edward Stanwood, *American Tariff Controversies in the Nineteenth Century* (Boston: 1903), Vol. I, p. 13, cited in Hudson, *Trade, Development and Foreign Debt*, p. 38.

[3] Witt Bowden, *The Industrial History of the United States* (New York: 1930), pp. 99ff. See also James E. Thorold Rogers, *The Industrial and Commercial History of England* (London: 1892), especially Part II, ch. x ("Home trade and international competition").

[4] Marx, *Capital: A Critical Analysis of Capitalist Production* [1867], Chapter 31: "Genesis of the Industrial Capitalist" (London: 1987), p. 782. https://www.marxists.org/archive/marx/works/1867-c1/ch31.htm. See also Marx, *On the Question of Free Trade* (1888), and *Capital*, Vol. III (Chicago: 1909), pp. 391ff.

of free trade shows that today, after the passage of over two centuries, this is not an innocent "error." It has become a foundational intellectual deception serving to weaponize neo-colonialist trade theory.

American protectionists were explicit in pointing out that rejecting protective tariffs and relying on Britain for America's manufactured goods instead of developing domestic industry would put it and other such countries in the position of what the Bible called "hewers of wood and drawers of water" like the Gibeonites, condemned to servitude to the Israelites.[5] The 20th century saw foreign trade "underdevelop" raw-materials exporters.

The "free market" status quo turns out to be shaped by the industrial nations, and helps global monopolists keep weaker countries poor and dependent. Bernard Semmel has called this "free-trade imperialism."[6] If it really were true that countries would do best by refraining from imposing tariffs or other public regulation, then America would have needed no government action to develop its industry.

How the United States gained its industrial advantage

When America's Civil War ended in 1865, Republicans sought to develop a pro-industrial policy in a world of steam-driven capital and rising labor productivity. That required a new economics curriculum to be created. Almost all the prestigious old colleges advocated free trade, having been founded to train the clergy in British-style moral philosophy. Land-grant colleges were founded across the United States, and their course of study was more secular and provided an alternative economics curriculum.

Alongside them, business schools were endowed, headed by the Wharton School at the University of Pennsylvania. Their role was to refine the logic of tariff protection and subsidies to enable industrialists to afford the capital investment needed to adopt the newest technology. They also advocated public infrastructure investment to lower the cost of living and doing business, by providing basic services freely or at subsidized rates, especially for public health, education and transportation.[7]

---

[5] Joshua 9:21: "Now therefore you are cursed, and some of you shall never be anything but servants, cutters of wood and drawers of water for the house of my God."

[6] Bernard Semmel, *The Rise of Free Trade Imperialism: Classical Political Economy, the Empire of Free Trade and Imperialism, 1750–1850* (New York: 1970).

[7] I review Simon Patten's argument for public infrastructure investment in "Simon Patten on Public Infrastructure and Economic Rent Capture," *American Journal*

A key recognition of the American School was that the progress of technology was leading mechanization to displace manual labor. The appropriate response was to upgrade the quality and productivity of labor.[8] In Grover Cleveland's two Democratic administrations (1885-89 and 1893-97) the State Department employed Jacob Schoenhof, who had immigrated from Germany in 1861, to travel around the world comparing wage rates and labor productivity. His statistics confirmed that favorable productivity advantages more than offset America's high wage levels. This was called the Economy of High Wages doctrine. "It is not by reducing wages that America is making her conquests," wrote Schoenhof in 1884,

> but by her superior organization, greater efficiency of labor conse-
> quent upon the higher standard of living ruling in the country. High-
> priced labor means better food and better living, and these supply the
> American workman with the energy and nerve-power for which he is so
> justly celebrated. High-priced labor countries are everywhere beating
> "pauper labor" countries.[9]

Instead of depicting pauper labor as winning the global industrial competition, the Economy of High Wages doctrine emphasized the need to accumulate mechanized capital operated by increasingly skilled labor. A feedback relationship existed between rising wages and pro-ductivity, increasing America's competitive advantage. As production became more capital intensive, profits would be reinvested under condi-tions of increasing returns. That would enable firms in high-productivity economies to undersell their rivals, whose relatively low living standards would prevent them from keeping pace with world-class capital produc-tivity. "The survival of the fittest," Schoenhof concluded, "is, therefore ... the result of a high wage rate; and a high standard of living in industrial countries, becomes a prerequisite to a low cost of production."[10]

Today's mainstream trade theory rejects this logic. There is no recog-nition of capital competing with manual labor and thus driving labor

---

of Economics and Sociology 70 (October 2011), pp. 873-903. Patten was the Wharton School's first professor of economics.

[8] See my "Obsolescent Factors in the International Economy," Review of Social Economics, March 1972.

[9] Jacob Schoenhof, Wages and Trade in Manufacturing Industries in America and Europe (New York: 1884), p. 19. See also Schoenhof's The Economy of High Wages (New York: 1892), p. 385.

[10] Jacob Schoenhof, Economy of High Wages, p. 39.

to move up the value chain to higher skill and productivity levels. The assumption is that labor in one country competes only with labor in other countries – presumably of equal productivity, as if there is no linkage between wage levels and productivity, and no role for public infrastructure investment. This oversimplified trade theory views some economies as inherently labor-intensive, as if that is their natural destiny under "free markets."

The "factor endowment" rationalization of the international status quo

Seeking to explain trade patterns simply in terms of the relative scarcity of labor relative to capital, with no adjustment for differences in the quality of labor, mainstream trade theory omits the role of tax policy and public subsidy. This approach remains stuck in the ideas put forth in 1919 by the Swedish economist Eli Heckscher and later elaborated by his student Bertil Ohlin. The Heckscher-Ohlin theorem describes any international status quo as being a natural result of the relative "endowments" of labor and capital, without explaining how these came to occur or how they might best be changed to improve economic prosperity.

Each economy is said to have its own distinct proportions of capital and labor "endowments," with each factor being paid according to its "contribution to production." The labor/capital proportion and productivity are assumed to be economy-wide, as if economies are homogeneous, not heterogeneous. There is no discussion of how the leading nations have self-endowed themselves with capital by protectionist policies and subsidies enabling their labor to "contribute more" to production. Most seriously, economic rent, debt levels and tax policy are not recognized as affecting cost structures.

These deficiencies – deliberate blind spots, not innocent oversights – make the definition of a country's capital/labor relations (that is, capital investment per employee) so abstract as to be meaningless. The reality is that economies have numerous sectors, which have a broad range of capital/labor proportions. Abstracting these variations into a single uniform national average diverts attention from which sectors are export-oriented and which ones are part of the domestic economy. Not all sectors are export-oriented – and those that are indeed export-oriented (and usually foreign-owned) have quite different capital/labor proportions from the rest of the economy. In fact, these proportions typically are more like those of the foreign investing-and-importing nation than those of the exporting economy.

The over-generality of thinking in terms of uniform national capital/ labor relations thus distracts attention from a distinguishing feature of today's specialization of world production: Most raw-materials exporters are "dual economies." Capital/labor proportions in the domestic sectors of "less developed countries" are much lower than those of the export sector – just the reverse of what one might expect. The explanation is simple: The export sectors of these economies tend to be foreign-owned (as noted above), and this foreign investment is concentrated in highly capital-intensive natural resource extraction, headed by oil and mining, and extending to plantation agriculture.

Recognition of this dual-economy structure invalidates Heckscher's claim that the incomes of identical factors of production (labor or capital) of equal productivity (his fatal oversimplification) will be equalized across countries as a result of free trade in commodities. "The prerequisites for initiating international trade," he wrote, "may thus be summarized as *different relative scarcity, i.e., different relative prices of the factors of production in the exchanging countries, as well as different proportions between the factors of production in different countries.*" "*Each region,*" Ohlin echoed, "*has an advantage in the production of commodities into which enter considerable amounts of factors abundant and cheap in that region.*"[11]

It all comes down to relative scarcity of capital and labor, Heckscher concluded: "If the conditions of production are the same in all countries," then "trade must continue to expand until an *equalization of the relative scarcity of the factors of production among countries* has occurred." Under free trade, world incomes are supposed to become more uniform as the products of highly paid "scarce" labor in one country are undersold by those made by relatively more abundant "lower-paid" labor elsewhere. This is the old "pauper labor" myth. It views poverty and an absence of public social services as a cost advantage, not a productivity disadvantage.

Only on the above "simplifying" assumptions would international incomes become more equal through free trade and its associated international investment flows. The fatal assumption is that "the conditions

---

[11] Eli Heckscher, "The Effect of Foreign Trade on the Distribution of Income" (1919), translated in Ellis and Metzler eds., *Readings in the Theory of International Trade* (Philadelphia: 1949), p. 274, italics in original. See also Bertil Ohlin, *Interregional and International Trade* (Cambridge: 1935), pp. 20, 22, and 24-29, also italics in original. Paul Samuelson mathematized the factor-endowment approach in what has become sanctified as the "factor-price equalization theorem." See his *Economics. An Introductory Analysis*, 7th ed. (New York: 1967), pp. 672 and 648.

of production are the same in all countries." All labor is assumed to be of equal productivity throughout the world, with no distinction between skilled and unskilled labor – or in national economic policy. An international convergence is promised to result naturally, if governments refrain from interfering with markets. The implication is that wages rise because of labor's diminishing supply relative to the availability of capital, not because of its higher productivity, or unionization, minimum-wage laws, or the high cost of living in financialized economies. This oversimplification is so unrealistic that it must be recognized as deliberate deception of students subjected to such indoctrination.

The reason why the relative incomes of labor and capital are not equalized by trade in the products they make is that productivity and economic policy differs among countries.[12] Capital is replacing labor in an expanding range of tasks. Manual labor is being undersold by new capital investment. But the Heckscher-Ohlin over-simplification treats labor as producing distinct labor services, which are assumed to be non-competitive with "capital services." The implication is that countries can succeed in exporting more "labor-intensive" products by lowering the price of their industrial labor, winning the race to the bottom by imposing austerity – as if poverty will make them rich.

While economists focus on the hypothetical conditions necessary to produce income convergence, world incomes are not equalizing. International income and productivity gaps have widened over the past two centuries, as capital has steadily increased its income over that of labor, despite large-scale international investment. So the "factor proportions" theory describes a world that does not exist. The reason for its academic success is not its explanatory power, but its political opposition to active government trade and social policy, especially protectionism and social spending to upgrade labor.

When a theory recommends that countries specialize in what they are "best" at producing at any given moment in time, it advises them to ignore the long-term gains they could secure by reforms to increase productivity and minimize *rentier* privileges. Such trade theorizing

---

[12] Free-trade theorists hedge their logic by acknowledging that in these hypothetical models trade is supposed to produce a *similarity* in income structures (that is, the same average *ratios* of wages to profits), although not necessarily absolute income equality, unless there is trade in common denominators such as raw materials and capital goods at a uniform world price. But there *is* such trade, and indeed a common world price for most raw materials and capital goods. That leaves the price of labor to be the only variable in *actual* costs throughout the world.

fails to recognize that the only way for less prosperous economies to raise their productivity and living standards to world levels is through structural reform of existing economic, financial and tax structures to minimize *rentier* privileges and upgrade labor, by protectionist measures and subsidy where appropriate. The "factor proportions" or "scarcity" theory seeks to lock in the inequitable status quo by belittling government policies that "interfere with free markets," accusing them of being ineffective in promoting prosperity.

Labor in the United States and other industrial nations also has suffered by national governments letting their industrial employers take the opportunity to offshore production by investing abroad and relying on lower-cost foreign labor to produce their nations' consumer goods. The claim is that wage earners will live better by obtaining cheaper imports. The trick is to try and make wage earners think of themselves as consumers, not workers, so that they will not ask what the benefit is in lower consumer prices if their job has been offshored. However, awareness of the offshoring and de-industrialization damage done to U.S. labor by President Bill Clinton's promotion of NAFTA (the North American Free-Trade Agreement) contributed strongly to the rejection of his Democratic Party in the 2000 presidential elections, much as Hillary Clinton's advocacy of the TPP (Trans-Pacific Partnership) doomed her in the 2016 election at the hands of protectionist Donald Trump.

Rarely acknowledging the role of government policy, debt service or *rentier* exploitation, free-trade models speculate about what *might* happen if all governments were to remain aloof from shaping the rules of trade and investment. Fiscal and financial systems are accepted as given, without discussion of how economic policy can transform them. Governments in the industrial nations certainly act to block less developed countries from subsidizing their own economic independence and replacing imports with their own production and foreign borrowing with their own money creation. This diplomatic activism by the leading industrial nations means that existing trade and investment patterns are *not* natural.

A satisfactory explanation for the rise of England, the United States, Germany, Japan and China would acknowledge the linkages among international trade, investment, financial diplomacy and military coercion. It would describe how economies that industrialized by protectionist "state capitalism" have monopolized the gains from trade and parlayed them into an investment position that has consolidated their control over world resources. It would trace how international credit has been extended far in excess of debtors' capacity to pay, keeping them on a tight debt leash to impose austerity and depress their terms of trade and wage levels, to the benefit of creditor-investor nations.

The impact of debt leverage and military coercion on international trade

Mercantilists pointed out that trade was the only way for nations lacking mines of their own to obtain silver and gold "money of the world." Domestic money and credit creation at that time were subject to the balance of international trade and payments, which determined exchange rates and hence whether exports and imports would be high- or low-priced in terms of world-money.

Lead nations have always held the ideal of using their trade surpluses (and tribute) to buy up the natural resources and, in modern times, industry and infrastructure monopolies of other countries, turning them into economic satellites controlled financially. This drive has polarized the world economy between wealthy creditor nations and countries whose failure to modernize their own industry and agriculture has led them into trade and debt dependency. A realistic trade theory must recognize the role of creditor/debtor relations that influence exchange rates and the terms of trade for imports and exports.

Pro-creditor interests claim that debt relations have no such effect. Ricardo argued that paying debt service is self-financing and hence cannot cause monetary deflation, because if an economy runs a balance-of-payments surplus, its monetary inflow and prices will rise. That will lead it to buy goods from the payments-deficit countries whose exchange rates are weakening, and who hence can sell enough additional exports to pay their debt service. In other words, what is paid abroad will come back, without a need for government trade and monetary (capital) controls.

A similar logic claims that paying domestic debt service cannot cause debt deflation, because creditors supposedly will spend their interest receipts back into the economy. But in reality they use their *rentier* income to make yet more loans and buy more property, not to buy more goods and services.

The blind spot in Ricardo's financial analysis is illustrated by the Ricardo Brothers' own underwriting of Greece's bond issue after it declared independence from Ottoman rule in 1829. The exorbitant debt service it paid was not recycled back into its economy. Greece suffered chronic austerity, leading it to default repeatedly over the rest of the 19th century.

Most international loans historically have been to finance war-making or help governments over fiscal emergencies, not for projects enabling debtors to pay by investing the proceeds productively. New loans were required to roll over the debts being run up, squeezing the debtor economies and their public budgets accordingly. Chronic debt-service tends to force governments to sell off rent-yielding natural resources or public enterprises.

No gunboats appear in mainstream trade theory, and nothing to reflect the extent to which natural resource rents have been secured by armed force, as in the Anglo-American overthrow of Iran's elected prime minister Mossadegh in 1953, and in the recent destruction and oil grabs in Iraq, Syria and Libya (and attempted in Venezuela).

In fact, the phenomenon of economic rent is not taken into account as a factor in international pricing and "gains from trade" calculations. Natural-resource rent, for example, is notably ignored, along with the typically related costs of military empire to protect rent-seeking investors. Nor are the environmental damages and their cleanup costs (discussed in Chapter 7) considered. Such "losses from trade" are not acknowledged, nor are the "externality" costs that can result from the politicized and militarized context of international investment.

Oil-exporting Venezuela, for instance, attracted U.S. companies. They were supported by U.S. foreign policy installing dictators to protect them (as was the case throughout most of Latin America). The country's trade deficit was financed by dollar bonds issued to U.S. and other foreign investors. A U.S.-backed client regime collateralized this government debt with the national oil company's assets, including its U.S. oil distribution system. When Venezuela elected a left-wing nationalist government, it was isolated by U.S.-sponsored trade sanctions, bondholders grabbed its foreign assets, and the Bank of England simply stole its gold stock on behalf of U.S.-based proxy politicians.

The World Bank's mega-engineering projects provide another example of the "externality costs" flowing from free trade and foreign investment. These projects are notorious for getting countries into debt, forcing them to borrow from the International Monetary Fund, which lays down "conditionalities" that say basically: "To pay your debts, you have to engage in a vicious class war against labor. You have to lower wages because they are the only variable in world trade. There's a common world trade [price] in raw materials: All countries pay the same price for copper, machinery and other materials. There is a common world price for oil, and for capital goods. The one variable in foreign trade is the price of labor. So you've got to prevent unionization and any other kind of pro-labor reform. Your only way of paying debts is to polarize your economy and impoverish your labor force."

Financial dependency has become the most destructive byproduct of today's monoculture trade dependency. Debtor countries are obliged to impose austerity that deters domestic capital investment. The IMF rationalizes its austerity programs by an "absorption approach" claiming that structural payments deficits can be overcome by increasing taxes, raising prices for public services and reducing public social spending. The idea is to tax ("absorb") so much domestic income that the population will not have enough revenue to spend on imports, while low wages ("pauper labor") spur exports. It is glibly assumed that paying labor less will leave output "free" to be exported – as if poverty and unemployment helps them earn more internationally!

The reality is that austerity shrinks the economy's productive power, and typically spurs emigration and capital flight. Squeezing out domestic income to pay foreign creditors and investors tends to leave debtor countries without the ability to break even. What the IMF calls "stabilization plans" have driven much of Latin America, Africa and Asia deeper into debt and trade dependency. The effect has been to "underdevelop" economies instead of modernizing them.

Free trade is claimed to eliminate poverty in low-wage countries by providing an "even international playing field" for manufacturing jobs, supposedly enabling the Global South's labor to undersell high-wage U.S. and European labor. The reality is that free trade locks in the existing, sharply uneven playing field that results from the advanced industrial nations' accumulation of large amounts of plant and equipment, public infrastructure and education that former colonialized countries have been blocked from developing.

Once this capital and social infrastructure investment is taken into account, it becomes clear why free trade is bound to favor the leading industrial nations over the world's "latecomers" – and indeed why accepting the productivity and above all ownership asymmetry aims to keep them from "coming" at all.

The aim is to persuade low-wage countries that they can rise into the middle class if they let U.S. and European investors establish factories for local labor-intensive production. A vocabulary of deception has been crafted to block them from recognizing that U.S. and European diplomacy aims at locking them into a foreign-debt trap that turns their domestic policy making over to their foreign creditors. This trap enables the IMF and related U.S.-centered diplomacy to "bail them out" by imposing austerity and debt deflation – capped by U.S. demands to control their rent-yielding natural resources and infrastructure monopolies.

The result is identical to that of traditional European colonialism and mercantilism. The pretense that an "open international economy" is a "level playing field" aims at keeping the Global South on a never-ending treadmill of poverty. Instead of turning low-wage labor into a middle class, they are to remain the most exploited victims of industrial and finance capital monopolized by the United States and Europe.

Trade dependency patterns have been backed up by brute force. In Latin America and Africa, American diplomacy has backed the assassination of advocates of land reform and of indigenous populations seeking to block logging and mining in their areas, and to redistribute the land of U.S.-owned export-crop plantations to local families wanting to produce food for their own livelihood and to provide a domestic alternative to having to import U.S. food crops.

Such use of force is not a "free market phenomenon," much less one of competition leading to greater international efficiency. Trade theory based simply on "factor proportions" overlooks how U.S. Dollar Diplomacy has created bloodbaths in Latin America and Africa, leaving them debt-strapped and calling it peace and democracy. It also overlooks the sanctioning and overthrow of local governments seeking more economic independence in other regions.

To cap matters, free-market economists claim that tariffs, quotas, capital controls and other actions to promote industry and raise productivity are synonymous with paving the road to serfdom. The reality is that a county's failure to protect, regulate and subsidize its key sectors leads to financial, trade and technological dependency locking it into chronic balance-of-payments drains to pay for imports and foreign loans. That is the real road to serfdom, and the context in which any analysis of trade policy needs to be placed.

How and why the United States lost its industrial advantage

Having failed to explain how the world's leading industrial and creditor nations gained dominance, mainstream trade theory has made no effort to explain why and how the U.S. economy has de-industrialized since 1980. With so much unemployment and so many unused factories, why doesn't American labor become "cheap," and hence employable, instead of American companies relocating industrial production facilities to East Asia?

It would be superficial to explain this simply as a shift to hiring labor in the lowest-wage countries. What is "the wage," after all? Is it what employers pay, or what labor obtains on balance from government and private employers together?

China has invested in a vast public infrastructure network to facilitate its industrial production by minimizing the cost of living and doing business. This has saved employers from having to pay higher wages for labor to afford privatized education, health care, transportation and other essential services. These basic needs are provided by public infrastructure, which Simon Patten called a "fourth factor of production."

Such public capital investment makes no appearance in the Heckscher-Ohlin-Samuelson world of "factor proportions." The government is seen only as overhead, not as a "factor of production." There is no recognition of the public sector's role in saving private employers from having to bear these costs themselves, or that making infrastructure public provides basic services at much lower costs than by privatizing them in the hands of rent-seeking monopolies in a Thatcherized neoliberal economy.

The reason why labor is so much less costly outside the United States is clear enough: The U.S. economy is the most financialized and privatized. As Chapter 5 has explained, American wage-earners are obliged to pay higher debt service, housing costs (either as renters or mortgage debtors), health insurance charges, education fees and charges for other basic services than workers in other countries. Even if food and other material needs were provided to labor freely, without any payment, American labor would be priced far out of world industrial markets in view of the afore-mentioned costs. U.S. housing now often absorbs from 30 to 40 percent of employee wages, while Social Security and Medicare siphon 15 percent of the paycheck off the top, and income and sales taxes account for perhaps another 20 percent, capped by privatized health insurance, financialized pension plans and personal debt service.

Explaining the shifting pattern of international trade thus entails taking the entire economy and its political setting into account and, most important in this regard, understanding how finance capitalism has undermined industrial capitalism by encouraging rent extraction and living in the short run. Industrial capitalism requires long-term planning to develop and market new products. But since 1980, economic management has sought short-term gains by financial engineering, making money by buying and selling assets (including financial securities and loans), not by creating new means of production to sell more goods and services. Investors calculate arbitrage opportunities in supply and demand conditions as they exist at a given moment in time.

What is so ironic is that China's policy has, as noted above, followed almost the same path that American protectionism did from 1865 through 1914: state subsidy for industry, heavy public-sector capital investment (but without creating predatory railroad land fortunes as became a U.S. economic curse), and social spending on education and health care to upgrade the quality and productivity of labor. This was not called Marxism in the United States; it was simply the logical way to look at industrialization, as part of a broad economic and social system. That frame of reference is now denounced as "the road to serfdom" and claimed to be autocratic, while the United States is itself moving into a financialized era of debt peonage.

U.S. attempts to domineer the international economy

Today's finance capitalism has left the United States mainly with agribusiness farm surpluses, and monopolies in information technology (largely developed as a byproduct of military research), military hardware, and pharmaceutical patents (based on public seed-money to fund research) able to extract monopoly rent while making themselves largely tax-exempt by using offshore banking centers. The U.S. economy is becoming more extractive than productive, a widening swath of it hollowed out.

The United States is increasingly left to rely only on its *rentier* and monetary power (Dollar Diplomacy, described in Chapter 10) to maintain a semblance of prosperity, which is becoming concentrated in the hands of the top One Percent of the population. Instead of trying to reverse the economy's polarization between a *rentier* FIRE sector and what remains of its industrial base (dominated by linkages to the military-industrial complex), U.S. diplomacy has imposed export and other trade sanctions against Russia, China and other countries to try to prevent them from becoming independent of U.S. control.

Attempts to prevent foreign technology from replacing imperial-center exports have usually been in vain, and typically are counter-productive. Trade sanctions imposed for strategic reasons likewise can produce results other than those desired. Against Russia, for instance, U.S. diplomats persuaded its NATO satellites to impose agricultural sanctions after Russia resisted the attempted U.S.-Ukrainian takeover of its Crimean naval base. The aim was to starve Russia into diplomatic submission. The actual effect was to provide Russia with the equivalent

of trade protection, which Russia's own economists had hesitated to legislate. A discussion between a Russian farm entrepreneur and President
Putin reflected the upshot:

> "I'm a farmer and cheesemaker from the Moscow region," Sirota told
> President Vladimir Putin during a public discussion in October 2018. "I
> make cheese. Let me begin by saying on behalf of the farmers, we have
> been telling you this repeatedly over the last four years...I wanted to
> thank you for the sanctions. In fact, we had a long discussion about this
> with experts at our session."
>
> Putin replied: "You should thank the Americans, not me." ...
>
> The farmer added: "Because it is delicious [continued Sirota]. Our
> cheese is tasty, hard and cheap thanks to the ruble rates. It is attracting
> investors, including international ones. Everyone has begun investing in
> Russia's agriculture. We have partners from Switzerland who relocated
> to Russia and are building farms. I was asked repeatedly during the
> session about what would happen if the sanctions were cancelled. What
> would I do? Would it be a disaster?"
>
> Putin: "Regarding cheese and what happens if sanctions are lifted.
> First of all, we are not seeing them readying to lift any sanctions so you
> can sleep tight."[13]

The effect of U.S. diplomacy has been to help – indeed, force – Russia
to nurture its own import-competing sectors, which normally would have
required protective tariffs. If the American strategists – or Russian officials, for that matter – had read Marx, they might have thought about
what he wrote to Engels in 1867. "What the Irish need," he said, was:

> (1) Self-government and independence from England.
>
> (2) An agrarian revolution. With the best intentions in the world the
> English cannot accomplish this for them, but they can give them the
> legal means of accomplishing it for themselves.
>
> (3) *Protective tariffs against England.* Between 1783 and 1801 every
> branch of industry began to flourish. The Union, which overthrew
> the protective tariffs established by the Irish parliament, destroyed all
> industrial life in Ireland. The bit of linen industry is no compensation
> whatever. The Union of 1801 had just the same effect on Irish industry
> as the measures for the suppression of the Irish woolen industry, etc.,
> taken by the English Parliament under Anne, George II, and others.
> Once the Irish are independent, necessity will turn them into protection-
> ists, as it did Canada, Australia, etc.[14]

---

[13] John Helmer, "Russia is now the big cheese," *Dances with Bears*, September 22,
2020. http://johnhelmer.net/russia-is-now-the-big-cheese/.

[14] Marx to Engels, November 30, 1867, in *Marx and Engels on Britain* (Moscow:
1962), p. 544.

A similar judgment applies to today's Russia. First, it needs a government independent of U.S. neoliberal advice and ideology, so as to sponsor an alternative to neoliberal free markets. The second need is to rationalize production and the tax and financial systems to replace the post-1991 *rentier* kleptocracy and help achieve the third need: domestic self-reliance against trade and financial dependency on the United States and its satellites, achieved by tariffs and other protectionist measures, and indeed even by U.S. trade sanctions forcing domestic self-reliance.

The degree to which China has mostly broken free by following this logic explains its greater industrial success to date. That success led the Trump Administration to impose sanctions to promote American Internet and related IT monopolies. U.S. diplomats have mobilized NATO and other allies to boycott China's 5G technology and its most successful companies, alleging privacy issues, a euphemism for China not permitting inclusion in its technology of U.S. spyware giving "backdoor" national security access for the United States.

Like ancient Rome, the U.S. economy has become dependent on foreign tribute for its survival in today's global *rentier* economy. Just as robbers fear retaliation from their victims, so *rentiers* and monopolists fear that their clients will revolt against a system that is basically unfair and provides a free lunch to the financially and militarily dominant nation ruling by force and legal "rights" that deprive other nations of *their* rights and opportunities for widespread prosperity. That is why the United States has surrounded Eurasia with 750 military bases.

This is more than just U.S. insistence on blocking foreign rivalry for its leading monopolies. What really is at issue is an opposition to government regulation of U.S.-centered finance capitalism in principle. U.S. policy is part of a class war against labor, and also a political and ideological war against mixed economies with government power – any government authority to regulate or tax American foreign investment, or to subsidize economic independence from U.S. suppliers and creditors. That is why U.S. opposition to today's post-Soviet Russia is as strong as it was during the Cold War, when the U.S. excuse was to counter the threatened spread of Communism.

The conflict indeed remains ideological. Today's renewed Cold War is a "libertarian" war. Backed by the U.S. financial sector and U.S. allies abroad, its aim is to shift planning and resource allocation away from governments to the world's financial centers, headed by Wall Street and the City of London. This fight is similar to what occurred in Rome when the oligarchic Senate defended creditor rights against popular demands for debt cancellation and land redistribution.

Through its belligerence, the United States is seeking to maintain its unipolar *rentier* dominance in a world that is becoming increasingly combative and militarized. This is yet another dimension of international trade that free-market academic models overlook. Foreign trade is part of an inter-connected system relying on security of supply. Interruptions, sanctions, boycotts or other forms of economic warfare can bring the entire supply chain to a halt. Such warfare is reminiscent of when U.S. strategists sought to ban food exports to China in the 1950s to oppose Mao's revolution. (Canada broke the embargo.)

President Joe Biden has declared China an enemy, and has appointed U.S. military leadership that in the past has endorsed pre-emptive war and nuclear confrontation. "When we join together with fellow democracies, our strength more than doubles," he announced. "China can't afford to ignore more than half the global economy. That gives us substantial leverage to shape the rules of the road on everything from the environment to labour, trade, technology and transparency, so they can continue to reflect democratic interests and values."[15] By "transparency," Mr. Biden means the ability of the U.S. National Security Council to eavesdrop on all foreign internet communications by means of the "backdoor" programs written into Facebook, Google, Apple and other U.S. information technology. That, as indicated above, is an added reason why U.S. trade negotiators seek to block Huawei, Tik-Tok and other applications from being used in Dollar Area countries.

The aim is to prevent China from creating a broad enough economy to defend itself from being wrecked by sanctions or more overt military attack. As Xi Jinping explained on April 10, 2020: "In order to safeguard China's industrial security and national security, we must focus on building production chains and supply chains that are independently controllable, secure and reliable, and strive for important products and supply channels to all have at least one alternative source, forming the necessary industrial backup system."[16]

Redundancy is a system built into nature and the biology of living beings. It is much the same in the international economy: Specialization of production to the degree that it leaves economies dependent for critical needs on a central supplier of resources ends at least in monopoly power, and at worst in the power to disrupt supply if the

---

[15] James Kynge, "China braced for lose-lose scenario in US election," *Financial Times*, October 15, 2020.

[16] Center for Security and Emerging Technology. https://cset.georgetown.edu/wp-content/uploads/t0235_Qiushi_Xi_economy_EN-1.pdf.

monopolist's demands are not met – demands that may be not only for high prices, but political demands to adopt the social system sponsored by the leading monopolists.

Government's support of U.S. industrial rivalry with China

What disturbs American Cold War strategists is that other countries have developed their own industry and agriculture instead of relying on U.S. exporters in a state of permanent dependency such as existed in 1945. Clyde Prestowitz, a conservative Republican trade advisor in the Reagan Administration, threw down the rhetorical gauntlet in 2021. After World War II, he explained: "The system arose out of the Pax Americana and a deep faith that the U.S. would always be the world's manufacturing and technology superpower, have the highest productivity, pay the highest wages, and always run a surplus or balanced trade account." Perpetuation of this unique status is "what the free world expected when it welcomed China into the free trade body [the World Trade Organization] in 2001. From the time of Deng Xiaoping's adoption of some market methods in 1979 and especially after the collapse of the Soviet Union in 1992, free world leaders believed increased trade with and investment in China would inevitably lead to the marketization of its economy, the demise of its state-owned enterprises."[17]

Instead, China has followed the classical mixed-economy policy that made the U.S., German and other industrial economies so successful. By 2021 the major U.S. rationale for protecting its large corporate monopolies from Chinese competition was the accusation that China's government was doing just what the U.S. government had been doing to support domestic industry since the late 19th century. At the root of the conflict, U.S. trade strategists claim, is neoliberal free market "democracy" threatened by Chinese autocracy. It is as if American industry had not itself grown strong by government support. Prestowitz framed the U.S.-China confrontation in terms of what is meant by a market-based economy. Is government support part of the market, or not? "China's economy," Prestowitz asserted,

---

[17] Clyde V. Prestowitz, Jr., "Blow Up the Global Trading System, *Washington Monthly*, March 24, 2021. The hypocrisy of the author's proposal is reflected in the fact that he took his MBA at the Wharton School, where Simon Patten had taught the virtues of public infrastructure and related support as a "fourth factor of production."

is incompatible with the main premises of the global economic system
embodied today in the World Trade Organization, the International
Monetary Fund, the World Bank, and a long list of other free trade
agreements. These pacts assume economies that are primarily market
based with the role of the state circumscribed ... This system never
anticipated an economy like China's in which state-owned enterprises
account for one-third of production; the fusion of the civilian economy
with the strategic-military economy is a government necessity ... to
be used for economic and political control; and international trade is
subject to being weaponized at any moment for strategic ends.

The United States, of course, also subsidizes aircraft producers,
Internet companies and other heavy industry with military orders and
contracts. Indeed, Prestowitz urged President Biden to "invoke the
Defense Production Act to direct increased U.S.-based production of
critical goods such as medicines, semiconductors, and solar panels."

The hypocrisy of U.S. foreign policy reached a new degree in the
accusation that China engages in "managing its currency." What Mr.
Prestowitz means is that China is doing just what European and other
countries are doing, stabilizing their exchange rates by recycling their
dollar receipts from U.S. imports and investment inflows into central
bank reserves held in the form of U.S. Treasury securities – the essence
of the U.S. Treasury-bill standard and U.S. monetary imperialism, after
all. And to cap matters, U.S. diplomacy has sharply expanded its use of
trade sanctions as a major economic weapon in its New Cold War, especially against Russia, Syria, Venezuela, Iran and other targeted countries.

Depicting American industry as being independent of government
support (when in fact it has largely captured the government and
receives enormous public subsidy and economic support) seems to be a
case of the pot calling the kettle black. Public subsidy was the doctrine
of industrial capitalism. But as America's economy has become financialized, it has de-industrialized and shifted production abroad. China
has succeeded by avoiding financialization and in fulfilling what had
been the U.S. ideal of providing low-priced basic infrastructure services.

Requirements for a modern theory of trade recognizing finance and the FIRE sector

For many centuries the key monopoly was money. That financial control
is still as much an issue today as was trade and military power in times
past. Although most trade theory is based on comparing direct production costs, debt financing, economic rent and tax policies have become
much more important, along with government infrastructure and sub-

sidies. As described above, Ricardo's depiction of comparative costs treated most outlays as being for consumer goods, whose prices could be resolved into labor costs. That seemed plausible enough in an epoch when food represented the major element in the worker's budget. But today, the major expense is housing costs (mainly rent and the servicing of mortgage debt), costs that are determined largely by the terms of mortgage credit, and by the presence or absence of land taxes to keep real estate prices down. These housing costs and charges for personal bank loans, credit-card debt and auto debt (and in America, student-loan debt) plus forced savings for Social Security, pension-fund contributions and health insurance typically push non-commodity costs to substantially over half the basic budget for labor.

A relevant trade theory therefore would need to take account of the fact that these non-production costs have risen. But the financial sector is the last interest group from which to expect policy realism in this discussion, because its prime directive is to deny culpability in causing economic problems and obtaining unearned income. Recognizing that what is not analyzed is less likely to be criticized and regulated, the financial sector prefers economic models in which money and debt don't matter. That leaves the financial dimension out of account.

By viewing the cost of capital goods only in terms of the labor time needed for their production, Ricardo sidestepped the credit terms on which they are financed, *e.g.*, interest rates and debt/equity ratios. Debt service accounts for a rising share of both labor and capital costs. A relevant international trade theory thus would recognize the degree to which financialization and related FIRE-sector *rentier* charges dominate the comparative costs of capital investment and labor. Interest and principal payments on home mortgages and education loans, health care costs, and forced saving for retirement pensions are overshadowing nominal wage payments and labor productivity in determining international competitiveness. The cost of health insurance and medical care in the United States, for instance, falls on individuals and their employers rather than being absorbed by the public sector.

An increasingly important consideration is how to treat debts that cannot be paid. That leads to a discussion of whether banking and credit should be made a public utility, as it is in China, or should remain privatized as in the West. Western firms do not have their debts written off when they cannot meet their scheduled debt service, but are declared insolvent and often dismantled. In China they are not closed down, thanks to the fact that the government bank extends credit to keep in business industrial facilities deemed to be in the national interest.

Governments throughout the world have shifted the tax burden off finance and property onto labor and industry. The effect has been to promote financial and real estate bubbles in which debt-financed purchases overshadow new capital investment. These developments make the concept of "cost of production" much more complex today than was the case in the formative centuries of trade theory. What now is appropriate is a "rent theory" of comparative disadvantage. Yet today's mainstream trade theory is blocked by the hard ideological wall excluding discussion of the role played by rent and indeed any challenge to the FIRE sector's role in domestic economies.

If protectionism is the trade policy of industrial capitalism, austerity and debt deflation are the policies of finance capitalism. Its "free market" message is, "Don't regulate your economies. Let our bankers and foreign investors take control of your economic planning and resource allocation." Like all good science fiction, this free-trade gospel requires a considerable suspension of disbelief to enter a world governed by unworldly assumptions.

7

Food, Oil, Mining and Natural-Resource Rents

The distinguishing dynamic of industrial capitalism is the exploitation of wage labor, but industrial nations also end up with most of the world's natural-resource rents. That is why the linkage between trade and foreign ownership is most visible in the food, oil and mining sectors.

Agricultural soil on top of the earth, and mineral wealth below the surface, always have attracted conquistadors and, most recently, corporate *rentier* appropriators. Standing behind them are their imperial-nation governments. That was the case from the silver mines of Spain in Roman times to those of Potosi in the Bolivian mountains, and from Roman *latifundia* in North Africa to American lands stocked with slaves while driving out the native occupants. More recent resource seizures have created plantation monocultures in Central America by United Fruit and other U.S. companies, client oil-country autocracies, and the copper mines of Chile, with the exploited nations suffering U.S.-imposed dictatorships. Raw-materials trade and client oligarchies have always gone hand in hand, oligarchy seemingly universally imposed on resource-rich countries as a kind of cosmic curse for their natural wealth.

Using financial and outright military power to prevent weaker countries from keeping possession of the natural-resource rents that 19th-century economists expected them to receive, the leading industrial nations dominate the international ownership of agriculture, oil and mining. The preferred tactic is to sponsor oligarchies and military dictatorships as local managers helping the industrial nations appropriate this natural wealth for their own companies so as to keep the world's resource rents flowing into their own economies. Host countries are left in poverty, often deprived of political autonomy and the basis for their own industrialization and prosperity. That is the "curse of oil," and indeed of rich land and other natural resources.

The *rentier* dynamic of natural-resource wealth means that possession of such wealth is not conducive to the development of industry. The Netherlands and Norway have retained control of their offshore oil, but have each seen their currency's exchange rate rise as a result of their vast rent-yielding asset, pricing their labor and exports out of world markets. That recently has been called the Dutch Disease.[1] A similar phenomenon occurred already in 16th-century Spain and Portugal, when silver from Latin America enriched their landed aristocracies but flowed through their hands to less autocratic economies to the north.

Even when nations remain in control of their agricultural, oil or mineral wealth, industrial nations control the marketing and sales of these products to siphon off their rents, and create tax avoidance schemes in offshore banking centers and "flags of convenience" to avoid paying income taxes on their privatized resource-rent. This is just the opposite of leaving such rent for the public domain as classical reformers advocated.

The curse of natural-resource wealth has long been analyzed as the Monoculture Syndrome, referring to national reliance on a few raw materials, creating dual economies: wealthy foreign-owned natural-resource sectors (typically capital-intensive) alongside impoverished domestic economies, which are kept under financial control by the leading industrial nations' ownership of the choke points of refining and marketing monopolies.

1) Agriculture

Ricardo's assumption of diminishing returns led him to believe that raw materials suppliers would become richer than industrial nations as the marginal cost of producing crops, mining and refining metals and other raw materials rose. With such products priced near their high-cost margin of production, the industrial nations' terms of trade would have worsened as recourse was made to poorer lands and raw materials. It would have made the most sparsely settled countries with the richest land and mines the greatest beneficiaries of international trade.

That obviously is not how matters have turned out. The foreign investment protected by U.S. and European diplomacy has helped create a sufficient abundance of raw materials to depress their prices toward their low-cost margin of production. And productivity has risen dramatically as increasing returns have become the norm. In agriculture, productivity gains were achieved by the fertilizers developed by Albrecht

---

[1] The *Economist* magazine coined this term in November 1977 to describe the decline of Holland's manufacturing sector after the discovery of the Groningen gas field off its Baltic coast in 1959. Oil economies are the major examples in today's world, followed by mineral-rich economies that tend to become "dual economies," having a wealthy *rentier* sector alongside a backward domestic economy.

Thaer (1752-1828) and Justus von Liebig (1803-73), and by the early 20th century Fritz Haber and Carl Bosch had developed their process of catalytic formation of ammonia, fixing nitrogen from the air. These latter innovations rendered Chile's guano supply largely redundant. Farm equipment vastly increased productivity with mechanized tractors, plowing and harvesting machinery, as well as pesticides and herbicides, and new seed varieties.

These productivity gains have been concentrated in the most industrialized nations, headed by the United States. Labor productivity in U.S. agriculture has exceeded that in almost any other sector in the world. This success has been promoted by protectionist measures, catalyzed by the Agricultural Adjustment Act of 1933 providing price supports and parity pricing subsidies, as well as import quotas. The EU has emulated America's example with its protectionist Common Agricultural Policy (CAP).

Environmental destruction as an "externality" of monocultures and agribusiness

Where diminishing returns did occur in Ricardo's day, it was on the same soils, which turned out to have no "original and indestructible" fertility as Ricardo had believed. A new term "mining the soil," exhausting "old" land, was applied to the cotton and tobacco plantation monocultures of America's southern slave states. This soil depletion kept slave-stocked plantations moving westward, led by Andrew Jackson driving the Native Americans off their land and replacing them with African slaves.[2]

A debate arose in the 1840s over how national economic accounts should measure environmental destruction. That debate is still going on today, so it is worthwhile reviewing how clearly the problem was recognized so long ago, along with free-trade opposition to acknowledging it. America ran a trade surplus in exporting plantation crops, but its soil was being depleted. "Productiveness of crops and destructiveness of soil are two most prominent features of American agriculture," wrote the

---

[2] The Native Americans chose to emigrate or die fighting rather than be enslaved. In the American Northwest, British land companies bought up vast land tracts to graze cattle, disrupting settler farmers. The fight between family farms and large absentee-owned *latifundia* of cattlemen – highlighted by the Battle of Powder River in Montana in 1876 – lasted for half a century. Similar conflicts occur today in Brazil and elsewhere in Latin America where loggers and agribusiness treat indigenous populations much like North Americans treated the native tribes and the homesteaders who displaced them.

Patent Office Report in 1852.[3] Advocates of industrialization calculated how much it would cost to replenish the minerals depleted by plantation farming. They found that these "public wealth" costs exceeded the private-sector's export proceeds. Modern free-trade theory excludes such costs as "externalities," that is, excludes them from its economic models.

Liebig controverted Ricardo's idea of land as having fixed and immutable powers in *Chemistry in its Relation to Agriculture and Physiology* (1840):

> Can the art of agriculture be based upon anything but the restitution of a disturbed equilibrium? Can it be imagined, that any country, however rich and fertile, with a flourishing commerce, which for centuries exports its produce in the shape of grain and cattle, will maintain its fertility, if the same commerce does not restore, in some form of manure, these elements which have been removed from the soil, and which cannot be replaced by the atmosphere? Must not the same fate await every such country which has actually befallen the once prolific soil of Virginia, now in many parts no longer able to grow its former staple productions – wheat and tobacco?[4]

The costs that someday would have to be paid to restore the soil's fertility were calculated by Daniel Lee when he became the director of the U.S. Patent Office's agricultural section from 1849 to 1852. For the year 1849, he estimated, the nation's exhaustive methods of cultivation entailed an annual loss averaging 10 cents per acre on 100 million of the 125 million acres of improved farmland then in use. This $10 million annual loss (akin to capital depreciation) was equal in magnitude to the proceeds of a capital investment of $166,666,000 at 6% annual interest.[5]

Ultimately responsible for impairing the nation's soil fertility, Lee asserted, was the nation's free-trade policy. "American statesmanship has

---

[3] *Report of the Commissioner of Patents for the year 1852, Part II: Agriculture* (Washington: 1853), p. 4. I summarize this literature in "Political Origins of the Department of Agriculture: Soil Chemistry and International Trade Theory, 1840-62," in *America's Protectionist Takeoff, 1815-1914: The Neglected American School of Political Economy* (Dresden: 2010).

[4] Justus von Liebig, "Familiar Letters on Chemistry," in *Complete Works on Chemistry* (trans. Lyon Playfair, Philadelphia: 1843), p. 32.

[5] "Statistics and Progress of Agriculture in the United States for the year 1849," in *Report of the Commissioner of Patents for the year 1849, Part II: Agriculture* (Washington: 1850), p. 25. In "Progress of Agriculture in the United States," in the above-cited Patent Office *Report* for 1852, p. 7, Lee estimated the implicit value of the minerals removed from the soil amounted to $300 million per year – that is, $3.00 an acre, or about 17 to 20 per cent of the crops' sales value, "by which remark we mean that complete restitution of the elements of crops removed, such as potash, soda,

adopted a system of political economy [free trade] which renders full and perfect restitution of the soil impossible so long [as] it shall prevail. This statesmanship, which ignores the very existence of agricultural science, and repudiates all its teachings, costs the country three hundred million dollars a year by needless destruction of its agricultural resources."[6]

Free-trade logic sidesteps these environmental costs of soil-depleting modes of cultivation. It also minimizes consideration of pollution, political consequences (racist slavery and genocide), and social abuses such as child labor and debt peonage for farm workers. That is why the U.S. Department of Agriculture had to be created over the opposition of southern plantation owners.[7]

Financial and marketing monopolies to exploit farmers

Marketing crops requires investment in transportation, storage and an array of other services including weather forecasting and agricultural education to promote the most efficient techniques and seed varieties. Marketing and transport services provide opportunities for monopoly control rents to be extracted at key choke points. Frank Norris's novel *The Octopus* (1908) describes the drive by railroads to extract the value of crop surpluses for themselves. As one survey summarizes the problem as it stands today, more than a century later:

> A handful of corporations control our food from farm to fork. Their unbridled power grants them increasing political influence over the rules that govern our food system and allows them to manipulate the marketplace – pushing down the prices paid to family farmers and driving them out of business. ... our corporate controlled food system damages rural communities, local economies, public health and the soil and water needed to sustain food production.[8]

---

lime, magnesia, chlorine, phosphoric and sulphuric acids, and ammonia, cannot be made short of an expense of three dollars per acre."

[6] 1849 *Patent Office Report*, p. 15.

[7] Paul W. Gates, *Agriculture in the Civil War* (New York: 1965), pp. 263f., observes: "By withdrawing from the Union in 1861, the Southern states removed the conservative element that had long prevented the adoption of important legislation affecting agriculture and the development of the West. In rapid succession congress enacted the Homestead Act with its free-land policy, the Pacific Railroad Act with its liberal aid for the building of a railroad to the Pacific, the act creating a Department of Agriculture, the National Bank Act, and the Morrill Act, all of which had been held up by the shrewd politics of a minority section."

[8] "Corporate Control of Agriculture," Farmaid (n.d.). https://www.farmaid.org/issues/corporate-power/corporate-power-in-ag/.

Most government aid now goes to the largest agribusiness corporations, not to family farms, whose number has been dwindling by about
10,000 farms each year, headed by midwestern dairy farmers. The
Farmaid report illustrates the concentration at work.

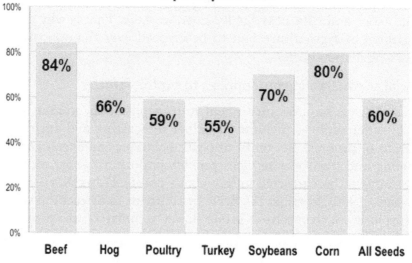

Concentration in Agriculture

Top 4 Companies' Share

Cargill, founded in Minnesota in 1865, has become America's largest
privately-owned corporation in terms of revenue. It controls one-quarter
of all U.S. grain exports, and nearly as much (22%) of the U.S. domestic
meat market. Former Congressman Henry A. Waxman calls it "the
worst company in the world" and accuses it of driving deforestation,
pollution, climate change and exploitation "at a scale that dwarfs their
closest competitors."[9]

The U.S. government has brought many charges against Cargill for
financially manipulating grain prices. Farmers typically sell their crop in
advance to Cargill and other grain companies, which organize market
contracts for each crop through the Chicago Board of Trade. During the
Great Depression the Board (along with the U.S. Commodity Exchange
Authority) accused Cargill of trying to corner the corn market to push
up crop prices to consumers, and in 1938 suspended the company and
three of its officers from the trading floor.

---

[9] Mighty Earth, "Cargill: The worst company in the world" (2019). https://stories.
mightyearth.org/cargill-worst-company-in-the-world/.

More recently, Cargill has been charged with illegally employing child labor and many other human rights violations throughout the world, as well as land monopolization in Colombia. The above-cited Mighty Earth report states that "perhaps Cargill's largest negative impact on the natural world is its role in driving the destruction of the world's last remaining intact forests and prairies," headed by deforestation of the Amazon to grow soybeans, and of Sumatra and Borneo to produce palm oil, one of the least healthy fast-food additives.

Pollution and related environmental problems are endemic to American agribusiness practice. "Feeding and raising meat consumes more land and freshwater than any other industry," the Mighty Earth report concludes, "and the industry's waste byproducts rank among the top sources of pollution around the world. Many of these impacts are concentrated in the United States, where factory farming has its stronghold, but are spreading rapidly to other parts of the world."

Cargill's international financial violations are in line with its earlier U.S. lawbreaking. When world grain prices spiked in 2008, Cargill – along with Archer-Daniels-Midland (ADM), Bunge and Louis Dreyfus Company (LDC) – manipulated their accounts in Argentina to report merely trivial profits by falsifying their sales contracts and records, using fictitious transfer pricing in selling grain at low production prices to their own trading affiliates in offshore banking centers and tax havens. (The practice was pioneered by the oil industry, as described below.) Argentina sued these firms for tax arrears of $1 billion in 2011. The head of its revenue service, Ricardo Echegaray, accused these companies of criminality, explaining that "2008 was when agricultural commodities prices spiked and was the best year for them in prices, yet we could see that the companies with the biggest sales showed very little profit in this country."[10]

Cargill's co-conspirator in the above case, Archer-Daniels-Midland, founded in Chicago in 1902, has been the next most complicit in financial abuses. It started as a specialist in linseed oil, helping form the National Linseed Oil Trust that was sued by the Department of Justice in 1920 for violating the Sherman Antitrust Act by creating a spike in linseed oil costs between 1916 and 1918, raising the price from $.50 per gallon to $1.80. The company also was prosecuted for price fixing in the international lysine market in 1993. Three of its officers were sent to prison, and the company was fined $100 million, at that time the largest anti-trust penalty on record. Kurt Eichenwald's novel *The Informant* (2000)

---

[10] Felicity Lawrence, "Argentina accuses world's largest grain traders of huge tax evasion," *The Guardian*, June 1, 2011.

was about the FBI investigation into this case, and a movie version (under the same name) was released in 2009.

A priority of U.S. trade diplomacy since World War II has been to secure foreign markets for U.S. farmers. Grain, soybean, pork and other farm exports have long been a mainstay in the U.S. trade balance, and hence of Dollar Diplomacy. U.S. officials have led the World Bank to lend for roadbuilding, ports and related infrastructure projects to promote plantation exports of tropical crops that do not compete with U.S. farm products. Countries run into foreign debt to hire mainly U.S. engineering and construction companies to facilitate these exports. Economies see their patrimony siphoned off as foreign-owned and export-oriented firms end up with their resource rents, aided by public infrastructure and transportation subsidies.

World Bank loan policy is concentrated on tropical plantation export crops such as rubber, palm oil, bananas and spices that do not compete with U.S. agribusiness, not on family-scale farming of domestic food crops. Its support for large-scale agribusiness over small-scale farming has been criticized by over 158 organizations and academics from around the world, especially for its Benchmarking the Business of Agriculture (BBA) program started in 2013 and its Enabling the Business of Agriculture (EBA) indicators backed also by the U.S. Agency for International Development (A.I.D.), the Gates Foundation and the British, Dutch and Danish governments. In response to accusations of encouraging "corporate land grabs and undermin[ing] smallholder farmers who produce 80% of food consumed in the developing world. ... the Bank made some cosmetic changes and dropped its controversial land indicator." However, a recent report summarizes, "its latest (2019) EBA still reflects its strong bias for commercial agricultural inputs and mono-cropping, undermining food security, sustainability as well as customary land holdings."[11]

At issue is who should benefit from agricultural land: the local population and family farmers, or plantation owners and biotech firms such as Monsanto-Bayer, Bunge (which also was expelled from Argentina), and Archer-Daniels-Midland, which oppose environmental regulation as

---

[11] Anis Chowdhury, "Is Development for the World Bank Mainly Doing Business," *Naked Capitalism*, November 15, 2020 (originally published at the Inter-Press Service). See also the Oakland Institute report, "Calling on the World Bank to End the Enabling the Business of Agriculture (EBA)," January 18, 2017. https://www.oaklandinstitute.org/calling-world-bank-end-enabling-business-agriculture.

well as restrictions on manipulative transfer-pricing of the sort that the oil sector has made most notorious.

2) Oil and gas

Throughout history labor productivity has largely reflected the rise in energy input per worker, from wind and water power to animal power, wood burning, coal, oil, nuclear, solar and geothermal power. Oil and gas remain critical to economic growth. Their control thus provides a chokepoint to control the world's geopolitics. That explains the over-whelming role of oil companies in Anglo-American diplomacy. The fight to block Russia's Nord Stream 2 gas pipeline by imposing sanctions on European companies aiding in its construction has been a focal point of today's New Cold War politics.

Financializing oil rents

Until OPEC countries took control of their oil production after 1974, all U.S. oil imports were from foreign affiliates and branches of U.S. firms. That kept the balance-of-payments costs minimal, because the nominal price of oil imports was offset by charges that were not paid to foreign producers. These offsetting charges included the profits that head offices retained, managerial fees, shipping and port charges, payments to U.S. managers and U.S. labor working abroad, U.S. exports of drilling equip-ment and other capital goods used in the oil-extraction process, and interest charges on advances and loans to foreign branches and affiliates.

U.S. companies still organize their oil production abroad as foreign branches of their U.S. head offices. Their oil production operations are consolidated into the parent-company balance sheet. That enables them to qualify for a U.S. depletion allowance – a tax-deductible credit supposed to reflect the cost of how much an oil company would have to spend in obtaining an equal amount of the oil being depleted! (No resti-tution is made by this allowance to countries whose oil resources actually are being emptied out.)

When the U.S. income tax was enacted in 1913 by the Sixteenth Amendment (following a four-year fight after Congress had passed the tax in 1909), it was intended to capture economic rents. But by the 1920s, oil and mineral rent extractors had lobbied to free themselves from income taxation. The oil depletion allowance was an accounting fiction that made the oil sector effectively exempt from both U.S. and foreign income taxation.

The next challenge was to avoid foreign taxes on oil production, refining and marketing. Oil industry lawyers and accountants created "flags of convenience" in the form of shipping and trading affiliates incorporated in offshore tax-avoidance centers. Liberia and Panama have no income tax, and use the U.S. dollar as their own currency, making themselves *de facto* parts of the U.S. economy.

For many decades U.S. oil majors sold the oil that they produced in Saudi Arabia and other Near Eastern countries at artificially low prices to their Panamanian or Liberian shipping and trading affiliates. These intermediaries then turned around and sold the oil they had bought at low prices to downstream distributors in the United States or Europe, at a transfer price high enough to leave no room for refineries or gas stations in Europe or other oil-consuming nations to report a profit to their own tax authorities. Earnings on the oil industry's foreign operations are reported as being made by the trading companies registered in countries where income is not taxed.

A basic criterion of a modern state is the ability to issue its own money, and to levy taxes to give value to it. "Flag-of-convenience" countries relinquish these inherent rights of states. Panama and Liberia are not "real" states, nor are the small Caribbean and Pacific tax-avoidance islands, Monaco and Liechtenstein. They are the neoliberal ideal of what a post-industrial state should be: no taxes on *rentier* income, no social spending, but existing simply to enable fictitious accounting to conceal where profits and natural-resource rents "really" are made.

Shifting the social costs of pollution off the oil polluters

Much like agribusiness, the oil and mining sectors are global polluters of land, water and air – and seek to avoid liability for the environmental problems they cause. The 1989 Exxon Valdez 10-million-gallon oil spill in Alaska is the most notorious oil tanker accident. It was followed by years of legal protest by Exxon to delay and ultimately evade having to make restitution for its pollution. Equally notorious is British Petroleum's 2010 Deepwater Horizon oil spill, resulting from the company avoiding the cost of having to properly seal its underwater well. BP's many misdemeanors and its felony count for lying to Congress reflect the industry's hardline opposition to environmental safety regulation.

On a smaller scale, thousands of oil leaks from abandoned wells and gas fracking operations in the United States have left massive local cleanup costs. Many of the operations (incorporated individually to avoid liability) are long gone, leaving local authorities no recourse for the costs of cleanup. Even on current operations, the vast amounts of water being consumed by gas fracking have led to widespread water pollution. Television news shows depict kitchen sinks whose flow of water can be lit with a match and turned into flame. Diversion of water causes lower water tables and small earthquakes and tremors, making the earth as unsafe as the local water supply.

These problems are capped by the oil sector's long-time refusal to acknowledge its role in causing global warming, extreme weather and rising sea levels. Government policy also is often to blame. Development of Canada's Athabasca tar sands in Alberta put the goal of U.S. energy independence ahead of environmental responsibility, at the cost of enormous pollution and oil spills through the pipelines laid to bring the province's dirty oil to the United States. It takes four gallons of water to make a barrel of tar-sand oil. Back in 1976, when I was a consultant to the Energy Research and Development Agency (ERDA) for its study of gas liquefaction, my protest over the cost of water being counted as zero was excluded from the official report so as to make it seem that tar-sand hydrocarbons were economic to exploit instead of needing subsidies of free water.

Isolating oil-producing countries that break from U.S. diplomacy

After 1973-74, oil-exporting countries (OPEC) sought a more equitable share in the gains from trade by taking control of their oil reserves and quadrupling their oil-export prices. But even industrial nations that have kept control of their oil have suffered from the Oil Curse, "Dutch Disease." Norway's North Sea oil has forced its currency up to such high levels that its industry is priced out of world markets. It ultimately solved this problem (as did Saudi Arabia) by recycling oil-export earnings into U.S. and other foreign financial and arms markets, which became the ultimate recipients of the oil-rents.

Libya sought independence from the Dollar Bloc. Muammar Qaddafi took the lead in using its oil to develop a national social-welfare and educational system. He hoped to create a gold-based African currency area, and kept Libya's foreign-exchange earnings in gold instead of dollars, ejected foreign military bases, and turned to China for construction instead of going to the World Bank. These actions led the United States, France and Britain to mount a NATO attack in 2011 that tortured and killed Qaddafi and destroyed Libya. Its gold reserves disappeared, and U.S. Secretary of State Hillary Clinton distributed its arms to ISIS fighters to attack Syria and Iraq to prevent these nations from using their oil for their own domestic growth.

On January 26, 2017, and again on February 26, 2018, President Trump insisted that the U.S. had a right to Iraqi and Syrian oil as reparations for the cost of attacking these countries![12] At a January 2020 campaign rally, Trump reiterated America's right to seize the natural resources of any country that it attacked, as compensation for the costs of mounting the attack, with no reparations to devasted countries unlucky enough to have resources desired by U.S., British or French investors:

> "People said to me, 'Why are you staying in Syria,'" Trump said. "Because I kept the oil, which frankly we should have done in Iraq," he added, to cheers and applause from the audience. The president has previously criticized his predecessors for not profiting off Iraqi oil wells.
> "So they say, 'Trump's in Syria,'..." the president continued. "We have the oil, really secure. We'll see what happens with it."[13]

Also under attack for its oil is Venezuela. For many decades the United States sponsored client dictators there and in neighboring Latin America. To protect against the threat of nationalist rejection of U.S. proxies, the oil industry located its refineries for Venezuelan oil offshore in Trinidad. The aim was part of the industry's strategy to prevent oil-producing countries from integrating their production with refining oil to produce gasoline and other fuels and marketing these products under their own control.

When U.S.-sponsored coups against Venezuela's president Nicolo Maduro failed, the United States rounded up its allies to impose sanctions to disrupt its economy and starve it into submission. When Venezuela tried to use its gold to pay for vital food, medicine and other urgent imports, Britain simply seized the gold reserves held in the Bank of England, holding them for whomever U.S. officials might decide should be the official leader of that country. "It would be unlawful to allow Mr. Maduro access to the gold, a British High Court judge said, because Brit-

---

[12] This was a long-standing position for Trump. "I still can't believe we left Iraq without the oil," he tweeted on January 23, 2013. And while campaigning for the presidency on September 7, 2016, he told *Today* show anchor Matt Lauer, "If we're going to get out, take the oil. ... It used to be, 'To the victor belong the spoils.' Now, there was no victor there, believe me. There was no victor. But I always said: take the oil." Bess Levin, "Trump Twice floated Plundering Iraq's Oil to its Prime Minister," *Vanity Fair*, November 26, 2018.

[13] David Brennan, "Trump Says U.S. Troops Stayed in Syria 'Because I Kept the Oil,'" *Newsweek*, January 15, 2020.

ain's government recognizes his rival, Juan Guaidó, as Venezuela's rightful leader."[14] Venezuelans did not support or accept the U.S. appointee.

The U.S. geopolitical strategy is to make the world dependent on U.S. oil suppliers and those in its diplomatic orbit. But a backlash has occurred as blatant U.S. use of its control of oil as a chokepoint to impose its economic and military diplomacy is prompting other nations to become energy-independent. The most recent showdown is the U.S. attempt to block Germany and other European countries from importing Russian gas. In December 2019, Congress imposed trade sanctions and financial penalties against companies helping construct Russia's Nord Stream 2 pipeline. U.S. Secretary of State Pompeo travelled to Europe to insist that Germany delay its completion and warning that importing energy from Russia would make Europe "trade dependent" and therefore potentially hostage to Russian influence. U.S. sanctions were imposed against "a Swiss company that supplied the ships to lower the pipes into the water," and in July 2020 "a bipartisan group of Senators moved to widen the sanctions in order to kill Nord Stream 2 altogether."[15]

On August 10, Russian foreign minister Sergei Lavrov held a joint news conference with his German counterpart Heiko Maas, and the two re-affirmed that Russia and Germany were determined to finish the Nord Stream 2 pipeline in the near future. Mr. Lavrov urged "that European states should determine their energy policy on their own."[16]

Germany tried to meet the Americans halfway by promising to invest about a billion dollars to build port facilities to import U.S. liquified natural gas (LNG) at much higher prices than those it was to pay for Russian oil, ostensibly to "diversify its supply." But the conflict continued to escalate steadily. On January 19, 2021, the final full day of the Trump administration, "the Treasury Department sanctioned the Fortuna, the Russian-owned barge that is now laying the Nord Stream

---

[14] Elian Peltier and Anatoly Kurmanaev, "Nicolás Maduro Can't Sell Venezuelan Gold at Bank of England, Court Rules," *The New York Times*, July 2, 2020. The article adds: "British officials have repeatedly sided with the United States in maintaining painful economic sanctions against Venezuela. President Trump's former national security adviser John Bolton ... recounted how in 2019, Britain's foreign minister at the time, Jeremy Hunt, was delighted to cooperate on steps they could take, for example freezing Venezuelan deposits in the Bank of England, so the regime could not sell the gold to keep itself going."

[15] Andreas Kluth, "Nord Stream 2 Could Sever Transatlantic Ties," *Bloomberg*, July 3, 2020.

[16] www.rt.com, August 11, 2020, from *Johnson's Russia List*, August 11, 2020, #8.

2 pipe on the Baltic Sea floor. A spokesman for Nord Stream 2 AG, the Swiss-registered, Russian-owned company building the pipeline, said, 'U.S. sanctions actions against companies conducting legitimate business in the [European Union] on the Nord Stream 2 project are contrary to international law and a violation of Europe's energy sovereignty.'[17] To U.S. policy makers, foreign energy sovereignty represented a threat to U.S. unipolar geo-economic sovereignty.

3) Copper and other minerals

Like oil and agribusiness, mining always has been destructive of the environment. Large public investment in road building usually is needed to reach the mountainous areas where metals tend to be located. Corporations seek to avoid having to bear these costs. That is where the World Bank comes in, lending resource-rich countries money to "nationalize" the costs of production "external" to corporate profit-and-loss statements.

Also like the oil industry, mining companies seek to minimize what they pay to the countries in which the natural resources are located. For many decades U.S. copper companies paid Chile royalties on long-term contractual supplies at "producers' prices" much lower than the spot prices set by the London Metal Exchange. As America's war in Vietnam expanded in the late 1960s, copper prices soared as each U.S. serviceman used about a ton of the metal each year to saturate the air with bullets. The London market price rose to 72 cents per pound, but the price that U.S. companies paid Chile remained fixed at 34 cents. The differential rent was taken by Anaconda, Kennecott and Cerro, so Chile was deprived of gaining export revenue from the boom.

The ensuing popular resentment contributed to Chileans electing the socialist Salvador Allende as president in 1970. When he announced his intention to sell Chile's copper to whomever he wanted, not necessarily to U.S. companies, he was overthrown on September 11, 1973, by a military coup backed by the Nixon-Kissinger White House. U.S. control

---

[17] Brett Forrest, "Biden Administration Reviews Nord Stream 2 Gas Pipeline," *Wall Street Journal.* For discussion of the Nord Stream 2 saga following the Trump presidency, the U.S goal of controlling Europe, and the dramatic escalation of the New Cold War in Ukraine in February 2022, see my articles "America's real adversaries are its European and other allies," February 8, 2022, and "America Defeats Germany for the Third Time in a Century," February 28, 2022. At https://michael-hudson.com/2022/02/americas-real-adversaries-are-its-european-and-other-allies/, and https://michael-hudson.com/2022/02/america-defeats-germany-for-the-third-time-in-a-century/, respectively.

was restored by installing General Augusto Pinochet, after the army's Commander in Chief, Rene Schneider, was assassinated for opposing military overthrow of a democratically elected leader.

A third similarity that minerals exporters share with oil and plantation monoculture exporters is their tendency to become dependent on foreign economies for their basic needs, even for food. Chile, whose guano deposits provide the world's highest natural supply of organic fertilizer, exports it instead of using it domestically to produce its own food. The problem is aggravated by Chile's extremely unequal land distribution, blocking it from growing its own food crops. The cost of its food imports (largely dependent on U.S. grain) often exceeds the net revenue that Chile receives by exporting copper, guano and other natural resources.

Chile's experience reflects a common political byproduct of export monocultures: their association with oligarchies led by dictators. Opposing sovereign governments strong enough to tax them by claiming that natural resources are national patrimony, the oil and mining sectors have become among the leading backers of the neoliberal reaction against social-democratic reforms and taxation. As discussed below, they were major backers of the proposals for the Investor State Dispute Settlement (ISDS) provisions that were included in the Trans-Pacific Partnership plan.

In Australia, an iron-mine heiress is the country's richest person, Gina Rinehart. She has thrown her immense fortune behind right-wing attacks on public regulation and taxation of *rentier* wealth. Her public-relations war against the government's short-lived 40 percent Mineral Resource-Rent Tax (MRRT) contributed to the downfall of the Australian Prime Minister who first proposed to tax such rents by a super-profits levy.[18]

Australia has succumbed to typical Dutch Disease features as a result of its iron ore exports. When I visited the country's central bank, I was informed that Australia was fortunate enough to live in the vicinity of China, which served as a customer for its iron ore exports. The resulting influx of foreign exchange helped inflate Australia's real estate bubble – on credit – to such high levels as to make any thought of competitive industrial trade unfeasible. The central banker explained that his country did not really need industrial employment, as it could simply

---

[18] Mining companies had spent some $20 million advertising against the Rudd Labor Government's more powerful Resource Super Profits Tax (RSPT) proposal. Labor Prime Minister Julia Gillard's watered-down version, the MRRT, was a backroom deal with the mining companies.

live off its natural-resource wealth, like Canada – presumably until all that would be left would be holes in the ground.

A fourth similarity of mining with agriculture and oil is the trend of increasing returns. The deterioration in ore quality has led to techno-logical improvements that enable countries whose mines contain only 1% copper to produce the metal at a lower cost than those with richer 3% ore. In countries like Canada and Australia, large earth-moving equip-ment has mechanized mining, replacing labor-intensive methods. Most challenges of lower richness of ore are met by technological responses that more than compensate.

The major cost that mining companies seek to shift onto their local communities is that of cleaning up the environmental and health damage they cause. The "external" costs of mining have obvious impli-cations for China's trade policy. It is the world's largest supplier of rare earth metals – 17 elements that are not really rare, but are so widely dis-persed in the ground that they require immense volumes of earth-mov-ing and chemical treatment to extract.[19] In 1992, Deng Xiaoping announced: "Rare earths are to China as oil is to the Middle East."[20] Yet for many years China let Taiwanese investors mine these elements, selling them on world markets basically for just the cost of their labor and machinery, with normal profit, subject to going world prices instead of charging what it would have cost U.S. and other industrial-nation pro-ducers to extract and refine these elements.

The result was that by 2002, Chinese sales drove Molybdenum Cor-poration to shut down its Mountain Pass mine in the American West, and China undersold its rare earths by so large a gap that by 2009 it accounted for 95 percent of the world's production. Its low export prices did not reflect the costs of cleaning up the soil and air pollution caused by their extraction.

China subsequently cut back its rare earth exports. That policy prompted foreign companies to obtain access to these elements by shifting industrial production to China. The United States mounted a

---

[19] Ambrose Evans-Pritchard, "World faces hi-tech crunch as China eyes ban on rare metal exports," *The Telegraph*, August 24, 2009, notes: "No replacement has been found for neodymium that enhances the power of magnets at high heat and is crucial for hard-disk drives, wind turbines, and the electric motors of hybrid cars. Each Toyota Prius uses 25 pounds of rare earth elements. Cerium and lanthanum are used in catalytic converters for diesel engines. Europium is used in lasers." Terbium is needed to produce low-wattage light bulbs, along with europium and yttrium.

[20] Javier Blas, "Commodities: In their element," *Financial Times*, January 29, 2010.

protectionist response to revive its own production to make sure that China cannot interrupt its supply by imposing the kind of sanctions that U.S. officials typically impose on other countries to force them to do its bidding. America's protectionist response will raise the marginal price of rare earths, offering substantial gains for differential rent-seeking.

4) The neoliberal fight against host-country democracy

The fact that so many natural resources are exploited in ways that pollute the land, air and water has led to attempts to charge private companies for damages and penalties in order to create less destructive behavior.[21] But corporations fight tooth and nail to maximize their profits by shifting the cleanup costs of their environmental or health damage onto the public sector. This drive to avoid any responsibility for pollution or other damage has produced a highly focused lobbying campaign to transform international law along neoliberal lines to block governments from acting in a way that the past few thousands of years of moral philosophy deems to be enlightened.

At issue is whether there is to be any constraint on private money-grabbing and exploitation. At the deepest level, the fight is about whether the world will be consigned to live in the short run, letting assets be stripped and the public damaged by what is much like a barbarian invasion, maximizing corporate and financial profits and resource rents at the expense of economic, social and environmental resilience.

A metaphor for this destructively short-term financial mentality is Brazil's destruction of the Amazon by loggers and slash-and-burn land grabbing, cutting down forests to expand cropland for planting or grazing. Government environmental and social policy is to be treated just like financialized corporate management, living in the short run and treating future consequences as "externalities." The entire world environment is to be treated simply as a space in which the natural-resource sector can operate to take what is most easy to extract with a minimum of protection against pollution and soil erosion, leaving poisoned soils and a stripped landscape in its wake.

Environmental destruction, like soil depletion and the extinction of species, is collateral damage in what is really a war against civilization.

---

[21] The classic pollution tax is the Pigovian tax on emissions, named for the British economist Arthur Cecil Pigou, who described his proposed tax in *The Economics of Welfare* (London: 1920). This has long been a liberal policy. See W. J. Baumol, "On Taxation and the Control of Externalities," *American Economic Review* 62 (1972), pp. 307-22.

That is what a military conquest looks like. In this case, the warlord leaders are financiers and their dukedom companions are the law-making politicians they sponsor to administer their takings.

Nowhere is opposition to public regulatory power more brutal than in relations between industrial nations and their raw-materials suppliers. The Trans-Pacific Partnership (TPP) and the kindred Transatlantic Trade and Investment Partnership (TTIP) sought to implement a legal strategy to prevent countries from fining or taxing companies to recover the cost of cleaning up the damage they cause.

The TPP was initiated in 2005 by New Zealand, Singapore, Chile, and Brunei as a mutual trade agreement. The United States jumped in to hijack discussions in 2008, and the Obama Administration sponsored about 300 corporate lobbyists to transform the TPP from a trade agreement into a full-blown anti-government legal philosophy to block public regulation of health, the environment, worker and consumer protection, and any other public interest that might interfere with corporate profit grabbing and rent extraction. The aim was nothing less than to prevent public regulation in principle.

The Investor State Dispute Settlement (ISDS) nullification of democratic law

Written by U.S.-backed lobbyists as if it were a free-trade act, the Trans-Pacific Partnership's actual aim was to create an Investor State Dispute Settlement (ISDS) court empowered to block governments from suing foreign investors to recover compensation for damages to their countries that these investors cause by their activities, from oil spills to tax avoidance. The ISDS tribunals could order a government to pay foreign companies any amount, without limit, for whatever profits they accuse public regulations of impairing. This would let investors damage public health and the environment without limit, "freed" of any public responsibility for uncivil behavior. As faculty members at the Global University for Sustainability summarized the TPP, under ISDS rules,

> if foreign investors consider certain measures of the host country –
> such as environmental, labor, or safety regulations – harmful to their
> present or future interests, they may bypass the legal framework of
> the host country to bring lawsuits against its government and demand
> compensation for "loss of profits." In other words, firms that invest in a
> country are quite literally outside the law. If disputes occur, arbitration

will no longer be sought based on the legal system of that country, but on the binding international standards of the TPP.[22]

One of the most notorious examples of bringing suits overriding a country's own legal framework occurred in Ecuador after Chevron caused a serious oil spill.

> In January [2016], an ISDS tribunal in The Hague overruled the Ecuadorian Supreme Court, which in 2013 confirmed the judgment of a lower Ecuadorian court that the oil firm Chevron would have to pay out $9.5 billion in damages for polluting the environment in the Oriente region.
>
> Texaco, acquired by Chevron in 2001, began drilling in the Ecuadorian Amazon in 1964. Billions of litres of wastewater were dumped in the rivers, contaminating food sources and exposing inhabitants to carcinogenic toxins responsible, inter alia, for elevated child leukemia rates. Indigenous Ecuadorians say that oil workers dynamited their homes and subjected them to sexual and other violence. Chevron says it 'is defending itself against false allegations that it is responsible for alleged environmental and social harms'.
>
> Ecuador has already been whacked by ISDS litigation initiated by petrol firms. In 2012 it was fined $1.8 billion plus interest – more than its annual healthcare budget – after it cancelled a joint exploration venture with the oil giant Occidental. Meanwhile, the Australian mining firm OceanaGold is suing El Salvador for withholding gold extraction permits from its subsidiary Pac Rim Cayman LLC – a result of government concerns that cyanide, used in early mining to extract gold from its ore, had polluted water supplies. OceanaGold is after $284 million, more than El Salvador's annual foreign aid income.[23]

The legal philosophy underlying these awards strips away the public's right to protect itself in any country signing onto such political, legal and economic surrender. Summarizing the extremes to which the ISDS had been pressed since its inception in the 1950s, one commentator observed: "In a little-noticed 2014 dissent U.S. Chief Justice John Roberts warned that ISDS arbitration panels hold the alarming power to review a nation's laws and 'effectively annul the authoritative acts of its legislature, executive, and judiciary.' ISDS arbitrators, he continued, 'can

---

[22] Sit Tsui, Erebus Wong, Lau Kin Chi and Wen Tiejun, "The Rhetoric and Reality of the Trans-Pacific Partnership: A View from China," *Monthly Review* (2016).

[23] Glen Newey, "Investors v. States," *London Review of Books* blog, April 29, 2016. http://www.lrb.co.uk/blog/2016/04/29/glen-newey/investors-v-states/. The article notes that "bilateral ISDS treaties have been around since the late 1950s, but ISDS litigation has rocketed in the last twenty years. Cases are now being filed at the rate of one a week," and typically cost governments $8 million each.

meet literally anywhere in the world' and 'sit in judgment' on a nation's 'sovereign acts.'"[24]

A *Financial Times* summary reported that "Australia has argued that this would weaken sovereign power in favor of multinationals. Anti-fracking activists say such a mechanism would allow oil companies to sue local authorities for imposing strict environmental guidelines. Canada has raised concerns that cigarette companies could use the provisions to take governments to court over anti-tobacco regulations."[25] Lori Wallach explained on *Democracy Now*: "Corporations are empowered to drag a sovereign government to a tribunal of three private-sector trade attorneys, who rotate between being the attorneys for the corporations suing the governments and being the judges. No conflict-of-interest rules. And these three private corporate attorneys can order a government to pay our tax dollars, in unlimited amounts, to a foreign corporation because they think that our domestic environmental, land-use, zoning, health, labor laws violate their new corporate rights in an agreement like TPP."[26]

A group formed to counter the TPP, *ExposeTheTPP.org*, noted:

> Even when governments win, they often must pay for the tribunals' costs and legal fees, which average $8 million per case. ... Some of the investor-state attacks now underway are:
> Chevron trying to evade liability for its Ecuadorian Amazon toxic contamination;
> Phillip Morris attacking Australia's cigarette labeling policy;
> Eli Lilly attacking Canada's drug patent policy; and
> European firms attacking Egypt's post-revolution minimum wage increase and South Africa's post-Apartheid affirmative action law.[27]

The TPP and TTIP would have handcuffed governments from regulating health standards and other areas of public interest, by what the economist Susan George characterized as "a sophisticated, toxic US-led corporate racket, a concerted assault across the spectrum, from the environment and animal welfare to labor rights." She pointed out that if Europe lowered its agricultural tariffs, "we will have a flood of American corn and basic grains flooding into Spain and that will ruin a

---

[24] Chris Hamby, "The Court that Rules the World," Buzzfeed.com, August 28, 2016.

[25] David Pilling and Shawn Donnan, "Ocean's Twelve," *Financial Times*, September 23, 2013.

[26] "A Corporate Trojan Horse: Critics Decry Secretive TPP Trade Deal as a Threat to Democracy," *Democracy Now!*, April 15, 2015, citing cases reviewed on www.isdscorporateattacks.org.

[27] David Swanson, "TPP: The Terrible Plutocratic Plan," *Counterpunch*, July 22, 2013

lot of farmers, exactly the way the *campesinos* in Mexico were ruined by the North American Free Trade Agreement, the NAFTA."[28]

The ISDS anti-government ideology was so abhorrent to modern social values that the public was kept in the dark. U.S. legislators had to read the text in a closed room on an "eyes only" basis, without being allowed to take notes, and were permitted only to vote to support or reject the entire agreement, without being able to propose any amendments to soften the text's corporate power-grab.

When the secrecy with which the corporate interests had wrapped their power grab began to be breached in the spring of 2015, Yves Smith wrote on *Naked Capitalism*: "What may have torched the latest Administration salvo is a well-timed joint publication by *Wikileaks* and *The New York Times* of a recent version of the so-called investment chapter. ... [The ISDS] allows for secret arbitration panels to effectively overrule national regulations by allowing foreign investors to sue governments over lost *potential future* profits in secret arbitration panels."[29]

Regarding the secrecy that *Wikileaks* exposed, Smith added:

> While the US Trade Representative technically allows access, in practice, that right is empty. The Congressman himself must read the text; no sending staffers or bringing experts allowed, and only staffers from the committees with direct oversight of trade bills (the Senate Finance Committee and the House Ways and Means Committee) are allowed to join their bosses. The USTR insists that the Congressman specify what chapter he wants to review in advance. The USTR then insists that the negotiator of those chapters be present. Since those negotiators travel, it usually takes three or four weeks to find a convenient time.

Hardly by surprise, popular opposition against the corporate takeover grab was directed largely against President Obama and the Democratic Party's designated successor, Hillary Clinton, culminating in their 2016 election defeat by Donald Trump running on a platform that included

---

[28] Raquel Paricio and Esther Vazquez, "Susan George on TTIP and new European movements," *Defend Democracy*, May 4, 2016. Ms. George added that: "The direct consequences for people, for individuals is that very likely the food we import would be chemically treated, would be genetically modified, would have no labels. You wouldn't know exactly what is in your food. You could buy chicken that has been rinsed in chlorine, you could have beef that was raised with hormones, you could have biosynthetic food made out of one gene of a plant another of an animal, and this would not be labeled."

[29] Yves Smith, "Thoughts about the Trans-Pacific Partnership," *Naked Capitalism*, March 27, 2015. She adds that the ISDS panels "have been proved to be conflict-ridden and arbitrary. And the grounds for appeal are limited and technical."

opposing the TPP. Immediately upon taking the presidency in January 2017, President Trump withdrew from the TPP, having won the midwestern states (Ohio, Indiana and Wisconsin) most seriously affected by the Democratic Party's neoliberal policies.

Instead of the TPP, the ASEAN countries, along with China, Japan, South Korea, Australia and New Zealand, signed a Regional Comprehensive Economic Partnership (RCEP) in November 2020.[30] The ISDS clauses had disappeared.

Even the *Financial Times* acknowledged that the Obama Administration's radically pro-corporate demands had the effect of isolating the United States from less oligarchic nations, but similar demands were renewed by the Democratic Biden-Harris Administration that took office in 2021. "President-elect Joe Biden wrote an article in *Foreign Affairs* in January 2020 promising that his incoming "foreign policy agenda will place the United States at the head of the table."[31] Congress, which must approve all final treaties, has remained firm that no foreign countries can set policy for the United States. It insists on not subjecting itself to any international law not drawn up by its own corporate lobbyists. In response, "the EU is pressing ahead with plans to increase regulation and taxation of U.S. tech groups, such as Google and Amazon," which the Biden Administration promotes as consolidating U.S. technological hegemony.

The looming global fracture is becoming a fight by the financialized United States against civilization's most basic organizing principles. All successful societies throughout history have been mixed economies. Any rule of law requires government power to enforce it. For any society to survive and prosper, it is necessary to subordinate private gain-seeking to public long-term objectives.

U.S. diplomacy is fighting against this principle, even more aggressively as its financialized de-industrialized economy is obliged to rely increasingly on overseas rent extraction and Dollar Diplomacy to avoid a crash. The earth is to be turned almost into a lunar landscape, with craters where coal and copper mines used to be, while the earth's vegetation and topsoil is stripped away. No longer will it be elected governments that are to write and enforce the laws, but warlord corporations, to which governments are to become administrative appendages. This is truly a struggle between socialism and barbarism.

---

[30] *Deutsche Welle.* https://www.dw.com/en/asia-pacific-natios-sign-worlds-biggest-free-trade-agreement/a-55604659.

[31] Gideon Rachman, "Biden's Flawed Plan for World Leadership," *Financial Times*, November 17, 2020.

Part II

The *Rentier* Counter-Revolution

8

How the *Rentiers* Diverted Politics away from Socialism

World War I was the great turning point of modern history, but not in the direction that economic observers had forecast. Most had anticipated that the logic of industrial growth would be to tax away or nationalize *rentier* income while increasing the planning and regulatory role of governments. In the United States, anti-trust legislation broke up the Standard Oil and American Tobacco Company monopolies in 1911, while the steeply progressive income tax (ruled constitutional in 1913) fell mainly on wealthy *rentiers*. In Europe, monarchies were overthrown, starting with Russia's Tsar Nicholas II and proceeding to Germany and Austria-Hungary. The aristocratic nobility lost its hereditary land rents, and the democratic Commons gained ground over the upper houses of parliament.

Wage earners and farmers were expected to elect politicians to represent their class interest, and socialist and Communist parties were created throughout Europe and North America. As unemployment soared in Europe, financially devastated by German reparations and Inter-Ally war debts to the United States, class conflict became violent. Fighting broke out from German cities in 1921 to Britain's General Strike of 1926.

But instead of socialism carrying the day, governments became repressive as fascism spread in Germany, Italy and Spain. And today, nominally social-democratic parties in the West have been hijacked to serve a small *rentier* layer, broadly characterized as the One Percent, controlling electoral politics even as it imposes austerity on most of the 99 Percent. Western economies are becoming *rentier* oligarchies, not democracies representing the economic interests of most of their citizens.

Why hasn't industrial capitalism fulfilled its seeming destiny of freeing economies from the *rentier* classes? How has rent seeking made a resurgence, accelerating since the 1980s to consolidate support for it in the U.S. and Europe's nominal democracies?

The middle-class aim of prosperity without an alliance with labor

Much of the explanation is to be found in the role of political parties in electoral politics. To win elections, labor parties usually have had to join with those of the middle class, whose ambition is to rise into the *rentier* class. Fearing socialist threats to property rights and wealth, much of the middle class has shied from making a common cause with labor and fears radical reform as threatening and intrusive. At issue therefore is how much of a compromise needs to be made with "centrists," meaning voters who fear disrupting existing trends even though these are polarizing and stifling economies, and hence ultimately their own interests. Insecurity, coupled with hopes for upward mobility, leads centrists to support the status quo, fearing that left-wing reforms would squeeze them.

The tacit assumption of mainstream political science is that democracy enables classes to vote in their self-interest, and hence will lead to an economy serving the majority – mainly wage earners. But the class consciousness of U.S. and European politics in the 1920s has been replaced in today's world by social-democratic and labor parties supporting, and indeed often leading, the enactment of privatization and financialization policies that ultimately are contrary to the economic interests of their own constituents.

Claiming that the middle class and even wage labor may benefit from a *rentier* economy, *rentier* lobbyists have played on the hope of wage earners to evolve into the middle class and share financially in *rentier* gains, by buying homes on credit, securing a retirement income by pension funds growing financially, and making capital gains by playing the stock market.

A second characteristic of pro-*rentier* rhetoric is its attack on Big Government, that is, one strong enough to regulate and tax economic rent. Any state power not in the hands of the *rentier* classes is viewed as an existential threat to *rentier* domination of society. Roman oligarchs accused reformers of "seeking kingship," much as Greek oligarchs accused them of an egotistical ambition to become tyrants. Although it was the oligarchs who were the most oppressive, they tried to turn the tables by depicting reformers as would-be tyrants. Yet the actual 7th- and 6th-century BC "tyrants" did just what popular reformers demanded throughout all antiquity: They cancelled debts and redistributed land as they overthrew warlord elites in Corinth and Sparta, as well as Athens (by Peisistratus, who followed Solon) to pave the way for classical democracy.

The Enlightenment doctrine of individual rights was opposed to the central authority of the Church, royalty and privileged nobility. By the late 19th century the Austrian School of individualism denounced state planning and regulatory power in principle, idealizing "free markets" (in the neoliberal non-classical sense) as if these were not controlled by the *rentier* class in an exploitative manner. As in antiquity, their doctrine attacked public planning and state enterprise when it began to be used to limit the power and privileges of the landed nobility as governments were democratized.

The conflict erupted in the battle of Red Vienna in the 1920s, and in due course Austrian individualism became full-blown fascism on its way to today's neoliberal ideology. Margaret Thatcher's privatizers and Ronald Reagan's deregulators in the 1980s demonized strong state regulatory power as antithetical to personal liberty, not as freeing individuals *from* the *rentier* interests seeking to monopolize the economic surplus for themselves while reducing the rest of the population to dependency and austerity.

Under cover of an anti-tax protest and an emotional anti-regulatory populism as opposed to socialist "interference" with markets, today's neoliberals have taken control of government power by re-directing the criticism that classical economists levied against *rentiers*. Governments are blamed for exploiting taxpayers and wasting money in bureaucratic administration and rulemaking, distracting attention from how creditors and other *rentiers* are breaking free of all public constraint to act in predatory ways through their own bureaucracies and donor-class lobbying organizations. The only proper role of government is said to be that of protecting *rentier* interests, above all the "property rights" of creditors against those of the increasingly indebted 99 Percent.

The problem, as Senator Bernie Sanders pointed out, is that "You can't be on the side of the wealthy and powerful if you are going to really fight for working families."[1] The stark opposition between the interests of the nominal pro-labor Democratic Party's voters and the pro-Wall Street loyalties of its political candidates became most glaring during the Obama Administration's wave of foreclosures on the homes of millions of victims of junk-mortgage fraud after the 2008 bank crash. This episode showed how the capture of government by high finance appeared to be quite natural and hence acceptable. Despite the popular resentment at the government acting on behalf of its political campaign contributors instead of its constituency of voters, President Obama and his Attorney General Eric Holder (coming from the elite oligarchic law firm Covington & Burling) defended banks rife with fraudulent "liars'

---

[1] "Axios on HBO," May 10, 2021. https://www.youtube.com/watch?v=G9I3cgFmvII.

loans" against their victims. The financial victims found themselves without political support or even an ideological defense.[2]

At work behind such governmental protection of *rentiers* is the rhetorical and conceptual Doublethink that inverts the classical definition of a free market to mean one free for rent-seeking, with minimal government regulation and public investment. The effect is to promote privatized monopolies in finance and basic social infrastructure. The pretense is that operating the economy's key sectors for profit will provide services more efficiently and hence at lower cost than government planning could do. In practice, the alternative to government planning has been monopolistic rent seeking and centralized planning by the financial sector.

As Chapter 4 has described, post-classical economic analysis erases the distinction between value and price, and hence the concept of economic rent and the contrast between earned and unearned income. All revenue is defined as being earned productively, with "value" attributed to "supply and demand." In practice, this is construed to mean any status quo, by a process of circular reasoning that diverts attention from whether income and wealth are obtained productively or by predatory means and privileges. The resulting political logic of economic individualism rejects any need for reforms and restrictions intended to protect labor and consumers.

Already in 1843, Thomas Carlyle, in describing this self-centered perspective, observed that "all this Mammon-Gospel, of Supply-and-Demand, Competition, Laissez-faire, and Devil take the hindmost begins to be one of the shabbiest Gospels ever preached."[3] In similar words two years later, Friedrich Engels denigrated the narrow trend of what he characterized as bourgeois economics as it appeared in market exchange:

---

[2] Reviewing Obama's 2020 memoir, *A Promised Land* (Penguin), Michael Kranish cites his "reverence for the status quo" as being to such a degree that the president worried that "stretching the definition of criminal statutes to prosecute banking executives" would have "required a violence to the social order," *Washington Post*, November 13, 2020. The refusal by President Obama and his Department of Justice to prosecute shows the degree to which the distinction between rent-seeking and outright fraud and financial crime has been thoroughly erased by Wall Street's regulatory capture not only of the Federal Reserve and Treasury, but of the Executive Branch of government itself. See also David Sirota, "Can Joe Biden Succeed Where Barack Obama Failed?" *Newsweek*, January 18, 2021.

[3] Thomas Carlyle, *Past and Present* (London: 1950 [1843]), pp. 189f., cited in Rajani K. Kanth, *Political Economy and Laissez-Faire: Economics and Ideology in the Ricardian Era* (Totawa, NJ: 1986), p. 16.

The huckstering spirit penetrates the whole language, all relations are expressed in business terms, in economic categories. Supply and demand are the formulas according to which the logic of the English bourgeois judges all human life. Hence free competition in every respect, hence the regime of laissez-faire, laissez-aller in government, in medicine, in education, and soon to be in religion too, as the State Church collapses more and more. Free competition will suffer no limitation, no State supervision: the whole State is but a burden to it. It would reach its highest perfection in a wholly ungoverned anarchic society, where each may exploit the other to his heart's content.[4]

By the late 20th century, this bourgeois economics would culminate in Chicago School "free market" economics.

Capital's resistance to reforms beyond checking the aristocracy's privileges

It was one thing to increase the power of the lower houses of parliaments to check that of the landed aristocracy, but once the Corn Laws were repealed in 1846, the last thing that industrialists and bankers wanted was for governments to enact policies favoring wage earners. Nonetheless, democratic reform was spurring class consciousness. The year 1848 saw social protests sweep across continental Europe, starting in February in France and in March in Germany, inspiring the *Communist Manifesto* among other writings. Serfdom was abolished in Austria and Hungry, but these revolutions stopped short of supporting labor.

The main political conflict was between industrial capitalists and the landlord class over who would get society's economic surplus: landlords, industrial capital or the government by a land tax. In 1848, John Stuart Mill's *Principles of Political Economy, with Some of their Applications to Social Philosophy* extended the Ricardian rent principle beyond free trade to fully tax land rent. Surveying the European political landscape in 1847, Marx wrote: "We understand such economists as Mill, Cherbuliez, Hilditch and others demanding that rent should be handed over to the state to serve in place of taxes. That is a frank expression of the hatred the industrial capitalist bears towards the landed proprietor, who seems to him a useless thing, an excrescence upon the general body of bourgeois production."[5]

---

[4] Friedrich Engels, *The Condition of the Working Class in England* [1845], in Marx-Engels, *Collected Works*, Vol. 4 (London: 1975), p. 564.

[5] Marx, *The Poverty of Philosophy* 2.4 (1847), available at www.marxists.org. The French anarchist Pierre-Joseph Proudhon coined the slogan "Property is theft" and

The program of industrial capital and the urban bourgeoisie stopped short of full-fledged socialism and public ownership of the means of production, but served as a catalyst for further reforms extending to labor's working conditions. In spring 1871, Parisians protested in the streets against the economic distress resulting from the Franco-Prussian German war. At first, Lenin later explained, the Paris Commune

> was supported by the small shopkeepers who were threatened with ruin unless there was a postponement of payments on debts and rent ... it had, at first, the sympathy of the bourgeois republicans, who feared that the reactionary National Assembly (the "backwoodsmen", ignorant land-lords) would restore the monarchy. But the chief role in this movement was of course played by the workers (especially the artisans of Paris) ...
>
> Only the workers remained loyal to the Commune to the end. The bourgeois republicans and the petty-bourgeoisie soon broke away from it, the former afraid of the revolutionary Socialist proletarian character of the movement, and the others dropping out when they saw that it was doomed to inevitable defeat. ... The entire bourgeoisie of France, all the landlords, the stockbrokers, the factory owners, all the great and small robbers, all the exploiters, combined against it. This bourgeois coali-tion, supported by Bismarck (who released a hundred thousand French soldiers who had been taken prisoner to put down revolutionary Paris), succeeded in rousing the backward peasants and the petty bourgeoisie of the provinces against the proletariat of Paris, and in surrounding half of Paris with a ring of steel (the other half was held by the German army).[6]

In May the French army killed six or seven thousand demonstrators to put down their attempt to obtain progressive social policies. By that time the middle class had withdrawn from the struggle.

The emergence of an anti-government individualism opposing socialism

A libertarian professional class supported what Proudhon called "order without power," idealizing independent producers free from government authority. Like socialists, they opposed the hereditary *rentier* class. But unlike socialists, they did not want any kind of strong government to replace it, especially state control dominated by the wage-earning class. Some libertarians withdrew into utopian communities (many in America) instead of fighting politically to gain control of the state with its lawmak-ing and economic powers, the powers that actually govern a nation.

---

advocated an idealistic cooperative movement.

[6] Lenin on the Paris Commune (April 1911), www.marxists.org, from *The Militant*, March 19, 1932, originally published in *Rabochaya Gazeta*, No. 4–5, April 28 (15), 1911.

The ideal was small-scale cooperative communities in which everyone went about their business without government taxes on their business strivings. There was little discussion of industrial capital as an employer of wage labor. This was Proudhon's approach in France in the 1840s, and in the United States, Henry George led this libertarian advocacy in the 1880s and '90s.

George's eloquent denunciation of English landlords in *The Irish Land Question* (1881) attracted many reformers to support his advocacy of a land tax. Many of his followers had been driven out of Ireland and emigrated to New York and other large cities. After he gained renown for his 1879 *Progress and Poverty*, labor groups ran him as a celebrity candidate for mayor of New York in 1886. But George disappointed them by insisting on re-writing the party platform to exclude all industrial and social reform. Turning on his erstwhile supporters, George stripped away all the proposed protections of labor's workplace safety and housing, claiming that a land tax would cure all of the economy's problems, with no need for laws to protect renters, consumers, workers or debtors.

The landlord interest, Catholic Church and pro-*rentier* academics denounced the land tax and similar laws as socialism. But George insisted that he also opposed socialism and formed his own political party, unwilling to join with allies whose concerns went beyond his own single-minded focus. He supported free trade against protective tariffs and indeed opposed all taxes apart from his Single Tax on land. Moving to the political right, he supported capital against labor unions, endorsed Illinois Governor Altgeld's police attack on the Chicago anarchists, and denied that interest-bearing debt was a problem or that interest was a form of unearned income. Even regarding land rent, he avoided relating his ideas about rents, profits and interest to the value and rent theory of Smith, Ricardo, John Stuart Mill, Marx and other classical socialists.

The scope of libertarian politics thus was much more narrowly focused than that of socialism. Yet this narrow-minded idea of individuals creating an economy without government had a simplistic logic more accessible than Marx's analysis of the economy as a complex evolving system. George's books sold millions of copies more than those of Marx, but as he became increasingly sectarian, the generation of reformers whom his early journalism had inspired shook their heads at how he rejected every reform except his Single Tax panacea.

Upon receiving copies of George's *Progress and Poverty* in 1881 (two years after its publication), Marx dismissed it as "simply an attempt, decked out with socialism, to save capitalist domination and indeed to establish it afresh on an even wider basis than its present one."[7] Rent was to be abolished only to swell industrial profits. Pointing out that the very first measure advocated by *The Communist Manifesto* included a land tax as a transitional measure, Marx criticized George on the ground that his "fundamental dogma is that everything would be all right if groundrent were paid to the state," without addressing capitalist relations with labor and finance, inheritance rights, education and other basic economic and social dimensions, or what the state would do with the land rent that it taxed away.

In contrast to his contemporary reformers writing in the tradition of classical value and price theory to isolate recipients of *rentier* income, George had no logic for extending the concept of land rent to other forms of unearned income. Wrapping his rent theory in libertarian rhetoric, his aim was to pry his readers away from socialism, not to cooperate with reformers to develop a common critique of rent, profit and interest.

The political blind spot in George's Single Tax campaign was his belief that the great fight throughout the 19th century – to enact a land tax – could be achieved without a government strong enough to check the power of vested interests. To overcome the power of landlords and legislate a land tax required an across-the-board set of alliances. But George refused to see the need for any financial or industrial reform. Opposing critics of the banking system as much as he opposed the socialists, he identified interest as a form of profit, and therefore justified as earned income. In 1883,

> when he visited England to lecture on the invitation of the Land Reform Union, the treasurer, Mr. Champion, and the secretary, Mr. Frost, both Socialists, waited on George and told him that, unless he advocated the nationalization of capital as well as land, the Socialists in the organization would be compelled to oppose his campaign. To this

[7] Marx to John Swinton, June 20, 1881, from *Letters: Marx-Engels Correspondence 1881*, www.marxists.org. I discuss Marx's views on land taxation and other critics of George in "Henry George's Political Critics," *American Journal of Economics and Sociology* 67 (January 2008), pp. 1-46. For a full bibliography of Marx's observations on George, see Hal Draper, *Marx-Engels Cyclopedia* (New York: 1985), *The Marx-Engels Glossary* (New York: 1986), p. 78, *The Marx-Engels Register* (New York: 1985), p. 104, and *The Marx-Engels Chronicle* (New York: 1985), pp. 217 (#23), 218 (#31), 220 (#61), 228 (#19), 229 (#27) and 245 (#47). On June 2, 1881, Marx described George as a "panacea monger," and on December 15 he noted that George had embarrassed himself as a "humbug" on his lecture trip to Ireland and England.

George sharply and justly replied that they should have been able to find
out from his books what he stood for before they invited him.[8]

Describing George's lecture tour to Holland in 1889, his major biog-
rapher notes that he "decided that European radicalism ... was too much
opposed to interest taking to suit his own position. Many think that
interest on capital is quite wrong, he wrote home, but none knows how
to capture it, except by the state operation of all business."[9] The upshot
was advocacy of a land tax without the aim of public investment of the
proceeds in infrastructure or other social spending, leaving infrastructure to private individuals and their financial backers.

After George died in 1897, Louis Post became the head of the
Single Taxers. George's followers and those of Marx went around the
United States debating each other. In a 1905 debate with socialists,
Post forecast: "The first really great labor contest at the ballot box is
going to be between the principle of the Single Tax on one side and
the principle of Socialism on the other." The socialists agreed, but as
Seymour Stedman (a socialist lawyer) argued: "The Single Tax is not a
philosophy," but only "a proposed patch work for the purpose of reme-
dying certain presumed abuses of the capitalist system."[10] Algie Martin
Simons (editor of the *International Socialist Review*) spelled out the crux of
the argument:

> We do not justify their landlord. We stand here to make no plea for
> him. But we ask them [the Single Taxers] do you justify the capitalist?
> That is the question. And by capitalist we mean not some man ... owning
> a little shop ... We mean those men that live by virtue of ownership and
> that hire other men to do the superintending, the bossing, the managing
> and the organizing; the men whom the French call the *rentier* class as
> distinguished from the entrepreneur class; the men who own stocks and
> bonds and mortgages ... Do they justify that? If they do, then Mr. Post
> was right when he said that the last great struggle was coming between
> Socialism and the Single Tax.

From Russia to Germany and other industrial economies, the political
question was whether the middle class, the bourgeoisie, would support
a socialist revolution or ally itself with landed and financial wealth

---

[8] Arthur Lewis, *Ten Blind Leaders of the Blind* (Chicago: 1910), pp. 39f. This book
too was published by Marx's co-operative Chicago publisher, Charles H. Kerr.

[9] Charles Albro Barker, *Henry George* (Oxford: 1955), p. 533.

[10] *Socialism vs. Single Tax. A Verbatim Report of a Debate held at Twelfth Street, Turner
Hall, Chicago, December 20th, 1905* (Chicago: 1905). The debates were also published
by Kerr.

to oppose reforms that would end hopes of entering the *rentier* class. Adolph Damaschke and other leading German followers of George became prominent Nazi supporters, and in New York City the Henry George School of Social Science became a gathering place for Nazi sympathizers and anti-Semites.[11] Frank Chodorov, who became the School's director in 1937, summed up its philosophy seeking to preserve George's libertarian evangelism:

> George is the apostle of individualism; he teaches the ethical basis of private property; ... he emphasizes the greater productivity of voluntary cooperation in a free market economy, the moral degeneration of a people subjected to state direction and socialistic conformity. His is the philosophy of free enterprise, free trade, free men.[12]

One of the most fateful byproducts of George's defense of capital was to so repel socialists that they left the issue of land taxation to his followers – and in so doing, socialists drifted away from rent theory. The socialist mainstream treated classical land and *rentier* problems as subordinate to problems between labor and industrial capital.

Middle-class parties tend to oppose anti-*rentier* reform and socialism in general

Fascism emerges when other parties demur from reforms that the population wants and is ready for. That is how Trotsky explained Hitler's National Socialists seizing the initiative in the post-1929 economic collapse. Although Germany's Communist Party had a million members under arms in 1930, Stalin directed its leaders not to fight against the

---

[11] I personally met a number of the School's teachers. I was told that by the 1940s, FBI agents had become a large part of the student body, seeking to track German agents working through the School. Ed Dodson, the School's former president, told me that an assistant head of the School was a Nazi German agent.

[12] Frank Chodorov, "Education for a Free Society," *Scribner's Commentator*, February 1941, pp. 36–7. Chodorov was removed in 1937 for opposing U.S. entry into World War II. George's major follower in the 1930s, the journalist Albert Jay Nock, became *persona non grata* as a result of his anti-Semitism. By the 1990s the school had become a feeder group for Ayn Rand's Objectivist cult. George's modern publisher, the Schalkenbach Foundation, was headed by a series of followers of Ludwig von Mises and James M. Buchanan. For background on its pro-business philosophy see Kenneth C. Wenzer, "The Degeneration of the Georgist Movement: From a Philosophy of Freedom to a Nickel and Dime Scramble," in *The Forgotten Legacy of Henry George* (Waterbury, CT: 2000), pp. 46-91.

Nazis but to form a common front with them. The party suffered a large exodus of members, and soon was wiped out.

Already at the Fifth Comintern meeting in 1927, Stalin had directed the Chinese Communist Party to join in a common front with Chiang Kai-Shek's Nationalists. That set the stage for the Shanghai massacre that wiped out most of the party's leadership.

Political hesitancy such as Stalin's was endemic to many left-wing leaders. The problem of party politics holding back on radical but popular and needed reforms was apparent already in 1917, when many Bolsheviks were active in February's Petrograd revolution. The party leadership was divided over whether to press for revolutionary change or join with the bourgeois parties seeking limited political gains – stopping the war with Germany, reforming post-serfdom rural landlordship, and improving wages and working conditions.

Trotsky describes Stalin, Zinoviev and other party leaders as lagging behind the more radical workers' groups, leaving Kerensky to form a moderate government. By April, he wrote: "The masses at the moment were more revolutionary than the Party, and the Party more revolutionary than its machine ... Compromisers yielded their power to the bourgeoisie." Stalin sought "not to frighten away" the Mensheviks and bourgeoisie. But as the war continued into autumn, "The masses were getting tired of waiting, of indecisiveness, of mere words."[13]

Middle-class party leaders advocated for their constituency's own relatively narrow concerns. They sought support of wage earners to win elections, but had little interest in enacting more than cosmetic policies to help them. "As a general rule," Trotsky summarized, "the confusion was most pervasive and lasted longest among the Party's higher-ups, who came in direct contact with bourgeois public opinion. The Bolshevik Duma faction at once made a sharp right turn by joining the Mensheviks in an equivocal declaration" over "whether the Party was to prepare to play the part of the Opposition in a bourgeois republic or whether it was to set itself the task of taking power by storm." Lenin was almost alone in insisting that the party should ally itself with the masses and move to overthrow the Kerensky government.[14]

---

[13] Leon Trotsky, *Stalin* (London: 2016 [expanded from the 1946 Harpers ed.]), pp. 236, 258, 243 and 290. His book initially was drafted as a planned biography of Lenin, but Trotsky adopted it for his biography of Stalin in response to a publication offer by Harpers.

[14] Trotsky, *Stalin*, pp. 214 and 289.

Russia's revolution turned out to become a tragic detour instead of a path to a socialist future. Communist parties around the world became pro-Russian organizations, fighting most passionately against the non-Stalinist left. Throughout the 1930s Stalin fought for "socialism in [only] one country" against Trotsky's internationalism, fearing that foreign socialist victories would shift the focus of world revolution away from his own leadership. The resulting internecine fight within the left became most blatant in the Spanish Civil War against Franco, as George Orwell and others have described so vividly.

The fact that many Communist parties were identified with Russia, and that many of their leaders were Jewish, along with their socialist ideology, led them to be attacked by the militaristic, nationalist and typically anti-Semitic right wing that emerged to oppose socialist reform in the decades leading up to World War II.

Political in-fighting among socialists left progressive politics mainly in the hands of social-democratic parties, most notably Franklin Roosevelt's Democratic Party with its New Deal in the United States. After World War II ended, it seemed that industrial capitalism had adopted enough reforms to support rising living standards alongside a growing *rentier* FIRE sector. From 1945 to about 1980, Western economies seemed to enjoy moderately stable growth, with high marginal income-tax rates, anti-monopoly regulation and an array of social reforms. (But as an undercurrent, to be sure, the United States and Britain fought covertly and often violently to prevent left-wing movements from emerging free of U.S. control in Greece, Italy and much of Latin America.)

To buyers of houses and investors in the stock markets, it seemed that banking, insurance and real estate indeed were providing productive services that worked together to create a vast increase in middle-class wealth, and indeed to elevate labor into the middle class as wage-earners became homeowners, on credit. Access to education was still available at non-punitive costs, and new adults were able to achieve higher living standards than their parents had enjoyed.

The post-World War II prosperity seemed to be working until about 1980, combining industrial growth with financial gains. The banking and financial sector seemed to be helping build up industrial capitalism. But the past four decades since 1980 have seen government investment in social services, regulation of prices and anti-monopoly legislation stripped away, deregulating and privatizing what seemed to be the proper role of government. This *rentier* resurgence has been led in the political realm primarily by parties identified with labor and small business, especially under Bill Clinton in the U.S. Democratic Party and

Tony Blair in Britain's Labour Party, along with continental European
socialist and social-democratic parties. (Chapter 9 will trace these
formerly social democratic parties in more detail.)

Anti-government strategists create an economic mythology to defend *rentiers*

The neoliberal ideological reversal since the 1980s has been bolstered
by a change in the way that voters, politicians and corporate managers
think about how economies work. Reversing the tradition of classical value, price and rent theory, neoliberal economics teaches that all
income is earned, and that all forms of economic rent are not merely
transfer payments but contribute to output, as measured by neoliberal
formulations and redefinition of Gross Domestic Product (GDP).[15] This
inversion of classical logic is so far-reaching and censorial that it has
influenced Chinese and Russian planning as well as that in the Western
economies.

The second contributing factor to post-industrial ideology is the political dimension of lawmaking, taxation and other government policy.
The financial sector has gained control of the leading political parties,
including those whose identity politics traditionally have aimed at labor
and minorities. The result is that instead of reflecting the economic
interests of these voters, today's party politics primarily reflect those of
the financial sector. What formerly was "left-wing" is now right-wing
neoliberal ideology.

To counter the prospect of more democratic or socialist governments
acting on behalf of labor and industry to tax and regulate *rentier* income,
the financial sector has sponsored three major censorial tactics to justify
a financialized corporate state: (1) a narrow-minded body of economic
theory that does not (as indicated above) recognize any productive role
for government regulation or public investment; (2) the denial (discussed
above and in Chapter 4) that any income or wealth is unearned, thereby
dropping the concept of economic rent; and (3) marginalist analysis
limited to the short term, excluding all structural economic change as
"political" and therefore "exogenous" to the economic logic being promulgated.

---

[15] In my *Killing the Host* I use the metaphor of thinking of this as a parasitic
takeover of the host's brain, to make the host imagine that the parasite (in this
case the *rentier*) is part of the body of industrial capitalism, not an intrusive and extractive free luncher.

As George Burns and others are reported to have described politics
and business: "It's all about sincerity. If you can fake that, you've got it
made." And from academia to politics, if you can fake plausibility, you
can convince students and the public. Crafting a seemingly realistic logic
by faking abstract plausibility is the task of *rentier* ideology. It presents
an internally consistent picture of how economies might operate without
government, simply by individuals producing and trading amongst
themselves, with no distinct FIRE sector, public infrastructure investment or economic rent-seeking. The rhetorical trick is to keep such prob-
lematic real-world phenomena out of the discussion. This tunnel vision
is the essence of today's academic neoliberalism.

The first tactic is to deny any productive role for government in
shaping markets. From Austrian economics through the kindred individ-
ualist schools that have followed it, the main thrust is that government
"interference" can only "distort" the presumably natural equilibrium of
private-sector markets, which are said to create the most efficient and
even equitable distribution of income and wealth.

As Margaret Thatcher famously put matters: "There is no such
thing as society." There is only "the market." She called it "the social
market," not because it was social but because "the market" was to
become society itself, stripping away everything social that does not
promote private profit and rent seeking. The resulting limited scope
restricts measurement and definition of "the economy" to private-sector
transactions. Public spending is counted as overhead – as if infrastructure investment, education and health and social services do not play
a productive economic role but merely absorb taxes and other transfer
payments – on the ground that they do not themselves make a profit, as
if that means they do not contribute to the economy's overall surplus.

James M. Buchanan's "public choice" theory distracts attention from
rent-seeking by re-defining it to mean what government bureaucrats
do: increase their power and wealth at the private sector's expense. The
only economic rent that is recognized is the revenue that governments
receive. (Their "choice" is just how to exploit the economy.) This view
depicts government officials as the real robber barons, not landlords,
monopolists and other *rentiers*. The solution to rent-seeking is claimed to
be to minimize government power, especially regulatory authority, not
to tax away *rentier* income.[16]

---

[16] For a review of how Buchanan's theories were sponsored by the Koch brothers
and libertarian public relations foundations, see Nancy Maclean, *Democracy in
Chains: The Deep History of the Radical Right's Stealth Plan for America* (New York:

The implication inherent in opposing government regulation, social spending, subsidies, taxes and resource allocation is that private-sector markets are not themselves planned. The reality is that every economy is planned. If governments do not set priorities, the financial sector takes over the planning role – planning in its own interest, not the interests of society as a whole. Where there is no public regulation, financial managers fill the policy vacuum by carving out monopoly privileges for themselves and their customers.

A second (and related) aim of pro-*rentier* ideology is to strip away rent theory, by claiming that all income is earned productively. That was asserted most glaringly by the American economist John Bates Clark (1847-1938), responding as much to the land-tax movement of Henry George as to Marx. His *Distribution of Wealth* (1899) claimed that everyone deserves what they earn, by assuming that all income is earned in proportion to its recipient's contribution to production. "It is the purpose of this work," Clark wrote, "to show that the distribution of the income of society is controlled by a natural law," namely that the revenue of each recipient is equal to the value they add to the "product" being sold, whether it takes the form of wages, profits, rents or interest. Land was depicted as simply a form of business investment, and rent and interest are payments for the landlord's or creditor's contribution to production, to be statistically reported as "the amount of wealth which that agent creates."[17] Robber barons, landlords and bankers are depicted as intrinsic parts of the economy's production process, while prices and incomes are assumed to settle at their cost of production, which is defined – by circular reasoning – to include whatever charges *rentiers* manage to obtain. This logic excludes any recognition that markets may work in unfair, inefficient or unproductive ways.

This claim that all income is earned productively is the foundation myth of the pro-*rentier* economics that has shaped today's National Income and Product Accounts (NIPA). Dropping the concept of economic rent as unearned income leaves no measure of exploitation, and hence no need for the reforms advocated by classical economics. Financial and *rentier* claims

---

2017). The politics legitimizing such "free market" tunnel vision is described in Avner Offer and Gabriel Södenberg, *The Nobel Factor: The Prize in Economics, Social Democracy, and the Market Turn* (Princeton: 2016). They describe how the prize single-handedly rescued the academic standing of Frederick Hayek and his attack on government regulation as "the road to serfdom," and hence the economic rationale for Mrs. Thatcher's dismantling of Britain's public sector.

[17] John Bates Clark, *The Distribution of Wealth* (New York: 1899), p. v.

on production are conflated with the basic technology of production. To Clark and subsequent free-market economists, a "market" is the existing status quo. The distribution of wealth and property rights is taken for granted as part of economic nature, no matter how inequitable. Any revenue-yielding asset is counted as capital, even if it is a *rentier* privilege.

This is the vantage point of financiers and investors, for whom land and other real estate, oil and mineral deposits, patents, monopoly privileges and related rent extraction opportunities are treated as capital investment. That erases the distinction between profit and *rentier* income. It is the approach followed by today's tax laws, which make no such distinction, and which, in practice, give tax favoritism to financial and real estate revenue.

A third arm of this supersession of classical theory is marginalism. It focuses on very small changes in a short-term time frame in which all variables are analyzed as working within a given set of economic and political institutions, because economic structures change in the long run. Sidestepping this reality rules out discussion of structural reforms as "exogenous," outside the narrow discipline of "economics" as compared to classical political economy and the 19th-century American Institutionalist school, which were all about how to improve existing institutions to minimize rent extraction. All consideration of change is avoided, because that would open the discussion to reform, which is excluded as being "political," not an economic topic as such.

In any case, the long run is irrelevant for financial managers. Their time frame is notoriously short-term, aiming to squeeze out as much revenue or capital gain as quickly as they can. The basic business plan is simply to take the money and run, for instance to use industrial profits to increase stock prices by buyback programs and dividend payments to stockholders instead of undertaking new capital investment, research and development.

The problem is that for a national economy, the result of living in the short term is to fall behind in the long run. Financial gain-seeking undercuts the overall economy when financial asset prices can be artificially increased by asset-stripping, shrinking tangible capital investment to produce financialized wealth in the form of price-inflated stock and bond claims on the economy.

The role of political parties in sponsoring neoliberal pro-*rentier* economics

History cannot be explained simply as the unfolding of a purely economic logic based on the dynamics of interest, land rent, monopoly rent, industrial capital and wages. All these dynamics unfold in the context of laws, public regulations and administration, and in a political regime usually characterized by at least two parties, although sometimes (as in China and the United States with its Democrat-Republican duopoly) a single policy-making regime. A party's platform and actions in office reflect an implicit body of economic theory, whose basic component concepts guide the understanding of political administrators.

Voters in Britain and the United States have had little alternative to what the dominant political duopoly has been offering. The reason for this, and for the limited ability of voters throughout the West to have a chance to elect a real alternative to the post-1980 trends of polarization and deepening austerity (debt deflation, rent-seeking, monopoly at home, and military support of client oligarchies abroad) lies mainly with the character of party politics in the West.

Popularization of the post-classical ideological changes described above was necessary to enable neoliberalism to secure control via Tony Blair's Labour Party and Bill Clinton's Democratic Party. Libertarian "free market" doctrine appeals to labor's wish to become prosperous members of the middle class. Mrs. Thatcher paved the way by offering small investors guaranteed quick gains (the "free lunch" that Milton Friedman claimed did not exist) by selling British Telecom customers (the entire adult population) underpriced shares of the monopoly on its way to being privatized. After a few follow-up financial giveaways, she promised occupants of Britain's publicly owned Council Housing quick real-estate gains by privatizing their homes, initially at low prices promising the traditional source of middle-class wealth.

Housing prices did soar for insiders (the initial buyers) who bought into the privatization. Indeed, they rose so far that few new workers could afford to rent or buy into London apartments. They had to live far outside of central London – and pay high prices for privatized rail transport to commute to their jobs. Buses also were privatized. Their central terminals were sold for quick real estate gains, and many routes were cut back, depriving low-income residents of access to jobs, shopping and other needs. That was libertarian democracy in practice.

The need for an alternative to democratic centrism in order to check *rentier* power

Today, the public policies that successfully guided U.S., German and other leading industrial economies during their industrial takeoff have been largely abandoned by them, but have been substantially adopted in China. That nation's success followed a revolution that cleared away landlordism and established state control of money creation and banking. Its remarkable economic growth since 1980 contrasts sharply with the decelerating growth of the United States, Europe and their associated "market democracies." Their economies have polarized and their cost of living and doing business has risen, contributing to their de-industrialization, while their privatized FIRE and infrastructure sectors and monopolies have seen their wealth soar since 1980. Looking back through history since classical antiquity, democracy rarely has managed to keep *rentier* interests in check. State-controlled economies have been more successful than democracies in checking *rentier* dominance.

The idea of a "*rentier* democracy" or "democratic oligarchy" would have seemed an oxymoron to 19th-century economists. The fight to reduce *rentier* legislative power, after all, had entailed a fight for democracy. Industrial capitalists sought to mobilize wage earners and the middle class to oppose post-feudal *rentier* power. Economic policy and organization were expected to follow the logic of industrial engineering to create prosperous domestic and foreign markets. This logic involved public subsidy of industry and social spending to increase economic productivity and create a prosperous domestic market. At least, that was the ideal that industrial capitalism promised.

The polarization and financial austerity of Western economies since the 1980s pose some hitherto unthinkable questions: Why have democratic party politics been unable to check the *rentier* interests, whose political and economic ideology contrasts sharply with the interests of wage labor, small business and even industry, by undermining the classical dynamics of industrial capitalism? Is the West doomed to austerity, debt deflation and privatized monopolies in what were expected to be public utilities in money and credit creation, banking, education, health care, transportation and communications, including today the Internet?

Have Western democracies reached an economic limit, a paralysis of growth as a result of their failure to prevent a new *rentier* sector from taking economic and even political control? Is a successful response to today's hereditary creditor class possible in the West, comparable to the 19th century's successful fight against the landed aristocracy? Or, must the West suffer the fate of the debt-ridden Roman Empire, dissolving into a Dark Age of *rentier* austerity, with culture and wealth surviving only at the top of the increasingly steep economic pyramid?

9

The Neo-*Rentier* Road to Serfdom

The great political question facing Europe's economies emerging from World War I was what would replace their dethroned monarchies and aristocracies. How much economic rent and natural resource wealth would be socialized by taxing *rentier* wealth more steeply, creating a classical rent-free market?

That era's widespread familiarity with the logic for taxing land and natural-resource rent has disappeared from today's policy discussion. Land rent, natural-resource rent and monopoly rents have been privatized in the hands of a *rentier* class, whose financial control is becoming as hereditary as that of Europe's post-feudal nobility as it breaks free of government regulation and taxation.

Locking in its dominance by inflating the Western economies' ratios of debt to income and wealth, today's neo-*rentier* revival cloaks itself in the vocabulary of democracy. But the business plan behind its rhetoric of free markets is to impose neo-feudal debt peonage and dependency by creating markets "free" from public regulation, sponsoring *rentier* monopolies that impose tollbooth charges for access to most basic needs, from housing to education and health care. The resulting rakeoff of payments for debt service and monopoly rents has led to an economic polarization not seen since the 1920s and the prewar Gilded Age.

Unlike the literal European serfdom that tied its subjects to where they were born and lived, people now have the freedom to move wherever they want. But wherever they live, they must go into debt and pay mortgage interest, or pay rent to a landlord who hands it over as interest for the credit needed to buy the property.

The most important choke point has become the political party system. The *rentier* sector's ability to control lawmaking is reflected in the fact that despite opinion polls reporting that most Americans want public health care, no party leadership does. Democracy as managed by the neoliberal Donor Class is a set of patronage relationships governed by wealth at the top. Characterizing any state strong enough to regulate business and finance as being inherently oppressive, financialized capital wants a strong state to serve its own interests, not those of labor, consumers, the environment or long-term social prosperity.

The West's former leftwing parties have adopted neoliberal policies relinquishing political control back to the financial and *rentier* elites that seemed on the brink of losing it when the 20th century's tax and regulatory reforms began to be put in place. Tony Blair's British Labour Party and Bill Clinton's U.S. Democratic Party in the 1990s have been followed by the German Social Democrats and French socialists in this regression, not to mention the Greek and Spanish socialist parties.

What began as a fight by Enlightenment reformers against the oppressive rule and privileges of the Church and governments controlled by the landed aristocracy has been transformed into a libertarian fight to block democratic governments from regulating and taxing *rentier* income and wealth. Instead of freedom from rent-seeking as envisioned by classical political economy, the slogan of free markets has been hijacked and redefined by neoliberals to mean *protection* of rent seekers. The classical freedom from rent seeking has been inverted to become freedom *for* rent extraction. Using a libertarian rhetoric, neoliberals warn that public regulation and spending is socialism, as if freedom from financial exploitation is something alien instead of a basic right.

Money, interest and debt as the crux of economic control

Aristotle described money as a product of law – nomos, the root of our word *numismatics*, the study of coinage. Debts and creditor rights also are created by laws. All money is debt, except for gold as a commodity. Historically, the power of creditors was based on their holdings of monetary metal – which they lent out at interest.

Today, commercial banks have the privilege of creating money as credit. They oppose governments creating their own money, because that would make economies less dependent on bankers and bondholders. Opposing Modern Monetary Theory (MMT), banks and bondholders demand that governments finance their budget deficits by borrowing at interest instead of simply creating their own money by fiat.

Monetary problems ultimately are debt problems. A key victory of neoliberal intellectual censorship has been to exclude both money and debt from economic analysis. Money is treated only as a veil or "counter," not as having its counterpart in debt on the liabilities side of the economy's balance sheet. The excuse is that it would be double counting to add the value of stocks, bonds and loans to the economy's underlying wealth. Financial liabilities and real wealth are seen as mirror images that cancel each other out because "we owe the debt to ourselves."

The problem, of course, is that the 99 Percent owe debts to the One Percent. Money creation in the form of rising debt ultimately leaves less disposable income to be spent on goods and services. The superstructure of debt and financial securities (claims on wealth) polarizes the distribution of income and wealth. That leads to debt deflation and increasingly widespread forfeiture or distress sales of property to creditors.

Near Eastern rulers kept the volume of debt in check for thousands of years by repeatedly proclaiming Clean Slates that cancelled debts, liberated bondservants and returned self-support land that had been forfeited to creditors. These acts prevented financial oligarchies from gaining enough power to rival the palace and indebt economies irreversibly. But subsequent Greek and Roman oligarchies rejected kings and wrote pro-creditor laws. Centuries of civil warfare failed to cancel debts and redistribute land to the citizenry.

Medieval European creditors obtained control over realms by lending them gold and silver to wage war, securing pledges of land and other royal assets as collateral. Similar creditor leverage is still forcing debtor countries to privatize public assets to pay off their borrowings from the IMF and foreign bondholders.

The United States is unique in being able to create its own fiat dollars (Treasury IOUs) as "money of the world." After the junk-mortgage crash in 2008, the Federal Reserve created trillions of dollars of fiat credit to bail out the banks that had made bad loans. And after the 2020 Covid-19 pandemic shutdown, it created a new wave of money to lower interest rates and raise prices for stocks and bonds. Establishing independent central banks under commercial bank control has shifted monetary and debt policy away from the national treasury, while fiat money creation (along with taxes on labor and consumers) replaces taxes on *rentier* income, giving *rentier* wealth priority over credit to build up the industrial "real" economy.

Interest as a transfer payment, not a "service" for credit as a real product

For thousands of years economies transacted their activities on credit. Exchange during the crop year was conducted on credit, *e.g.*, by Babylonians running up tabs at ale houses. The major early use of money – initially, grain or other crops – was to settle debts after the harvest was in. Interest typically was only charged for late payments.

Aristotle noted the seeming irony that creditors charged interest despite the fact that metallic money itself was "sterile." As Shakespeare put matters, interest was "a breed of barren metal." The problem was that interest-bearing loans did not create the means of production to pay the debt service, but had to be paid out of what debtors were able to pay by producing or earning income elsewhere.

Pro-*rentier* economists characterize interest as being "earned" by creditors filling a basic economic need. From the medieval Schoolmen to 19th-century Austrians, interest rates were justified by reference to the creditors' cost of doing business, headed by taking risk. But in practice creditors shun risk, and demand public bailouts when their solvency is threatened, even after the massive bank fraud that caused the 2008 junk-mortgage crash. Creditors also expand their power not only by charging interest, but by foreclosing on collateral when debts cannot be paid.

Today's central banks administer interest rates by supplying or withdrawing money from the banking system. For most of the 20th century their main aim was to stabilize foreign-exchange rates. But since 2008 their aim has been to protect the FIRE sector and the rest of the One Percent from losing wealth as the economy suffers from debt deflation. The U.S. Federal Reserve and European Central Bank have inflated asset prices for stocks, bonds and packaged real estate loans through Quantitative Easing. Their "helicopter" only drops money on Wall Street and other financial centers, not over the rest of the economy.

The Austrian School has treated interest as a reward for creditors making the personal sacrifice of being "patient" and abstinent, saving their money instead of spending it on consumption. That prompted Marx to quip that the Rothschilds must be the most abstinent family in Europe – as if their wealth was obtained by consuming less, not by moneylending that ultimately limits the ability of their debtors to spend and consume.

As individuals become richer, they succumb to wealth addiction. Creditors – and indeed the rest of finance capital – are notoriously impatient. It is the height of hypocrisy to turn the tables and blame debtors for being "impatient." The doctrine of personal responsibility holds the poor to be responsible for their poverty, as if their indebtedness reflects a choice to "consume now," not simply to survive. The problem is market and debt relations in a polarizing economy.

A related Austrian speculation depicts interest charges as a fair sharing in profits made by the debtor investing loan proceeds productively. A false-historical fable is hypothesized in which the practice of charging interest might have originated among individuals lending and borrowing grain or cattle at interest, which the borrowers supposedly would have paid out of the crop surplus or calves produced by the grain or cattle obtained on credit. This "productivity theory of interest" included compensation for risk of non-payment because of crop failure, cattle dying and so forth. But no such lending of cattle or grain is attested either by anthropologists or Assyriologists. The risk historically has been placed on the debtors, who often lost the cattle that they were obliged to pledge to creditors, or which creditors simply seized. Debtors also lost their personal liberty or that of their family members, and ultimately their land rights and hence their means of self-support. The effect was to turn free owner-occupants into renters

Crops did indeed sometimes fail back in the Bronze Age (3500-1200 BC). When drought, floods or disease occurred, debts could not be paid. But thanks to the fact that most debts were owed to the palaces, temples and their collectors, Near Eastern rulers were able to maintain stability by proclaiming the Clean State amnesties described above that wiped out the rent and debt arrears. Since most of these debts were owed to themselves, there was no strong vested financial interest to protest, as would be the case by classical antiquity in Greece and Rome. These Clean Slates prevented crop failures and other interruptions from destabilizing economies, minimizing the transactions costs of human bondage and monopolization of the land.

None of these adverse effects of creditor-debtor relations have deterred pro-financial apologists from depicting finance-driven economies as minimizing transactions costs, while government regulations and taxes are said to increase such costs, by definition (that is, by an Orwellian circular reasoning). Douglass North was awarded a Nobel Economics Prize for this anti-government Thatcherite approach. His view would oppose government policy maintaining resilience by cancelling debts as increasing the risk to creditors. This aim of deregulating *rentier* wealth-seeking turns a blind eye to how cancelling bad debts minimizes risk and transaction costs to debtors, and hence to society at large inasmuch as most of the economy is indebted.

Western civilization since classical antiquity has replaced financial Clean Slates with pro-creditor laws. Medieval creditors demanded that governments pay debts by selling off their natural resources and mines, or by creating public monopolies to sell off or trade for government debt. That is why Europe's East and West India Companies were created, as well as Britain's South Sea Company and the Bank of England.

Today's financial sector likewise shifts the risk of inability to pay onto the public sector. Yet neoliberal economics refuses to treat this as a "transaction cost," or to see any negative consequence of today's creditor privileges. Yet the major cost burden plaguing today's post-1980 *rentier* economies in the West is the proliferation of private-sector credit and the resulting economic polarization. Financial and related *rentier* overhead has been the most disruptive and polarizing cost throughout most of history, impoverishing societies as the One Percent increases its wealth by holding the 99 Percent in deepening debt. The objective is to monopolize society's wealth and income for itself, as if this is a natural right, not a product of acquired financial dominance.

Celebrating wealth addiction as the economy's driving force

Milton Friedman claimed that corporate managers should ignore all social responsibility and aim simply at benefiting stockholders.[1] The implication is that governments should not impose any such responsibility. Left out of account is the fact that corporations originally were granted charters for performing services helping the economy on behalf of government policy. The 19th century saw corporations break free of any such responsibility.[2] They have no social responsibility in their charters, and according to the Chicago School, *should* not have any conscience. As Friedman claimed in his 1962 book *Capitalism and Freedom*, each attempt to limit corporate gain-seeking is a step along the road to totalitarianism! He rejected the logic for governments to set social priorities for the environment, infrastructure, education and leisure, worker safety and public health.

The degree to which his doctrine of greed has been able to gain firm control over nominal democracies is documented almost daily. For instance:

> Gina Rinehart, Australia's richest person, lashed out at politicians for their high levels of spending in response to Covid-19 and warned

---

[1] Milton Friedman, "A Friedman Doctrine: The Social Responsibility of Business is to Increase its Profits," *The New York Times Magazine*, September 13, 1970. "Insofar as [a business executive's] actions in accord with his 'social responsibility' reduce returns to stockholders, he is spending their money. Insofar as his actions raise the price to customers, he is spending the customers' money. Insofar as his actions lower the wages of some employees, he is spending their money." Herman Kahn's wife Jane Kahn told me that when she asked Friedman whether orphans should be supported, he answered, "Why do you want to subsidize the production of orphans?" All price rises are held to be an "incentive" to produce more, and all taxes a disincentive.

[2] For a good popular review, see Maurice Wormser, *Frankenstein, Incorporated* (New York: 1931).

the mining industry could face future tax increases as a result. ... Ms. Rinehart criticized Australia's political establishment for spending policies that have pushed debt levels to new highs. ... "And guess whose money they are spending? Their own? Of course not. It's the taxpayers ... which is why our taxes continue to be too high."[3]

The *rentier* worldview seeks to disable the ability of governments to tax and regulate *rentier* income and wealth, on the ground that taxing it or spending public money to prevent global warming or other social disruptions would be steps along Hayek's road to serfdom.

To defend their ideology, *rentier* interests use their economic rents to buy control of public media and sponsor a self-serving academic curriculum to influence government policy makers and to shape the perceptions and value judgments of voters with regard to how economies actually function, by indoctrinating students with the worldview of finance capital. Public-relations "think tanks" are funded, such as those endowed by Ms. Rinehart, along with award-giving institutions such as the Nobel Economics Prize committee. The most notorious funder of such propaganda is Charles Koch, who has used his net worth (estimated to exceed $50 billion) to finance a phalanx of lobbyists, think tanks and university programs including Americans for Prosperity (a grass-roots army of political activists), the Cato Institute, the American Enterprise Institute and the Ayn Rand Institute. One recent journalist summed up their common philosophy:

> In 1974, Mr. Koch gave a blistering speech to a libertarian think tank, called the Institute for Humane Studies, in which he outlined his vision of the American regulatory state, and the strategy he would employ over the ensuing decades to realize that vision. On the list of government interventions he condemned were "confiscatory taxation, wage and price controls, commodity allocations programs, trade barriers, restrictions on foreign investments, so-called equal opportunity requirements, safety and health regulations, land use controls, licensing laws, outright government ownership of businesses and industries." As if that list were not exhaustive enough, he added, "... and many more interventions." In

---

[3] Jamie Smyth, "Iron magnate rails at Australia's Covid Relief," *Financial Times*, November 24, 2020. The report adds: "She reported a 55 percent year-on-year increase in profits to A$4.07 bn, thanks to a boom in iron ore prices – pushing her wealth to $21bn in 2020, thanks to her successful drive to ax the Australian Labor Party's mining tax via her rightwing Institute of Public Affairs, a think-tank that promotes climate change scepticism."

short, Charles Koch believes that an unregulated free market is the only sustainable structure for human society.[4]

The degree to which this worldview threatens the resilience of Western civilization is indicated by the remarks of Thomas Hobbes in Chapter 29 of his *Leviathan* (1651), "Of Those Things that Weaken or Tend to the Dissolution of a Commonwealth":

> A fifth doctrine that tendeth to the dissolution of a Commonwealth is that every private man has an absolute propriety in his goods, such as excludeth the right of the sovereign. Every man has indeed a propriety that excludes the right of every other subject ...
> ... there is sometimes in a Commonwealth a disease which resembleth the pleurisy; and that is when the treasury of the Commonwealth, flowing out of its due course, is gathered together in too much abundance in one or a few private men, by monopolies or by farms of the public revenues; in the same manner as the blood in a pleurisy, getting into the membrane of the breast, breedeth there an inflammation, accompanied with a fever and painful stitches.

Hayek's anti-government *Road to Serfdom* failed to recognize that the actual road to serfdom is that which is occurring in the West today as a result of the financial sector gaining control of the government. Thomas Jefferson warned against that prospect already two centuries ago, complaining in 1825 about the "vast accession of strength from their younger recruits, who ... now look to a single and splendid government of an Aristocracy, founded on banking institutions and monied in corporations under the guise and cloak of their favored branches of manufactures commerce and navigation, riding and ruling over the plundered ploughman and beggared yeomanry."[5]

Franklin D. Roosevelt made a similar point in his 1938 Message to Congress on Curbing Monopolies:

> The first truth is that the liberty of a democracy is not safe if the people tolerate the growth of private power to a point where it becomes stronger than their democratic state itself. That, in its essence, is fascism – ownership of government by an individual, by a group, or by any other controlling private power ... Among us today, a concentration of private power without equal in history is growing ... And industrial empire

---

[4] Christopher Leonard, "Charles Koch's Big Bet on Barrett," *The New York Times*, October 12, 2020. He was a major supporter of James Buchanan, as well as "Tea Party" Republican politicians.

[5] Jefferson to William Branch Giles, December 26, 1825. https://founders.archives.gov/documents/Jefferson/98-01-02-5771.

building, unfortunately, has evolved into banker control of industry. We oppose that.

To the extent that governments refrain (or are prevented) from regulating economies, life will be shaped by financial wealth overpowering the ostensibly democratic state as well as industry. The Supreme Court's Citizens United ruling of January 21, 2010 treated corporations as "persons," letting them and their owners become the Donor Class contributing unlimited amounts of money to buy control of election campaigns. The result is to make voting power proportional to wealth, which defends its *rentier* income by asserting libertarian property rights against public taxes.

The most successful exercise in mobilizing populist opposition to taxing *rentier* income is California's Proposition 13, passed in 1978 to freeze taxes on all real estate, commercial as well as residential. The result has been an enormous price rise for real estate. Not collecting rising site values as taxes has provided a bonanza for commercial property owners and for banks as the rising rents have been paid as interest – while state and local authorities have had to cut back public services.

In 2020, some 42 years after this neoliberal tax revolt, Proposition 15 was put on the state's ballot to end the tax freeze and raise an estimated "$6.5 billion to $11.5 billion a year for public schools, community colleges and city and county governments," explained one advocate. "We can't afford to continue to give large corporations a tax break they don't need when we desperately need to invest in infrastructure, first responders, public health and public education."[6] But Californians voted not to repeal the tax giveaway.

They also rejected a law that would have obliged Uber and other cab companies to treat their drivers as employees and pay for health insurance, Social Security and other workplace benefits. Treating them as self-employed contract workers "freed" Uber from what had been normal employer obligations. Wage labor thus finally has made its way into what appears to be a professional class – as piece workers, excluded from protection under what used to be viewed as the social contract.

Paved by the steady decline in union membership since 1980, wage rates have remained stagnant while *rentier* income and wealth has soared. That is the financial sector's business plan: to roll back the 20th century's democratic reforms and lead economies down the road to serfdom and debt peonage.

---

[6] Conor Dougherty, "California Tax Revolt Faces a Retreat, 40 Years Later," *The New York Times*, October 28, 2020.

Evangelistic ideal of a (U.S.-centered) corporate global state

When the Louisiana demagogue Huey Long was asked in the 1930s whether fascism could come to America, he replied: "Sure, only we'll call it anti-Fascism."[7] As Bertolt Brecht explained: "The intellectuals cast a veil over the dictatorial character of bourgeois democracy not least by presenting democracy as the absolute opposite of fascism, not as just another natural phase of it where the bourgeois dictatorship is revealed in a more open form."[8]

Neoliberal policy sees democratic laws as intruding on liberty if they oblige business to take the common weal into account, *e.g.*, by holding corporations liable for damages that they cause. The ideal is the ISDS court discussed above in Chapter 7, denying nation-states the power to enact their own democratic laws. The kind of "government interference" that neoliberals applaud is the World Bank's recent urging that governments attract foreign investment by guaranteeing profits by socializing the risks.[9]

What was needed to create a full-blown new pro-*rentier* international economic order was a proselytizing idealization of the corporate state. The logic was couched in modern liberal terms by Democratic official George Ball, who served as Under Secretary of State for Economic and Agricultural Affairs in the Kennedy and Johnson Administrations, 1961-66. Explaining that "the nation state is a very old-fashioned idea and badly adopted to serve the needs of our present complex world,"[10] Ball urged that the modern age required a more modern planner, the multinational corporation, to replace governments as the new organizers of global markets. At a Joint Economic Committee hearing he attacked the very notion of sovereignty, complaining that governments made policy "based on parochial (local or selfish) considerations." Proselytizing the virtues of transferring the power to allocate resources and shape markets to multinational corporations, he advocated that:

---

[7] "Some of the Voices of Hate," *Life Magazine*, March 6, 1939.

[8] Bertolt Brecht, *Journals, 1934-55* (London: 2016), p. 387 (for March 16, 1948), quoted in Gabriel Rockhill, "Liberalism and Fascism: Partners in Crime," *Counterpunch*, October 14, 2020.

[9] Jomo Kwame Sundaram and Anis Chowdhury, "World Bank urges Governments to Guarantee Private Profits," November 23, 2020. https://www.ksjomo.org/post/world-bank-urges-governments-to-guarantee-private-profits.

[10] "The promise of the Multinational Corporation," *Fortune Magazine*, June, 1967, p. 80.

> to fulfill its full potential the multinational corporation must be able
> to operate with little regard for ... restrictions imposed by individual
> national governments. ...
>
> Implied in this, of course, is a considerable erosion of the rigid
> concepts of national sovereignty ...What I am recommending is nothing
> so unreal and idealistic as a world government ... But it seems beyond
> question that modern business – sustained and reinforced by modern
> technology – has outgrown the constrictive limits of the antiquated polit-
> ical structures in which most of the world is organized, and that itself is
> a political fact which cannot be ignored. For the explosion of business
> beyond national borders will tend to create needs and pressures that can
> help alter political structures to fit the requirements of modern man far
> more adequately than the present crazy quilt of small national states.
> And meanwhile, commercial, monetary, and antitrust policies – and
> even the domiciliary supervision of earth-straddling corporations – will
> have to be increasingly entrusted to supranational institutions....[11]

A global corporate state thus was depicted as an idealistic alternative
to the nation-state, whose rivalries had led to World Wars I and II. But
in practice, this has turned out to be an American nationalism direct-
ing other countries to create *rentier* economies to serve as spokes in the
U.S.-centered global economic wheel.

The cover story for turning control over to the corporate state was a
promise that companies would sponsor rising living standards by investing in technology to raise productivity. But despite soaring productivity
gains since 1980, wages have stagnated and American employees are
being worked even harder as their workplace conditions have become
more harsh. Most are being driven deeper into debt as the financial
sector monopolizes and appropriates the economic surplus. As the satir-
ical publication *The Onion* put matters in a comic headline: "Cost Of
Living Now Outweighs Benefits."[12]

---

[11] Matt Stoller, "'Free Trade' Pacts Were Always About Weakening Nation-States
to Promote Rule by Multinationals," repr. *Naked Capitalism*, February 21, 2014,
https://www.nakedcapitalism.com/2014/02/matt-stoller-free-trade-never-trade-
eroding-nation-states-advance-rule-multinationals-stealth-colonialism.html, citing
the Congressional Record transcript of the July 20, 1967 hearing on "The Future
of U.S. Foreign Trade Policy," available at http://obamatrade.com/wp-content/
uploads/1967-NAFTA-discussion.pdf, pp. 272-73. Stoller makes the point that
pressing for the reduction of trade barriers with the Kennedy Round – and by
extension, the 2016 push for the TPP and TPIP – was less about free trade than
about reorganizing the world so that corporations could manage resources for what
Ball characterized in his Congressional presentation as "the benefit of mankind."

[12] *The Onion.* https://www.theonion.com/cost-of-living-now-outweighs-bene-
fits-1819567799.

Disabling the ability of democratic party politics to check the *rentier* interests

In practice, only the two official parties can play a significant role in the U.S. Congress. Independent candidates such as Bernie Sanders are obliged to caucus and vote either with the Democrats or Republicans. The aim is to prevent any alternative party from gaining proportional representation such as occurs in Europe's parliamentary systems. Corporate control of the two official parties allows voters to select only those candidates vetted by the elite – at best, to choose who seems to be the lesser of two evils.

Two journalists recently discussed how the Democratic Party leadership blocked Massachusetts Senator Elizabeth Warren from becoming Treasury Secretary after she campaigned for consumer financial protection against bank abuses and urged a wealth tax on America's ruling One Percent.

> Paul Jay: I sat with Tom Ferguson, who does a lot of "money in politics" research. I asked him once, "Would finance rather go with a kind of fascism that Trump's heading towards or would they put up with a Warren?" And his answer was, "As long as the wealth tax is on the table, they'll go with fascism." And maybe it actually was a tactical mistake of hers. Maybe the wealth tax – it's just not the time to do that, given how strong the rightwing forces are.
>
> Matt Taibbi: I think it's obvious that they would have preferred Trump over a Warren because they didn't see Trump as a terribly dangerous figure. He gave them everything they wanted in the pandemic bailout and his tax policy and military spending. And, yeah, Warren's wealth tax was a problem because there was no way to loophole your way out of it. That was the whole point of the proposal. It was designed to make sure that companies just paid taxes on what they actually earned as opposed to what they reported or where they reported it.[13]

In 2016 the Democratic National Committee preferred to lose the presidential election to Donald Trump with Hillary Clinton as their candidate than to win with Senator Sanders. Again in 2020 they manipulated the presidential primary elections to stack the deck for the second time against Sanders, putting forth the decrepit Joe Biden (along with the equally unpopular Vice-Presidential candidate Kamala Harris),

---

[13] A Dangerous Moment for the Democratic Party – Matt Taibbi, theAnalysis. news, November 10, 2020. https://theanalysis.news/interviews/a-dangerous-moment-for-the-democratic-party-matt-taibbi/.

just sneaking to a win over Mr. Trump while losing congressional seats threatening their majority.

Biden's election was followed by the Democrats' Night of the Long Knives to marginalize the left-wing "Squad" in the House of Representatives. The Democratic National Committee simply purged them from funding and from appointment to meaningful positions.

The revival of *rentier* political power threatens a regression of Western civilization to one controlled by a narrow finance-based class lording it over the economy and the rest of society. The political crisis has been most blatant where neoliberals had the freest hand to create their ideal market from scratch – namely, in advising Soviet Russia to use shock therapy after 1991 to create a crisis enabling natural-resource rents to be privatized and the selling off of public utilities for token amounts to compliant insiders, who dollarized the value for their takings by selling a large part of their shares to Western buyers. This was applauded as wealth creation, and it certainly did create wealth for U.S. investors in the post-Soviet stock market and real estate. The neoliberalized post-Soviet states became an object lesson in what to avoid in the Western model, as Chapter 11 will describe.

Unlike the situation in the 1920s, force has not been necessary in the United States, Europe and the post-Soviet economies to prevent industrial capitalism from evolving toward socialism. A distorted narrative of history and economics has clouded public understanding of where today's *rentier*-based finance capitalism is leading.

So we are brought back to how Rosa Luxemburg summarized matters: the choice is between socialism and barbarism. Creating privatized kleptocracies to serve as client oligarchies is a basic aim of U.S. diplomacy, locking in its power by controlling the international monetary and financial system. That is the topic of Chapter 10.

10

Dollar Hegemony: The Privilege of Creating "Paper Gold"

Imagine that you could go to the store to buy groceries, eat out in restaurants, pay your rent, and buy automobiles and furniture simply by writing IOUs to the sellers. People cannot do this in practice, because nobody would accept their IOUs for long – unless they had legal recourse to seize the income and property of whomever has signed the promissory note, as banks do when they make loan agreements.

But what if the grocery store or other businesses just accepted your IOU, and indeed paid *their* suppliers partly with it, circulating it like real money?

That is the kind of free monetary ride that the United States enjoys in its foreign relations. Most of the excess dollars that its military and civilian economy spend abroad end up in foreign central banks. Foreign exporters receiving these dollars exchange them at their central banks for their own domestic currency to conduct their business. The central banks have no real recourse other than to recycle these dollars by purchasing U.S. Treasury IOUs. They are not permitted to use their dollar inflows to buy the commanding heights of the U.S. economy. OPEC countries, for instance, have been told that they can use their surplus dollars to buy into the U.S. stock market as junior partners, but not to buy any real control over vital U.S. assets. China likewise is blocked from buying important information technology companies.[1]

Every empire in history has drawn money and resources into itself from its dependencies. This power always has been backed by military force, and most of the tribute has been spent on this military force. America's 750 foreign military bases around the world are in this tradition, requiring foreign financing, while its domestic military-industrial complex is the major drain on the domestic Treasury budget.

---

[1] This chapter summarizes my *Super Imperialism: The Economic Strategy of American Empire* ([1972], new ed., Dresden: 2021).

What sustains this military power is U.S. control of the international financial system, giving it a free ride and enabling it to spend over $1 trillion annually to field military operations that would collapse the exchange rate of any other nation, and which indeed drove the dollar off gold in 1971. Despite its widening balance-of-payments deficit beginning with the Korean War in 1950 and accelerating with its subsequent military spending on the Vietnam War, U.S. diplomacy has been able to retain its financial domination over the world economy – no longer by its power as the world's major creditor, but as its largest debtor. The dollars that the U.S. Government and private investors spend abroad to pay for America's military and economic encirclement of the world pile up as monetary reserves in foreign central banks, whether countries want these dollars or not, and despite rising concern about the U.S. military adventurism that these dollar outflows finance.

This financial arrangement is what makes America "the exceptional economy." When other countries run deeply into debt, the IMF and bondholders bring financial pressure to dictate their economic policy, privatize their natural resources and public enterprises, and impose austerity on their labor force. But U.S. officials have always rejected foreign attempts to dictate its domestic or foreign policy.

In being exempt from reliance on having to earn foreign money in order to conduct its military policy, the United States enjoys a fortunate monetary position akin to that of classical Athens described in Chapter 3. Athens was able to build expensive trireme ships, hire mercenaries and support military allies with silver "owls" minted from its own silver mines at Laurion. The U.S. Treasury does not have to produce or sell silver or gold, but can simply print dollars as "paper gold," Treasury IOUs to spend abroad.

Unlike the foreign debt of other countries, nobody expects the United States to pay off its IOUs. In fact, official U.S. dollar debts have virtually no likelihood of being paid off. That, indeed, is what makes the United States so exceptional. The United States has now enjoyed this self-financing unconstrained free lunch for the past fifty years.

However, in the face of growing foreign disagreement with the aims of Dollar Diplomacy, a rising number of countries are seeking to break free and de-dollarize their economies to stop funding the U.S. military encirclement of their territory, and to limit the ability of U.S. investors to buy up their most profitable industries and natural resources.

Inter-governmental imperialism contrasted with private-sector imperialism

Prior to World War I, government intervention in foreign lands followed the path of private trade and investment. Governments used force to seize lands rich in minerals, tropical crops and other raw materials, and to expand the interests of their nationals in these areas. Private capital took the initiative; government policy followed.

But the debt settlements imposed in the wake of World War I saw inter-governmental debts far exceed the value of private foreign investment, and governments to have strategic objectives quite distinct from those of private investors. Government demands for payment crowded out private investment opportunities. And for the first time in modern history, international finance became dominated by a single government. The U.S. Government emerged as the overwhelming world creditor – mainly to its allies for their arms debts incurred prior to U.S. entry into the war. Its monetary claims far overshadowed private loans and investments.

The priority of government over private interests was assumed to be natural, and hence that debt payments to the U.S. Government should take precedence over private-sector concerns. This view was held even to the point of imposing unemployment and the Great Depression, setting the stage for World War II. The world sacrificed its growth and stability by agreeing to satisfy the demands of public as well as private creditors so large that debtor countries could pay only by subjecting their economies to austerity. Foreign governments siphoned off economic surpluses to pay debts to the U.S. Government.

No writer had anticipated that the main destabilizing and exploitative factor would be government, not private capital. During the war Lenin's *Imperialism: The Highest Stage of Capitalism* (1917) had anticipated that private capital and its growing concentration would become the major cause of future conflict. To many observers, the main hope for world peace seemed to be inter-governmental cooperation to restrain commercial and financial rivalries.

Within the emerging postwar finance capitalism, however, private and government policies were indeed at cross purposes. The overriding concern of U.S. diplomacy was for its own world power, even to the point of disrupting prosperity, and hence the profits of its bankers and investors. That is why President Herbert Hoover's 1931 announcement of a moratorium on U.S. Inter-Ally debt demands and German reparations made stock markets jump throughout the world. Debt relief suspending inter-governmental claims restored foreign-exchange stability, more than repaying the United States for the loss of the nominal $250 million in foregone debt service.

Wall Street bankers wanted the government's creditor claims out of the way so as to leave room for a renewal of private credit. A conflict broke out on the eve of the 1933 London Economic Conference as incoming president Franklin Roosevelt replaced Hoover, who – along with Republican Treasury Secretary Ogden Mills – supported the Eastern banking interests. Led by Morgan partner Russell Leffingwell, the Wall Street internationalists tried to promote Norman Davis, a State Department Democrat, to a position of influence. But Roosevelt's advisor Raymond Moley expressed his mistrust, writing that Davis "wanted to get the debts out of the way to facilitate reviving private lending to Europe." Roosevelt rejected Davis's advice.[2]

The U.S. aim was to subordinate foreign interests to those of its government's creditor claims, while escalating America's protective tariffs and quotas. Critics complained that the Roosevelt Administration's "America first" policy was rejecting world leadership and even world recovery, by blocking debtor countries from earning the dollars to pay by exporting more to the United States. But Roosevelt and his advisors did not want an altruistic internationalist leadership that would have rehabilitated British, French and other governments and their economies to act as equals of America. In the U.S. view, freeing Europe from having to pay its war debts to the United States would simply leave its governments with more money to re-arm and threaten the world once more with war.

War did occur, of course. And the U.S. Government organized the aftermath to gain an even stronger position vis-à-vis Europe and Japan. In 1944-45 it moved to absorb the Sterling and Franc areas into its own dollar-centered financial system. In the U.S. nationalistic view, no other country or grouping of countries should be in a position to dictate economic or foreign policy to the United States. Insisting on retaining unilateral national autonomy, U.S. diplomats did not want to create a grouping of equal nations. They wanted America's own unipolar dominance, and have sought that goal ever since.

Setting to work on global planning in the closing years of World War II, U.S. officials once again used the government's creditor power as a lever to shape postwar diplomacy. With the Axis powers vanquished,

---

[2] Raymond Moley, *After Seven Years* (New York: 1939), pp. 96-100, and *The First New Deal* (New York: 1966), pp. 52ff.

it was now time for the United States to subdue its allies. But instead of seeking direct repayment of its wartime loans (which would have repeated the post-World War I debt tangle), U.S. officials set about to conquer America's allies in a more enlightened manner, demanding concessions of a commercial and political nature, above all to open foreign markets to U.S. exporters and investors.

Viewing British imperial interests in particular as being antithetical to those of the United States, the first postwar objective was for the dollar to replace sterling as the world's leading currency and indeed, as the basis of the global monetary system. America's creditor power remained its key leverage. Early in the war Treasury Secretary Henry Morgenthau Jr. "started putting pressure on the British to sell off their big American companies – Shell Oil, Lever Brothers and Brown & Williamson Tobacco." On January 28, 1941, the Senate Foreign Relations Committee reported that: "If Lord and Lady Astor own real estate in New York their assets will be on the auction block with the rest."[3]

Lend-Lease and Bretton Woods: Blocking alternatives to U.S. economic dominance

The first fight was over America's Lend-Lease loans to finance Britain's war effort. The basic principle of Lend-Lease was free trade. Called "multilateralism," it was nationalistic from the U.S. vantage point, calling for a strict commitment to non-discriminatory foreign trade and the end of British Empire Preference, the preferential tariff arrangements between Britain and its colonies and former colonies within the British Commonwealth.

Ending that protectionist system opened up British and European colonial raw-materials resources and import markets to all comers, naturally led by the United States. Whereas Britain had opened up China by force, America opened up Britain and its empire by a "Your money or your life" offer at a time of British wartime neediness. Paragraph (2) of Article VII the Lend-Lease agreement called for "the elimination of all forms of discriminatory treatment in international commerce; and (3) the reduction of tariff and other trade barriers."[4] When Keynes was

---

[3] Robert Skidelsky, *John Maynard Keynes*, Vol. III: *Fighting for Freedom, 1937-46* (New York: 2001), pp. 99 and 102f.

[4] Hal Lary and Associates, *The United States in the World Economy* (U.S. Department of Commerce, Economic Series No. 23, Washington, D.C.: 1943), p. 12. Britain asked that Lend-Lease be made retroactive so as to recoup the heavy expenditures it had made in the United States before the Lend-Lease program had begun. Its

handed a draft of Article VII of the Lend-Lease agreement on July 28, 1941, he noted that it said "nothing at all about the essential counter-parts in American policy – the lowering of tariffs and the avoidance of a serious post-war depression."[5]

Harry Truman, then head of the Senate's War Investigating Commit-tee, demanded in November 1943 that when it came time for repayment of Lend-Lease and other American credits to Britain: "if Britain cannot pay us dollars for petroleum needed by her and cannot, by reason of a shipping shortage or other situation, procure the petroleum she needs from the petroleum resources she controls in Asia, South America, and the Dutch East Indies, consideration should be given as to whether she might not pay for the petroleum obtained from us by transferring to us her ownership of an equivalent value of foreign petroleum reserves or of the Englishheld securities of the corporations having title to such reserves ..."[6]

The U.S. Government insisted that Lend-Lease support stop with the end of hostilities, and by 1945 its Lend-Lease claims on Britain amounted to $20 billion. U.S. negotiators set the stage for the $3.75 billion British Loan of 1946 by terminating Lend-Lease to Britain upon the declaration of peace ending the war. That threatened its economy with insolvency, leaving Britain with little alternative but to agree to the terms of the loan, which served as a lever to pry open Britain's Empire Preference system, with its nearly $10 billion in blocked sterling wartime accounts accumulated by India, Egypt, Argentina and other countries by the end of 1944. These sterling balances (debts owed by Britain to Sterling Area countries for supplies they had provided during the war) were restricted to be spent on British exports.

It is natural for the economic theory and diplomacy of every country to reflect its immediate situation and self-interest. And the rules that U.S.

---

request was rejected, leaving substantial sums owed for the military and economic support Britain had obtained prior to that date.

[5] Richard N. Gardner, *Sterling-Dollar Diplomacy* (Oxford, 1956), p. 57. The British Empire Preference or "Imperial Preference" system of relatively low tariffs among Commonwealth members was developed in 1932 at the Ottawa Conference to maintain some degree of payments stability within the British Empire in the face of the Inter-Ally debt disruptions.

[6] Arthur D. Gayer, "Economic Aspects of Lend-Lease," in Jacob Viner *et al.*, *The United States in a Multinational Economy* (New York: 1945), p. 140, referring to *Additional Report of the Special Committee Investigating the National Defense Program*, Senate Report No. 10, Pt. 12, 78th Cong., 1st Sess. (Washington, D.C.: 1943), pp. 13f.

diplomats drew up for the International Monetary Fund (which Britain was required to join as a condition of the British Loan) sought to free these sterling balances to be spent on foreign (largely U.S.) exports. From the American vantage point, access to foreign markets was deemed to be a precondition for achieving full employment at home. But U.S. exports would be constrained if foreign countries were permitted to insulate their economies to promote their own growth. To prevent them from enacting protective tariffs, quotas or financial barriers such as competitive devaluation, multiple exchange rates, bilateral clearing agreements or blocked currency practices beyond a brief transition period, the United States took the lead in forming the IMF to ensure a postwar system of fixed currency parities.

Britain and other countries receiving U.S., IMF or World Bank aid (which was an added incentive for countries to join the Fund) were obliged to relinquish concepts of self-sufficiency and reject a return to protectionist policies and controls. Any nation wishing to join the Bank had to agree to join the Fund and to service all its outstanding and future official government and government-guaranteed debt to foreign creditors. The Fund was to be financed by member-country subscriptions in their own currencies, with voting rights proportional to their subscription quota. The United States had the largest vote (giving it veto power), on the logic that its dollars were expected to be the most in demand by war-torn countries.

The terms of the British Loan precluded Britain from devaluing the pound sterling until 1949, keeping it overvalued and forcing Britain's balance of payments into deepening deficit. It also prevented Sterling Area reserves (including the sterling balances) from being spent on British and British Empire goods. Sterling became a satellite currency of the U.S. dollar, reversing the situation that had existed in the 19th century. Keynes saw that the U.S. plans for an open international economy "sacrificed domestic employment to free trade and the gold standard," locking Britain into a high exchange rate that required it to impose domestic austerity to prevent spending on imports.[7]

By surrendering to these terms, Britain joined the United States in a united front vis-à-vis Continental Europe to negotiate the operational philosophy of the Bretton Woods institutions and the proposed International Trade Organization. Then the developed nations as a group, having accepted the U.S. terms in the face of their own economic duress, confronted the less developed countries with a *fait accompli*. That opened

---

[7] Skidelsky, *Keynes*, pp. 130f.

war-devastated markets to U.S. exports and established the postwar order for most of the world on principles locking in U.S. leadership and domination.

U.S. opposition to international money independent of the dollar and U.S. gold

As U.K. Treasury representative, Keynes went to the 1944 Bretton Woods Conference with a plan for an International Clearing Union to settle multilateral payments by putting pressure for adjustment on creditor economies (mainly the United States), not deficit economies (such as Britain). His plan was for the IMF to issue a fiat international currency, the bancor, to finance balance-of-payments deficits. The Clearing Union would provide credit to help countries invest in productive economic expansion.

Unlike the U.S. plan for a fund of dollars and other national currencies, Keynes's plan did not require governments to pay their subscriptions in their own currency. The bancor was to be a blanket overdraft facility. International payments would be effected by the Clearing Union debiting the paying country and crediting the receiving country.

Most important, Keynes sought a Scarce Currency Clause. Its basic philosophy was that creditor nations had an obligation to make debts payable by importing goods from the debtor countries. If the balance of payments of creditor nations became unmanageably high, these credits might be canceled altogether, freeing the deficit countries from obligations that had become unpayable. That would prevent creditor nations from monopolizing the world's money.

But such a financial monopoly was precisely what U.S. officials desired. By providing new dollar credits to supplement Europe's depleted gold reserves, America enabled the metal to be maintained as the basis of international finance instead of the managed paper credit standard that Keynes proposed. The dollar was made as good as gold, convertible into the metal at the rate of $35 an ounce under the gold-dollar exchange standard. U.S. policy thus was determined to ensure that no alternatives to the dollar and its own near monopoly of gold holdings emerged.

Europe, running balance-of-payments deficits, lost gold rapidly to the U.S. Treasury, which increased its holdings steadily. When the war ended in 1945, it held about $20 billion, accounting for 59 per cent of world gold reserves. U.S. holdings rose by $4.3 billion by 1948, and by 1949 its gold stock reached an all-time high of $24.8 billion, reflecting an inflow of nearly $5 billion since the end of the war.

Neither the World Bank's reconstruction loans nor the IMF's balance-of-payments stabilization loans were sufficient to meet the financial needs of European recovery. France lost 60 percent of its gold and foreign exchange reserves during 1946-47, and Sweden's reserves fell by 75 percent. The effect was to concentrate in U.S. Government hands most of the major decisions as to how much, to which countries, and on what conditions international loans would be extended.

Foreign wars push the U.S. balance of payments into deficit

From outbreak of the Korean War in 1950 onwards, the U.S. balance of payments moved steadily into deficit. The private sector's trade and investment were in close balance, and U.S. foreign aid was tied to the purchase of U.S. exports and so actually produced a payments inflow. The deficit resulted entirely from U.S. military spending.

Europe and other countries initially welcomed the net outflow of dollars. It helped them increase their international reserves and afford pro-growth policies. As the U.S. deficit widened, Europe and other countries began to rebuild their gold stocks. That freed them from pressures to prevent their exchange rates from declining by slowing down their economies in order to limit imports.

By the 1960s the Vietnam War and related U.S. military spending in Asia made U.S. gold losses serious. Every Friday the Federal Reserve Board published statistics on the gold cover – the degree to which paper U.S. currency was backed by the Treasury's monetary gold stock. U.S. law required at least 25 percent gold cover. The gold drain was reducing this legal gold cover toward the point where insufficient bullion would remain available to pay foreign countries turning in their surplus dollars for gold.

General de Gaulle was most vocal in cashing in the surplus dollars flowing into France from its banks in Vietnam, Laos and other former French colonies, where there were few U.S. banks. Chase Manhattan was asked to help solve this problem by setting up a branch in Saigon, which was built like a fortress. That was not a business decision, but a show of patriotism by David Rockefeller. He had taken over the bank from George Champion, who had been one of the most outspoken critics of the Vietnam War and its associated military spending, accusing it of not being fiscally responsible. Political support for U.S. military policy did not come from Wall Street, but from the labor movement and Cold War advocates of the national-security state. In Europe, large anti-American demonstrations were organized in response to the atrocities reported from the war.

Matters reached crisis proportions by January 1965, when President Lyndon Johnson announced a set of "voluntary" balance of payments controls. U.S. banks and companies were told not to increase their total foreign loans or investments by more than 5 percent during the coming year. That disrupted business plans. Banks make their profits by increasing their lending, and that was limited. The oil industry also was strongly affected, fearing that foreign rivals would gain an edge in new investment.

The war in Southeast Asia was conducted with almost no understanding of how it affected the U.S. business sector. Companies pointed out that much of what was reported as foreign "investment" did not really constitute a balance-of-payments outflow. When oil companies (or airlines or manufacturing firms) moved U.S. equipment and machinery or lent dollars to their foreign branches or affiliates to pay U.S. management, interest charges and other expenses, including for imports of U.S. equipment, these dollars never really left the U.S. economy. The trade and GDP figures reported trade and investment "as if" it were all paid in cash rather than being largely balance-sheet entries with little actual outflow after accounting for countervailing exports of U.S. goods and services. As a result of industry lobbying to explain these facts of international life to Congress, the oil industry was made exempt from the Johnson "voluntary" program.

But banks and civilian industry suffered. American business continued to be boxed in by the financial effect of U.S. military policy. Interest rates rose, and after public opposition to the war forced President Johnson to announce in 1968 that he would not run again for office, the Democrats lost overwhelmingly to Richard Nixon, who promised a plan to end the war.

However, Secretary of State Henry Kissinger persuaded Nixon to extend the war to Laos and Cambodia, hoping to "bomb the enemy to the peace table." As the U.S. military buildup escalated, other countries stepped up their gold purchases. Germany kept pace with France in turning in its excess dollars, although without the public verbal confrontation expressed by the Gaullists.

U.S. tactics to create a free lunch to finance its military payments deficit

By the late 1960s, U.S. diplomats revived Keynes's idea for the IMF to create a fiat bancor, proposing Special Drawing Rights (SDRs). The idea was to give member countries overdraft facilities in proportion to their IMF quotas. SDRs would enable the United States to use the IMF as a means of financing its international military spending responsible for its balance-of-payments deficits. The difference was that Keynes's plan aimed at financing economic recovery and expansion of Europe's economies to create means of production, not military spending to destroy it in countries deemed to be U.S. adversaries. Understandably, foreign countries balked.

Finally, by August 1971 it became apparent that the price for continuing U.S. military war-making was for the Treasury to either lose its shrinking gold stock or cut the dollar loose from gold. President Nixon chose to stop supplying Treasury gold to the London Gold Pool to hold down the gold price – which quickly soared. That effectively ended the dollar's convertibility into gold at $35 an ounce.

Many politicians worried that this would mean the end of America's diplomatic leverage over the world's financial system. Ever since World War I the United States had dominated world diplomacy by its creditor position, monopolizing most of the world's gold and therefore the global monetary base. Other countries suffering gold outflows had to impose austerity. "Hard money" economists forecast that continuing to run a balance-of-payments deficit would drive the dollar down and cause inflation. And indeed, Treasury Secretary John Connally started the decline by depreciating the dollar's exchange rate by 5 percent at the same time that he stopped gold sales. When that reduced Europe's valuation of its dollar reserves as measured in its nations' own domestic currencies, Connally quipped to Europeans: "It's our dollar, but your problem."

However, what followed the 1971 delinking of the dollar from gold turned out to be quite unanticipated. It opened the way for a new form of dollar hegemony – one based on America's leverage as the world's major monetary debtor.

The dilemma that America's Dollar Diplomacy poses for foreign central banks

Central banks had little option regarding what to do with the surplus dollars being pumped into the world monetary system by U.S. military spending and investment buyouts of foreign companies. Central banks did not buy stocks, and they were not going to buy U.S. companies or real estate, as sovereign wealth funds had not yet come into being. So the great question was how Europe and other economies would cope with the glut of new dollars, now that they no longer were able to cash them in for gold.

Until quite recently, what central banks have bought usually has been limited to the bonds of other governments. The only major supply of such securities in the 1970s and indeed down to fairly recent times were U.S. Treasury bonds and IOUs. So that is what foreign central banks bought with their surplus dollars. In the absence of the gold standard, the world moved onto a U.S. Treasury-IOU standard.

Here's the problem that foreign economies faced: If their central banks did not recycle their dollar inflows into the U.S. economy – by buying Treasury securities – their exchange rates would rise against the dollar. That would raise the price of their exports to Dollar Area economies. To prevent the dollar glut from giving Dollar Area exports a price advantage, nations receiving a surplus of these dollars used them to buy Treasury securities, supporting the dollar's exchange rate.

This recycling meant that contrary to usual experience, America's largely military balance-of-payments deficit helped finance the domestic budget deficit. Both deficits stemmed largely from spending on the military-industrial complex.

This was a new kind of international circular flow, and it tended to lock in foreign central banks. The more U.S. securities they bought, the more they stood to lose (as measured in their own domestic currencies) if the dollar depreciated. U.S. officials encouraged recycling by inviting central banks to buy U.S. stocks and private-sector bonds as well as Treasury securities – but not majority ownership of leading U.S. companies. Only the United States as the world's "exceptional nation" could do this to other economies (subject to occasional nationalistic pushback abroad).

American demands that foreign countries recycle their dollar inflows into U.S. bond markets became explicit by late 1973 and early 1974, when OPEC oil producers responded to the quadrupling of U.S. grain prices by quadrupling their oil prices so as not to lose purchasing power. State Department officials told their counterparts in Saudi Arabia and other Arab oil-producing countries that they would agree not to oppose the price increase as long as these countries agreed to recycle their surplus dollar inflows to U.S. financial markets. Failure to do that would be an act of war. (I was invited to a number of White House and Defense Department meetings where officials elaborated the details of this agreement.)

U.S. dollar outflows ended up in the oil-exporting countries and Europe, and were returned to the United States as liquid financial investments in corporate stocks and bonds, Treasury securities, and an unprecedented inflow into U.S. commercial banks. Much of this inflow was lent to Third World countries to pay for their increasingly costly grain and oil imports, as well as to pay debt service on their mounting foreign debts incurred to finance their own balance-of-payments deficits.

The Washington Consensus aims to create an international *rentier* economy

U.S. officials deftly played both sides of the emerging creditor and debtor diplomacy. While using the new debtor-based Dollar Diplomacy against trade-surplus nations, they took a pro-creditor position when dealing with Third World countries and others running balance-of-payments deficits. The post-1980 Washington Consensus called for the IMF and bondholders to impose austerity on these countries, forcing privatization sell-offs and an ongoing devaluation of their currencies – and hence, depreciation of the price of their labor.

The effect was as destructive and predatory as overt European colonialism had been. Much as European imperialism had turned colonies and dependencies into trade and monetary satellites, grabbing the natural resources and rent-extracting monopolies for Europe's own investors, the neoliberal Washington Consensus guiding IMF policy has had a similar effect. The foreign-currency debt overhead of Third World and other payments-deficit countries blocks their ability to develop industrial capitalism along the lines followed by the United States and Western Europe. The Washington Consensus turns these countries into *rentier* economies, as well as financializing the advanced Western economies in which wealth also is obtained increasingly by rent extraction.

This is welcomed as ushering in a "post-industrial society." But it is precisely what classical economists from Adam Smith through John Stuart Mill, Marx, Alfred Marshall and Thorstein Veblen hoped to avoid. In their mind the dynamic of industrial capitalism was to free economies and markets *from* rent-seeking. The expectation was that wealthy nations would invest in less developed countries and help them catch up, spreading democratic politics and public investment to modernize colonial and other less developed economies. But instead of helping these countries join the industrial economies, the effect of U.S. diplomacy and the Washington Consensus has been to aggravate their inequality and impose dictatorships run by oppressive client oligarchies. This is not progress; it is a new form of backwardness, almost a retrogression back toward a feudal property-owning creditor class.

U.S. officials take a pro-creditor stance toward Third World debtor countries, defending U.S. bondholders and foreign client elites holding their countries' dollarized bonds. Vulture-funds pick up what institutional bondholders sell off, at pennies on the dollar, hoping to foreclose on whatever government assets they can grab. That has occurred most notoriously with Paul Singer's moves against Argentina.

The 2020-22 Covid-19 pandemic has slashed industrial production throughout the West, leaving little or no way for many Third World debtors to pay their scheduled debt service. So we are back in the kind of Latin American debt crash that followed Mexico's announcement in 1982 that it could not pay its foreign debt. The result then was a cessation of international lending, leading Argentina and Brazil to pay 45 percent annual interest on their dollar debt by 1990 (owed mainly to their domestic oligarchies operating out of tax-haven accounts, to be sure), and Mexico to pay over 22 percent on its medium-term dollar bonds. In the wake of the world economic slowdown resulting from the coronavirus, demand for raw materials and other exports has declined, creating new Third World balance-of-payments deficits.

The question confronting today's indebted Third World countries is whether they once again will be forced into austerity that prevents their economies from recovering. Will they be forced to privatize their natural resources and public enterprises, for sale to payments-surplus countries and U.S. investors?

Such economic demands in the past could only be imposed by military conquest. Today they are being imposed by financial conquest – just as destructive, taking into account the decline in population resulting from shortening life spans, suicide rates and emigration. The destruction is financial and intellectual, not military. Dollar Diplomacy enables the United States to use the deadly monetary weapons of austerity and financial sanctions to gain economic control – and to obtain the free lunch that goes with it.

That is the international dynamic of *rentier* finance capitalism. Indebted countries cannot "inflate their way out of debt," because it is denominated mainly in dollars or other foreign currency, which their central banks cannot print. They can create domestic currency, but not the dollars and other hard currencies necessary to pay these foreign debts. Increasing domestic taxes will not help to pay their foreign-currency debts, because taxes are levied in local currency.

That is what Keynes called the Transfer Problem in the 1920s, when the European allies demanded that Germany wreck its economy to pay reparations. The pro-creditor assumption is that higher taxes will impoverish labor and business by enough to slow imports of consumer goods and capital goods. But this is only a cover story, an excuse to make debtor countries even more dependent on creditors. The reality is that poverty is never a way to grow. It only pays the looters, and even in such cases only in the short run.

Attempts to enforce Europe's unpayably high foreign debts after World War I were in vain. Keynes showed that unless the allies would agree to buy German exports, there was no way the Reichsbank could create or tax the dollars to pay. Yet today's IMF and U.S. foreign diplomacy follow this destructive "hard money" policy, insisting that fiscal austerity, along with asset sell-offs, can pay foreign debt service. The effect can only be to strip and impoverish debtor countries.

Chronic austerity is now also being imposed on Eurozone members, making the euro a satellite currency of the dollar. Limiting budget deficits to no more than 3 percent of Eurozone GDP prevents euros from being issued in large enough amounts to rival the dollar as a vehicle for central bank reserves. This rule also prevents Eurozone members from Keynesian spending to revive their economies from stagnation. The result is a monetary strait-jacket that limits social spending to promote economic growth. Probably national populations and living standard will have to drop substantially in order for voters to become aware that this limitation is needless and that austerity is not necessary.

If European governments continue to refrain from creating their own money in more than marginal amounts and no other alternative currency bloc emerges, that will leave global money creation to American military spending and other U.S. balance-of-payments deficits ending up in the world's central banks. That is the essence of today's dollar standard and the United States' almost unipolar dominance of global money creation.

Today's contrast between nationalism and globalism is occurring in a completely different context from what it was in the 1940s and '50s when discussions were framed in the aftermath of World War II and when it seemed to be a good idea for Europe to integrate so as never again to suffer intra-European wars. Seven countries formed to create the European Common Market, with special focus on creating its Common Agricultural Policy (CAP) to make itself independent of reliance on foreign (mainly U.S.) food producers.

The United States kept trying to break down the CAP and sponsored the creation of a rival European Free Trade Area (EFTA) led by Britain (as usual acting as U.S. foreign-policy proxy) and Scandinavia. The U.S. hope was that this free trade area would provide an alternative to progressive social democratic or socialist continental Europe.

Today, the English-speaking and Scandinavian sphere is part of NATO's right-wing alliance. Now that NATO and the Eurozone have expanded eastward to include the Baltic states and Poland, the result has been to block the EU politicians in Brussels from following policies at odds with U.S. plans, particularly in relation to Russia, China and other countries the United States treats as adversaries or potential trade rivals.

The response by nations that are sanctioned or otherwise treated as antagonists to U.S. neoliberal policy is to revert to settling their balance-of-payments surpluses or deficits in ways that existed prior to the U.S. Treasury-bill standard.

Resisting Dollar Hegemony

Every economy needs foreign exchange reserves. Dollar reserves are U.S. debt, supplied mainly by U.S. military spending, Cold War diplomacy and investment takeovers of foreign economies, headed by investment in natural-resource rent extraction and monopoly rent opportunities that arise from privatizing public infrastructure.

The problem for foreign countries is how to protect themselves from being flooded with dollar inflows stemming from U.S. military and investment takeovers, for which they receive merely "paper dollars." As noted above, countries that do not approve of the combination of U.S. military policies and U.S. takeover of their economic assets face a dilemma: If they do not recycle their dollar inflows into U.S. capital markets, their currencies will rise, threatening to price their exports out of world markets.

The path of least resistance taken by Russia, China and some other payments-surplus nations is to de-dollarize. One element of this policy is to revive gold as a means of settling balance-of-payments deficits. Gold is a pure asset, having no liability on the opposite side of the balance sheet, and hence does not fund the U.S. budget and payments deficits that finance dollar hegemony. Gold's use to settle payments deficits is likely to be the smoothest route in any transition to an alternative currency bloc.

For Third World debtor countries, the problem is how to avoid letting creditor demands destroy their economies in the way that German reparations and Inter-Ally arms debts destroyed Europe's economies in the 1920s. IMF and U.S. diplomacy offer only marginal palliatives such as lower interest rates, slower amortization payments and simply lending countries enough to pay their scheduled debt service. But as the underlying debt volume keeps accumulating, debt writedowns are the only solution in the end. That requires a new principle of international law, stipulating that no country should be forced to destroy its economy to pay foreign creditors. That principle recognizes that pro-creditor laws are a tributary demand similar to an act of war.

Ultimately at issue are the criteria for nationhood, as a modern corollary to the 1648 Treaty of Westphalia that ended Europe's bloody Thirty
Years War. The Treaty ruled that nations should not interfere in the
government or internal politics of other nations. At issue is political and
economic independence, whether to be in control of one's own destiny
by preventing foreign interference in domestic affairs, or to be faced with
today's financial "market" dilemma: "Your money, or your life."

U.S. financial diplomacy rejects the long-standing 1648 principle of
international relations, replacing it with unilateral U.S. demands for
controlling world trade and investment diplomacy, while refusing to
join any international institution unless it has veto power to be exempt
from any foreign control or censure over its own policies. That is why
it refused to join the League of Nations after World War I, and agreed
to join the United Nations only on condition that it have veto power.
Similar U.S. power was assured in 1944 over the World Bank and IMF
by setting the U.S. quota high enough to veto any policy decision that U.S.
representatives did not feel reflected U.S. national interests. That logic
also led the United States not to join the World Court.

In a travesty of the traditional rules-based order, U.S. officials insist on
their unilateral right to dictate the rules of other countries' domestic as
well as foreign policies. Matters came to a head on March 18, 2021 when
U.S. and Chinese officials confronted each other in Anchorage, Alaska.
Secretary of State Antony Blinken in effect depicted U.S. sanctions,
political meddling in other countries' elections, and military belligerence backing dictators, client oligarchies and neoliberal kleptocracies as
being the essence of the world's new "rules-based order." In substance,
he accused China's domestic policy of threatening this U.S.-centered
neoliberal order by subsidizing its industry and refraining from privatization. "The alternative to a rules-based order," he claimed, "is a world
in which might makes right and winner takes all and that would be a far
more violent and unstable world."[8]

There was no acknowledgement that the main purveyor of military
confrontation, violence and global rule-breaking and instability for
decades has been the United States. China's representative Yang
Jiechi, a member of China's Communist Party Politburo, replied that a

---

[8] U.S. Department of State, "Secretary Antony J. Blinken, National Security
Advisor Jake Sullivan, Chinese Director of the Office of the Central Commission
for Foreign Affairs Yang Jiechi And Chinese State Councilor Wang Yi At the Top
of Their Meeting," March 18, 2021. https://hk.usconsulate.gov/n-2021031801/.

rules-based order imposed unilaterally by the United States in its own national interest was unacceptable:

> I don't think the overwhelming majority of countries in the world would recognize that the universal values advocated by the United States or that the opinion of the United States could represent international public opinion, and those countries would not recognize that the rules made by a small number of people would serve as the basis for the international order.

Yang urged his audience to uphold the United Nations-centered order underpinned by international law, not what is advocated by a small number of countries of the so-called "rules-based" international order of U.S.-backed neoliberal principles.

Referring to this China-U.S. exchange, Russian Foreign Minister Sergei Lavrov backed China's position that the U.S. aim was not to create a common and symmetrical order, but to ensure its own unilateral dominance. U.S. diplomats, he stated, "want to replace international law with their own rules, which have nothing in common with the supremacy of law globally, on a universal scale." He noted that when he had complained to former Secretary of State Rex Tillerson about U.S. support for anti-Putin movements in Russia and the Ukraine Support Act: "He told me that was totally different. I asked him why, and he said because we promoted authoritarianism, and they spread democracy. That was it."[9]

In contrast to the U.S. insistence on non-interference in its own affairs, its diplomats insist that they have a right as "the exceptional nation" to dictate the policies of other countries, removing elected leaders who advocate political and economic policies that do not serve America's New Cold War aims. Also exceptional is America's insistence (voiced most proudly by President Trump) that the United States must be the net gainer in any trade agreement. This demand for unipolar world domination rejects the traditional norms of equity and symmetry, prompting a reaction to create a more multipolar world economy.

U.S. diplomats like to describe their policies by sanctimonious biblical quotes. More appropriate is what the Christian Father Lactantius (c. 250-325) wrote in the *Divine Institutes*, describing the Roman Empire. His

---

[9] Russian Ministry of Foreign Affairs, "Foreign Minister Sergey Lavrov's interview given to Channel One's Bolshaya Igra (Great Game) talk show, Moscow, April 1, 2021," Johnson's Russia List, April 2, 2021, #20, from https://www.mid.ru/en/press_service/minister_speeches/-/asset_publisher/7OvQR5KJWVmR/content/id/4662534.

description might well describe that of the United States and indeed, the inherent dynamic of today's finance capitalism.

> In order to enslave the many, the greedy began to appropriate and accumulate the necessities of life and keep them tightly closed up, so that they might keep these bounties for themselves. They did this not for humanity's sake (which was not in them at all), but to rake up all things as products of their greed and avarice. In the name of justice they made unfair and unjust laws to sanction their thefts and avarice against the power of the multitude. In this way they availed as much by authority as by strength of arms or overt evil.[10]

---

[10] Lactantius, *Divine Institutes* 5.6:7-9 (1964: 72).

11

The War against Nations that treat Money and Land as Public Utilities

Nearly half a millennium ago Niccolo Machiavelli's *The Prince* described three options for how a victorious power might treat states that it defeated in war but "have been accustomed to live under their own laws and in freedom: ... the first is to ruin them, the next is to reside there in person, the third is to permit them to live under their own laws, drawing a tribute, and establishing within it an oligarchy that will keep it friendly to you."[1]

Machiavelli preferred the first option, citing Rome's destruction of Carthage. That is what the United States did to Iraq and Libya after 2001. But in today's world it also wreaks lethal destruction in ways much less costly than military warfare, by trade blockades and financial sanctions such as it has imposed on Cuba, Iran and Venezuela, and with less success against Russia and China. The idea is to deny adversaries essential technology and information processing ability, raw materials, and access to credit.

The second option is to occupy rivals. This is done only partially by the troops stationed in America's 750 military bases abroad. The more efficient and remunerative occupation is by corporate takeovers of their basic infrastructure, land and natural resources, banking and public utilities. The effect is to siphon off economic rent, profits and interest for the imperial core.

President Trump said that he wanted to seize Iraq's and Syria's oil as reparations for the cost of destroying their society. His successor Joe Biden, upon taking office in 2021, sought to appoint Hillary Clinton's loyalist Neera Tanden to a high government position. She had urged that America should make Libya turn over its vast oil reserves to fund its Cold War spending. "We have a giant deficit. They have a lot of oil. Most Americans would choose not to engage in the world because of that

---

[1] Niccolo Machiavelli, *The Prince* (1532), Chapter 5: "Concerning the way to govern cities or principalities which lived under their own laws before they were annexed."

deficit. If we want to continue to engage in the world, gestures like having oil rich countries partially pay us back doesn't seem crazy to me."[2]

U.S. strategists usually focus on Machiavelli's third option: leaving the defeated adversary nominally independent but ruling via a client oligarchy, backed by the above-mentioned corporate occupation and local military base. President Jimmy Carter's national-security advisor Zbigniew Brzezinski referred to them as "vassals," in the classical meaning of owing loyalty to their U.S. patron, sharing a mutual interest in privatizing and financializing the subject country's economy.

These latter two options often are initiated by ruining the adversary to begin with. Shock therapy in the former Soviet republics after 1991 cleared the slate for privatization by a client oligarchy, created by a grabitization that utterly disrupted the economic interconnections that had integrated the former Soviet economies. The effect was to block national self-reliance keeping the economic surplus at home to promote domestic prosperity. "To put it in a terminology that harkens back to the more brutal age of ancient empires," Brzezinski explained, "the three grand imperatives of imperial geostrategy are to prevent collusion and maintain security dependence among the vassals, to keep tributaries pliant and protected and to keep the barbarians from coming together."[3]

Having defeated Germany and Japan in World War II, U.S. diplomacy reduced Britain and its imperial Sterling Area to vassalage by 1946, followed by the rest of Western Europe and its former colonial systems (as Chapter 10 has described). The next step was to isolate Russia and China, while keeping these "barbarians from coming together." If they were to join up, warned Mr. Brzezinski, "the United States may have to determine how to cope with regional coalitions that seek to push America out of Eurasia, thereby threatening America's status as a global power."[4] That is the logic underlying today's Cold War 2.0.

---

[2] Neera Tanden, "Should Libya pay us back?" memo to Faiz Shakir, Peter Juul, Benjamin Armbruster and NSIP Core, October 21, 2011. Mr. Shakir, to his credit, wrote back: "If we think we can make money off an incursion, we'll do it? That's a serious policy/messaging/moral problem for our foreign policy I think."

[3] Zbigniew Brzezinski, *The Grand Chessboard: American Primacy and its Geostrategic Imperatives* (New York: 1997), p. 40. See Pepe Escobar, "For Leviathan, It's So Cold in Alaska," *Unz.com*, March 18, 2021.

[4] Brzezinski, *ibid.*, p. 55.

Neoliberalism's ideological conquest to promote *rentier* kleptocracies

Marx did not write a blueprint for how to manage a socialist economy on its way toward communism. His writings focused on how capitalism was laying the groundwork for socialism by organizing industry and banking, in ways that in the natural course of affairs would become socialized, simply on grounds of efficiency. In Russia and then in China, to be sure, this evolution toward the most efficient organization of industry, labor and agriculture required a revolution to free economies from control by the old vested interests. That is what occurred in Russia in October 1917.

But Russian officials read less of what Marx wrote about capitalism as they focused on how to create their own economy, starting with electrification and the logic of industrial engineering. State companies acted as public utilities, responsible for feeding their work force, providing leisure and other obligations. Housing, education, health care and other basic needs were treated as public utilities, not opportunities for rent-seeking requiring families to run into debt to a banking sector. Although housing supply remained limited and crowded, at least it was free of real estate speculators.

Money and credit also were treated as public utilities. State credit was provided to build factories, electrify the economy and provide other basic needs. Interest was not charged, because the state did not seek to make a profit. This is what the classical economists had urged. Soviet leaders also limited labor's work week, and provided paid vacation time and education to raise literacy and make labor more productive.

The largest Soviet companies were governments in miniature, providing housing, meals and entertainment. Some entire cities, such as Russia's largest auto manufacturing site, the AutoVAZ plant in Tolyatti, Samara Oblast, were local corporate states. Privatizing such enterprises stripped away the social functions they had provided, leaving employees without compensation to make up for the loss of these corporate obligations.

What Soviet Russia did not have was market feedback, or opportunities for innovation of new products such as China has allowed since the reforms of Deng Xiaoping (1982-87) and his successors Jiang Zemin, Zhu Rongji, Hu Jintao, and Xi Jinping since 2012. By the late 1980s the inefficiency of Soviet central planning led its officials to become demoralized by their failure to match America's consumer prosperity. They saw a need for a market, but did not anticipate how financialization and rent seeking would distort market prices, income and wealth distribution. There was no recognition of the most positive Soviet achievement: the abolition of rent and interest charges on real estate and industry.

It may have been this freedom from *rentier* income – and from a *rentier* class – that led Soviet officials not to understand the pitfalls of financialization and landlordship when they agreed to introduce Western finance capitalism by neoliberal shock therapy (without any real therapy), as if that were the only alternative to Soviet bureaucracy.

Pulling out the Soviet Union's economic interconnections and mutual obligations was promised to lead to a survival of the fittest in which the most efficient and productive businessmen would create an economy like that of the United States. Giving away state property to insiders was supposed to create a managerial class motivated to maximize profits by running business along economically rational lines. Neoliberals claimed that "freeing" Russia from central planning would make it richer in consumer goods, housing and living standards – without any need for anti-monopoly legislation, workplace protection for labor or progressive taxation such as was common in the West before the 1980s. Such policies were claimed to be "intrusive" into the neoliberal "free markets" presented to Russia as the new Western economic ideal.

This advice turned Russia's wealth and accumulated capital investment into a market free for a U.S.-oriented client *rentier* class to extract land and natural resource rents, monopoly rents and interest. The alternative to centralized Soviet industrial planning turned out to be kleptocratic rent seeking. Much of this *rentier* revenue quickly found its way into the hands of foreign investors and banks. The result was a collapse that Naomi Klein described in *Shock Doctrine: The Rise of Disaster Capitalism* (2007).[5]

The neoliberal "reforms" following this shock therapy sharply raised the former Soviet Union's cost of living and doing business. Goods and services that were not privatized simply stopped being produced. Soviet planners had distributed production facilities across the Soviet Union's member states, and these interconnections were pulled up from East Germany to the Pacific Ocean. All that Russia was left with to export were its natural resources – whose rents were privatized, not used to support post-Soviet public spending. Russia lost as much of its population as had perished in World War II. While prices soared, labor went unpaid as factories were closed or simply stopped paying salaries or providing the basic services, meals, health care and other social obligations that

---

[5] The most thorough discussion is by Peter Reddaway and Dmitri Glinski, *The Tragedy of Russia's Reforms: Market Bolshevism Against Democracy* (Washington, D.C.: 2001).

had been built into the Soviet industrial system. Birth rates and health standards fell as AIDS cases spread from the classic response to poverty: a combination of drug addiction, prostitution and rising suicide rates.

The decade of the 1990s in Russia stands as an object lesson demonstrating the economic and social damage resulting from the Washington Consensus promoting asset grabbing by privatization. The kleptocratic class sponsored by neoliberals registered Russia's natural resources and land in their own names and went untaxed. It was a very narrow class.

There was method in this madness. Cold War planners recognized that the narrower an oligarchy in control of a nation's wealth, the more cosmopolitan its members behave and the larger its capital flight tends to be. The more easily this privileged class gained a free lunch via privatization, the more eager its members were to cash out by selling their shares abroad. Using the proceeds to buy foreign real estate and financial assets was the easiest way for Russian kleptocrats to avoid domestic tax collectors (and prosecutors).

Today, three decades later, the destiny of Russia and other post-Soviet states remains shaped by the way in which their land, mineral resources and public enterprises have been privatized. Unlike the Norman invasion of England and Spain's conquest of Peru and Mexico, there was no need for military invasion to grab ownership of formerly public assets. The Soviet Union's major assets were stripped by financial means – and like the land grabs of the Norman Conquest and Spain's conquest of the New World, the post-Soviet asset grab created a new aristocracy empowered to extract land and natural-resource rents for themselves – and increasingly for their U.S. and other foreign shareholders and backers.

Russians called this "grabitization," while Western neoliberals celebrated it as a success story. It made Russia the world's most lucrative stock market during 1994-97. Insiders registered companies in their own names, and the Seven Bankers obtained key natural resources for pennies on the dollar (paying largely with deposits from Russia's own central bank). But they could only "cash out" their takings at a high price by selling their shares to Western buyers, because domestic savings had been wiped out by the hyperinflation caused by the U.S.-sponsored shock therapy. So the new grabitizers relied mainly on U.S. financial institutions to market their shares.

The Russian government could have maximized its return from its privatizations by following the normal practice that privatizing governments and venture capitalists in the West use in Initial Public Offerings (IPOs): issue only a small proportion of the shares to private buyers at first, to establish a realistic price for the remaining shares. That is what Saudi Arabia did when it started to privatize Aramco shares. But Western consultants and brokerage firms advised Russia not to protect itself by holding off. To keep almost all the price gains for U.S. investors, the American advisors insisted that all the shares of new natural-resource companies and monopolies be sold at once, meaning at a distress price instead of waiting for the new managers to show a profit (or economic rent) that could be capitalized into asset-price gains. The underwriters wanted their own clients and money managers to grab as much rent-yielding privileges as possible, by underpricing the entire stock issue in one quick asset grab, snapping up the shares for a fraction of what they soon would bring as U.S. investors piled in and bid up their prices.

What privatizers and foreign investors want most are raw materials and real estate, not industrial enterprise. That is where quick and easy economic rents can be made, in contrast to profits made by investing to restructure industry to make it more efficient. Russian industry was dismantled, undercutting its military potential by turning the economy into what Senator John McCain called "a gas station masquerading as a country." This industrial dismantling and sell-off of land and natural resources was precisely the neoliberal aim – a Western fast-buck ideal.

While factories were closed down and sold for scrap, the former Soviet Union experienced the largest real estate bubble in modern history. New housing, office buildings, stores and hotels were built for privatizers and foreigners, not for the population at large. Employment was plummeting while Russia suffered an estimated $25 billion in annual capital flight throughout the 1990s, which continued well into the 21st century.

The Soviet tragedy was the inability of its leaders to imagine an alternative to the drastic restructuring urged by Western neoliberals. Soviet leaders thought that U.S. advisors would help Russia replicate the kind of capitalism that had made America prosperous, not loot it and turn it into a tributary satellite ruled by a local client oligarchy. They did not understand that there are various kinds of capitalism, and that U.S. finance capitalism itself was nearing the end of its great post-1945 expansion, an end accelerated by its own embrace of neoliberalism since the 1980s.

Privatizing post-Soviet economies by pulling out their interconnections

What is so remarkable in retrospect is how clearly the scenario for uprooting Soviet industry was spelled out in advance. On December 19, 1990, the IMF and World Bank, the Organization for Economic Cooperation and Development (OECD) and the European Bank for Reconstruction and Development (EBRD) produced a joint report on *The Economy of the USSR. A study undertaken to a request by the Houston Summit.*[6] Published by the IMF, the report imposed on the Soviet Union what the Treaty of Versailles had done to Germany after World War I. It delivered the coup de grace ending the Cold War that had lasted since Russia's 1917 Revolution.

Russia's demoralized leadership accepted the neoliberal insistence that there was no way to reform or "enhance performance under the old system." Describing social democracy as a misguided attempt to shape a fair society, the Houston report claimed: "There is no example of a successful modern centrally planned economy." Government planning has "proved to be counterproductive" seemingly everywhere – as if only a kleptocratic oligarchy can create a truly free market!

The reality throughout history is that no *rentier* economy can be deemed successful except for the predatory class at the top. Only mixed economies with checks and balances have prevented economic polarization and concentration of wealth from impoverishing society. Yet the report's free-market tunnel vision claimed not to know of any "path of gradual reform ... which would minimize economic disturbance and lead to an early harvesting of the fruits of economic efficiency." Only a radical shock would do the trick – endowing an oligarchy of insiders with virtually free ownership of privatized enterprises, without being constrained by laws and regulations.

Neither employees nor government agencies were given a role to play in the resulting "free market." Warning that "workers' ownership in enterprises ... would run counter to the desired objectives of enterprise reform," the Houston report opposed democratizing ownership, claiming that maximum efficiency could be obtained by avoiding employee constraints on management. A largely symbolic "voucher" scheme provided opportunities for asset grabbing. Most vouchers were said to have been sold for the price of a glass of vodka, because at least that was something tangible.

The Houston report insisted that an optimum market economy "must be accompanied by rapid and comprehensive price liberalization." The ensuing hyperinflation wiped out Russian savings, pensions and related social support systems, which were characterized as "the overhang problem." Capital flight crashed the ruble's exchange rate, making

---

[6] I discuss this in "How Neoliberal Tax and Financial Policy Impoverishes Russia – Needlessly," *Mir Peremen* (The World of Transformations), 2012 (3), pp. 49-64 (in Russian). МИР ПЕРЕМЕН 3/2012 (ISSN 2073-3038), Неолиберальная налоговая и финансовая политика приводит к обнищанию России, pp. 49-64.

imports more expensive, while the IMF's demand to restrict the money supply shrank employment and production. Progressive taxation was rejected in favor of a flat tax on income, with almost no property tax. The word "reform" took on a negative connotation to most Russians.

Neoliberals thus achieved in the former Soviet bloc what they could not completely bring about in the United States and Europe: a corporate *rentier* state. The resulting austerity was even more drastic than that which the IMF, Chicago Boys and U.S.-sponsored Operation Condor had imposed on Latin America in the 1970s. The false promise was that rising prices would cure shortages by eliciting more output, while reducing the population's purchasing power (by wiping out Soviet-era savings) would leave more output to be exported. What actually happened was that Russia's industry was closed down, leaving no industrial output to export.

The government could have generated at least as much revenue – and much more foreign exchange – by operating these enterprises itself. Instead, Russia suffered a lost decade and lost half a trillion dollars in capital flight and tax evasion. In the face of this industrial dismantling and its lost opportunities, the overhead cost of a bureaucratic state seems to pale. By 2020, three decades after the reforms started, Russians recognized how drastic a mistake they had made:

> Praised in Washington, President Gorbachev's 1985 flagship Perestroika policy was welcomed with open arms by the West. Now, in 2020, almost half of Russia believes that the country would be better off if it had never happened. According to a poll by the Levada Center, 47% of Russians believe that life in the country was better before Perestroika, with just 39% disagreeing. When isolating the responses of those over the age of 55, all of whom were adults when the reforms began in 1985, almost two-thirds (61%) agreed that life was better before.[7]

The neoliberal plan to turn countries into U.S. economic satellites

Selling mineral rights, land, public infrastructure and industrial companies to foreigners was supposed to increase efficiency, on the theory that foreign management would raise productivity, and thereby supposedly generate more foreign exchange for Russia. Instead, the new managers bled their enterprises and sent their takings abroad as U.S. and other Western buyers bought their ownership rights.

---

[7] Jonny Tickle, "Would life be better if Gorbachev's Perestroika reform never happened? Almost half of today's Russians say yes, reveals new poll," www.rt.com, November 3, 2020, from *Johnson's Russia List*, November 4, 2020, #15.

Privatizing financial, real estate and other rent-yielding assets, "freeing" these *rentier* chokepoints from public regulation and even untaxing their income has become the capstone of a U.S.-centered "rule of law" legitimizing rent seeking, sponsored by the U.S. Agency for International Development (A.I.D.), the World Bank and IMF. The resulting dynamic has indebted foreign economies to U.S. banks and bondholders in the absence of local public banks, leaving the host economies to collapse under a deepening financial and fiscal burden – which acts as a lever to force yet further privatizations, sell-offs and new indebtedness.

This neoliberal policy involves eleven major aims:

(1)   *Privatization* to remove assets from the public domain. Privatizing the banking and credit system is the key to transferring real estate, natural resources and basic infrastructure mainly to political insiders. These appropriators are expected to find their interest to lie in selling their shares to buyers in the United States and Western Europe, at prices that leave substantial leeway for capital gains.

(2)   *Privatization of basic public utilities*, typically starting with the highly capital-intensive transportation and communications sector, whose services can be provided at inflated prices, including monopoly rents. Health care and education likewise can be privatized and monopolized. Political support for capturing public regulatory agencies can be gained by a symbiosis of the infrastructure privatizers with the financial sector by using mutually remunerative debt financing.

(3)   *Minimal regulation* to protect labor and consumers and the environment, permitting creditors, landlords and employers to maximize rents and profits, and to transfer the proceeds abroad in capital flight to London, New York and Delaware, Cyprus and other tax havens.

(4)   *Dependency* on U.S. and European banks to create credit for domestic governments, banks and companies – credit that domestic central banks could create themselves – at a cost of foreign-exchange outflows of debt service and income in years to come.

(5)   *A debt burden*, especially one denominated in foreign currencies (dollars, euros or other) for real estate, corporate and financial debt, whose burden grows proportionally with the local currency's depreciation.

(6)   *Merely nominal taxes on real estate and other rent-yielding property*, inverting the classical principle of progressive taxation falling mainly on land rent, natural resource rent and monopoly rent.

(7)   *A regressive flat income tax* that falls on labor, increasing its cost and thus helping price it out of foreign markets and in time the home market, while favoring the *rentier* income and wealth of client oligarchies and their foreign investors.

(8)   *A real estate bubble* raising access prices for housing and commercial space, and hence the economy's cost structure but increasing the

mortgage market for banks. This obliges the domestic economy to take on rising mortgage debt, raising the cost of living and doing business.

(9)   *De-industrialization*, resulting from financialization, that is, from financial short-termism and privatization, regressive income and consumption taxes instead of taxes on economic rent, and high debt burdens (all of which raise the cost of living and doing business, thereby pricing domestic labor and industry out of world markets), euphemized as progress toward a post-industrial economy.

(10)   *Rising trade dependency* resulting from de-industrialization and the tendency of monocultures to lack basic economic self-sufficiency, leading to structural balance-of-payments deficits. The resulting foreign debt causes deepening dependency on the IMF and foreign bondholders, which insist on yet more neoliberalization in a vicious economic circle.

(11)   *Capital flight* and emigration of labor, especially skilled labor.

Reversing the Progressive Era reforms of the late 19th and early 20th centuries, the above prescription for economic suicide aims to make populations and businesses increasingly indebted and dependent on financial and property-owning *rentiers* within the U.S. orbit.

How Russia could have laid the ground for post-Soviet prosperity

Most Soviet resources were spent on industry and the military. There was a chronic housing shortage and overcrowding, but at least housing charges were much lower than those in the West, with no speculative market. Russia left its assessed land valuation unchanged since 1928. Rents remained fixed at low rates that "were absorbing less than 3 percent of household income"[8] by 1991. There was no mortgage debt or absentee landlordship, because housing was treated as a public utility, a natural right.

If the former Soviet Republics had maintained this principle and turned over their housing and office space to its existing occupants and users after 1991, that would have endowed their populations with the hallmark of middle-class status, with minimal housing costs. Instead, prime real estate was indeed turned over at giveaway prices, but only to insiders and corrupt opportunists. Post-Soviet governments could have taxed away the rise in property prices so as to recapture what was obtained corruptly. A land tax would have minimized leeway for banks to create credit (debt) to bid up real estate. Instead, real estate prices soared to levels that made post-Soviet cities the world's most expensive.

---

[8] Reddaway and Glinsky, *The Tragedy of Russia's Reforms*, p. 179.

In the Baltics, Swedish banks provided most credit for buyers to obtain ownership of their own homes. They aggravated the debt problem by persuading borrowers to obtain slightly lower interest rates by denominating their mortgage debts in dollars, euros or Swiss francs. It was a bad option, because hard-currency exchange rates rapidly rose against the post-Soviet currencies, increasing the debt burden of for-eign-currency loans.

The military and political aftermath

A major reason why Mikhail Gorbachev accepted the U.S. offer of "advice" to help the Soviet economy privatize was his hope of ending the Cold War spending that was weighing it down. Ending the military confrontation was seen as making possible a "peace dividend" by redi-recting government spending to social and economic investment. U.S. President George H. W. Bush (1989-92) and Secretary of State James Baker promised Mr. Gorbachev that NATO would not move eastward if Russia dissolved the Warsaw Pact and agreed to let East and West Germany integrate. But the incoming administration of Bill Clinton (1993-2000) broke this promise, reminding the Soviet leader that he had not gotten anything in writing. Gorbachev had naively trusted the United States, neglecting the most basic rules of international agreement making. Breaking treaties has been U.S. policy since the nation's incep-tion, as shown by its dozens of broken treaties with Native American tribes in the 19th century down to its withdrawal from the Joint Compre-hensive Plan of Action with Iran in today's world.

Claiming to be protecting democracy, U.S. Cold Warriors demanded that Russia remove the strong Yevgeni Primakov from office as a condi-tion for getting IMF loans.[9] Then, disappointed at President Putin for ending the Yeltsin era's giveaways, Mikhail Khodorkovsky was lionized as a hero of democracy. Formerly Russia's richest oligarch (Forbes esti-mated his fortune to be $15 billion in 2003, the year in which he was arrested for tax fraud and embezzlement), he had used profits made from import trading to buy privatization vouchers and helped found the Menatep bank to finance further acquisitions, topped by the vast Yukos

---

[9] Kevin Murphy, "Stephen F. Cohen Helped Us Understand the Russian Revolu-tion and Nikolai Bukharin," *Jacobin*, December 5, 2020. He adds: "When Prime Minister Yevgeny Primakov made moves toward state regulation and deficit spending in the late 1990s, the IMF refused financial help, only to renew it once he was unceremoniously ousted after only eight months in office."

oil reserves in Siberia. When he prepared to sell the company to Exxon, Vladimir Putin drew the line.

Supporting Bill Browder, former head of the Hermitage Fund when it was the largest foreign stock investor in Russia, President Obama sponsored the Magnitsky Act, named for Browder's lawyer-fixer Sergei Magnitsky, imprisoned for financial fraud.[10] Western sanctions were imposed against Russia, ostensibly to defend "democracy," implicitly defining it as including freedom for tax evasion and money laundering by client kleptocracies.

Like wartime isolation or tariffs, the effect of these U.S. and NATO trade sanctions on Russia was to spur domestic production. In agriculture, for instance, Russia developed its own cheese production to replace imports from Lithuania and other foreign dairy producers, and became the world's leading grain exporter. American-backed sanctions also have been mounted in an attempt to block Russia's main exports, oil and gas. As discussed in Chapter 7, U.S. officials pressured Germany in an attempt to block the Nord Stream 2 pipeline from supplying Germany with low-priced Russian gas, and insisted that Europe earmark an estimated $1 billion to build shipping terminals to import U.S. liquified natural gas (LNG) at much higher prices.

America's hopes to subdue China much as it had defeated Russia

In the wake of Russia's economic dismemberment and that of other ex-Soviet republics, former National Security Adviser Brzezinski crowed that "the economic and even political destiny of what was not long ago a threatening superpower is now increasingly passing into *de facto* Western receivership." That was the setting for the U.S hope that China might be as gullible as the Soviet Union and adopt neoliberal policy privatizing its wealth and selling it off to Americans. As Chapter 6 describes, Clyde Prestowitz, former trade advisor in the Reagan Administration, recently spelt out that hope: "what the free world expected when it welcomed China into the free trade body [the World Trade Organization] in 2001," was that "from the time of Deng Xiaoping's adoption of some market methods in 1979 and especially after the collapse of the Soviet Union in 1992 ... increased trade with and investment in China would inevitably

---

[10] Lucy Komisar provides an ongoing narrative of U.S. support of Browder and Magnitsky in her blog: https://www.thekomisarscoop.com.

lead to the marketization of its economy, the demise of its state-owned enterprises."[11]

When America invited China to join the World Trade Organization (WTO) in 2001, membership was expected to transform China to accept "democracy," a euphemism for U.S. financial takeover of its commanding heights. After all, China already had sold or reorganized some of its unprofitable state-owned companies after the 1997-98 Asia Crisis.

The WTO imposed hard entry conditions on China, particularly regarding patent and "intellectual property" rights. But China insisted that foreign manufacturing affiliates share their technology if they were to set up domestic production facilities.[12] Having few national loyalties, U.S. and other international firms agreed to do this, seeing an opportunity to replace American workers with China's vast pool of lower-priced labor. The labor-cost gains were so large that companies were willing to de-industrialize their own economy in order to get rich on the China trade, benefiting from international "labor rent" by selling its products in the United States for as near as possible to the price that it would cost American labor to make them.

American banks were expected to accompany U.S. foreign investors to China and create credit to finance local business, real estate and even government budgets. In this scenario, China was to relinquish the gains from trade to foreign investors and American banks. Its balance of trade and payments would fall into deficit, enabling the IMF and foreign lenders to insist that China sell off its public infrastructure, as occurred in Russia and other post-Soviet economies and in a replay of the 1997-98 Asia Crisis, with client Chinese billionaires turning its economy into a Yeltsin-style kleptocracy.

Instead of following the neoliberal lines imposed on the former Soviet economies after 1991, China's government kept control of industrial investment, and also kept money and debt in state hands. This was "at odds with the liberal, rules-based global system," complained Prestowitz. "More fundamentally," he summed up (to repeat the quote in Chapter 6):

> China's economy is incompatible with the main premises of the global economic system embodied today in the World Trade Organization, the International Monetary Fund, the World Bank, and a long list of other free trade agreements. These pacts assume economies that are primarily

---

[11] Clyde Prestowitz, "Blow Up the Global Trading System," *Washington Monthly*, March 24, 2021.

[12] See my article "China in Thirty Years," in *China in the Next Thirty Years* (Beijing: 2011), pp. 2-29.

market based with the role of the state circumscribed and micro-eco-
nomic decisions largely left to private interests operating under a rule
of law. This system never anticipated an economy like China's in which
state-owned enterprises account for one-third of production; the fusion
of the civilian economy with the strategic-military economy is a government necessity; five year economic plans guide investment to targeted
sectors; an eternally dominant political party names the CEOs of a third
or more of major corporations and has established party cells in every
significant company; the value of the currency is managed, corporate
and personal data are minutely collected by the government to be used
for economic and political control; and international trade is subject to
being weaponized at any moment for strategic ends.

This is jaw-dropping hypocrisy – as if the U.S. civilian economy is not
fused with its own military-industrial complex and does not manage its
currency or weaponize its international trade as a means of achieving
strategic ends. And as for the fantasy that American industry is independent of government, Prestowitz urged President Biden to "invoke
the Defense Production Act to direct increased U.S.-based production of
critical goods such as medicines, semiconductors, and solar panels."

The U.S.-China conflict between *rentier* finance capitalism and socialism

Seeing the Pax Americana unravelling, Brzezinski by 2016 acknowledged that the United States "is no longer the globally imperial power."[13]
That is what is making so urgent its antagonism toward China and
Russia, along with Iran and Venezuela. The conflict is deeper than
just national trade rivalry. The underlying issue is whether money and
credit, land, natural resources and monopolies will be privatized and
concentrated in the hands of a *rentier* oligarchy or used to promote
general prosperity and growth. This is basically a conflict between
finance capitalism vs. socialism as economic systems.

When U.S. trade strategists juxtapose Free World "democracy"
against Chinese autocracy, the major conflict in reality concerns government control of money and credit. China avoided foreign dependency by
not turning its infrastructure investment into rent-extracting tollbooths
on roads, phone systems and other natural monopolies such as characterize Western *rentier* economies. It has kept basic infrastructure services
low-priced via public enterprise.

---

[13] Brzezinski, "Towards a Global Realignment," *The American Interest*, April 17,
2016. For a discussion see Mike Whitney, "The Broken Checkboard: Brzezinski
Gives Up on Empire," *Counterpunch*, August 25, 2016.

Most important, China also has kept the Peoples' Central Bank and its subsidiary banks in the hands of the state, not leaving them to be privatized and to eventually gain control over the non-financial economy. As the U.S. economy has become financialized and de-industrialized, China has shown itself to be aware of the risks of financialization and has taken measures to contain it. State control has enabled the government to alleviate debt strains instead of letting these lead to close-downs and labor layoffs such as those that are now plaguing North America and Europe, particularly in the aftermath of the Covid-19 pandemic.

China has increased the productivity of its labor and capital in the same way that the United States and Germany did to overtake British industrial leadership in the 19th century: by public investment in education, health, transportation and other infrastructure, providing their services at subsidized prices or freely.[14] That, along with public control of money and credit, was the classical doctrine of industrial capitalism. It has enabled China to avoid the Washington Consensus that carved up the post-Soviet economies and which indeed has been applied by Western nations to their own economies since the 1980s. The resulting contrast between shrinking Western growth and China's state-sponsored takeoff is the reason why today's world is being plunged into an economic and quasi-military Cold War 2.0.

In its broadest terms the conflict between *rentier* oligarchies and an overriding central power seeking to maintain economic resilience is found already 2500 years ago, in the contrast between Near Eastern kingship and the Greek and Roman oligarchies. Since classical antiquity, Western economies have been dominated by private owners of rent-yielding assets: money and banking (with creditor-oriented rules governing debt foreclosure), land and natural resources.

Rentier oligarchies historically have fought against the concept of kingship and, most recently, against democratic or socialist government power. Greek and Roman oligarchies feared that royal power – or that of domestic "tyrants" and democratic reformers – might cancel debts to save populations from being reduced to debt bondage and dependency (and ultimately to serfdom), and redistribute land to prevent its owner-

---

[14] There was no conscious attempt to emulate U.S. experience. Indeed, that era of the American takeoff finds no mention in Western economic history books, because it was protectionist and largely state-directed, in contrast to the present-day neoliberal mainstream. I describe this school in *America's Protectionist Takeoff, 1815-1914: The Neglected American School of Political Economy* (Dresden: 2010).

ship from becoming concentrated in the hands of creditors and wealthy landowners.

Having managed largely on a pragmatic *ad hoc* basis to uplift the welfare and productivity of its population, China has not sought to proselytize the logic that has made it so successful. Its logic is much like that of Soviet Russia when it started out, with central planning by industrial engineers, starting with electrification and extending to water systems and other basic public utilities. This was purely pragmatic, not ideological, except to the extent that official Marxist policy emphasized the political and moral ideals of social equity and avoidance of a *rentier* class receiving interest and rents.

All economies are planned. The key to understanding their dynamics is to ask who is doing the planning, and in whose interest. Will decision-making be placed in the hands of elected or state officials with a primary concern for their nation's development and a realistic economic understanding to guide their national laws, or in the hands of special interests to create a dysfunctional system that polarizes and impoverishes society? Will labor and industry control the state, or will finance and real estate monopolies do so? Will it be run for a narrow elite, or the population at large? And in today's world, will it be U.S.-centered, or multipolar?

For all economies, the major internal threat to general prosperity is that a *rentier* class will develop, above all a financial interest fueling a real estate bubble. Everyone should have a home, without having to spend a lifetime going into debt. The Soviet states were able to avoid the "Western disease" of rising housing prices, which increase nominal wealth for those who already own their homes, but raise the cost of living and hence the basic wage that new buyers require and ultimately employers have to pay, as Chapters 4 and 5 have described.

Why *rentier* capitalism treats China's socialist economy as an existential threat

Since taking the lead in restructuring the world economy in 1945, the United States has obliged other countries to reshape their economies to accept Washington's control as the price of remaining in its unipolar Free World monetary and trade orbit. Financial dependency was locked in by the gold-exchange standard until 1971, and then by the dollar standard (the Treasury-bill standard), while trade dependency obliged countries to rely on the United States for essential imports, from grain to information technology.

Many nations are today moving to create an alternative to U.S. *dirigisme* over their economies. That breakaway was beyond the scope of the Non-Aligned Nations in the 1960s and 1970s. They had large populations, but lacked the diversification and self-sufficiency to become independent. But since the 1990s, especially since China's membership in the WTO, the only leverage left to the United States is gunboat diplomacy, "regime change" coups and manipulation of NATO satellites to impose sanctions against Russia, China and other nations whose policies do not follow the Washington Consensus. Meanwhile, instead of supplying credit to the world, the United States demands that foreign central banks support it by accepting dollar IOUs (U.S. Treasury securities) without limit. And U.S. and other investors and bankers seek to undermine and isolate what they cannot control.

Finance capital wants a strong state to serve itself, but not to serve labor, consumers, the environment or social progress at the cost of eroding profits and rents. That is why U.S. diplomacy sees China and Russia as existential threats to the global expansion of U.S.-centered *rentier* wealth, and therefore aims to deter them and neighboring members of the Shanghai Cooperation Organization (SCO) from socializing their financial systems, land and natural resources, and from keeping infrastructure utilities public to prevent their being monopolized in private hands and siphoning off economic rents.

The increasingly aggressive and military tone of this conflict is fracturing the world's trade and monetary relations, even between the United States and Western Europe. Germany's subjugation to U.S. natural-gas rivalry opposing the Nord Stream 2 pipeline has strongly contributed to Russia's pivot to Asia, mainly to China. As Russian Foreign Minister Sergey Lavrov explained on December 8, 2020: "apparently, the European Union has given up any attempts to become one of the centers in the emerging multipolar world order and is now simply taking its cues from the US."[15]

The U.S. economy is de-industrializing regardless of Chinese competition. Its policy seems bound to be self-defeating in that it is opposing China's successful system on the one hand while supporting a financialized rent-seeking privatization of its own economy – the very same policy that it has used to control "vassal" countries. Former U.S.

---

[15] Foreign Minister Sergey Lavrov, remarks at the general meeting of the Russian International Affairs Council, Moscow, December 8, 2020. https://www.mid.ru/en/press_service/minister_speeches/-/asset_publisher/7OvQR5KJWVmR/content/id/4470074.

Treasury Secretary and Goldman Sachs head Henry Paulson noted the
U.S. policy dilemma: its own economic power is waning while that of
China is increasing. In 2001 when China was admitted to the WTO, U.S.
companies saw that shifting their production facilities abroad would
increase their profits. That did occur, but at the cost of turning what
had been America's industrial heartland into a rust belt.

The U.S. response has not been to rebuild its economy, but to become
more belligerent toward countries not following neoliberal financialization and its race to the bottom when it comes to their own labor force.
"While investors from around the world are benefiting from investing in
equity securities from China, Washington is making it more difficult for
U.S. investors to do so. ... unless something changes dramatically, China
will remain the world's fastest-growing major economy, surpassing the
U.S. in size in the foreseeable future," while at home, "Washington won't
be able to pay its bills."[16]

To cap matters, U.S. economic warfare and sanctions are driving
China, Russia and other countries to protect themselves by de-dollarizing their economies. That threatens to end the Treasury-bill standard's
balance-of-payments free lunch.

China also is protecting its economy from U.S.-backed trade and
financial sanctions by aiming at self-sufficiency in essentials. That
involves technological independence and the ability to provide enough
food and energy resources to support its economy in isolation from the
U.S. bloc. It also involves creation of a computerized alternative to the
SWIFT bank-clearing system.

Likewise, the task confronting Russia since the late 1990s has been how
to invest its wealth in the national interest rather than see it disappear in
asset-stripping and capital flight to London and the West. The problem is
that President Putin is obliged to deal with wealth that is concentrated in
just a relatively few hands. It may take another revolution to create a regulatory and tax policy to achieve a broadly grounded prosperity.

The age-old policy challenge of preventing a *rentier* class from cor-roding prosperity

China and indeed all countries face a threat from domestic or for-
eign-backed families seeking to get rich financially, using their power
to exploit populations by usury, landlordship and kindred patronage

---

[16] Henry M. Paulson Jr., "China Wants to Be the World's Banker," *Wall Street Journal*, December 10, 2020.

arrangements. This threat has characterized civilization for thousands of years. It traditionally has been countered by government control of credit and debt relations, land tenure and infrastructure.

That control is the basic principle of socialism, but it has a millennia-long pedigree extending back to the palace economies of the Bronze Age Near East. Rulers prevented an oligarchy from emerging to threaten their palace-centered economies by taxing or redistributing large aggregations of wealth to prevent rivalry with the palace, which found its interest to lie in protecting a broad distribution of self-support land and prosperity so as to maximize tax revenue and population growth.

Western history broke from this tradition when it started its distinct trajectory in the Aegean and Mediterranean in the 7th and 6th centuries BC. There was no legacy of "divine rulership," but spontaneous early revolutions addressed the threat from the wealthy domineering families early on. Reformer leaders ("tyrants") mobilized support to overthrow local warlords who dominated archaic city-states, and they took steps to protect themselves from being overthrown by oligarchic families. A key step was to bring the people (*demos*) into their camp by supporting democratic checks and balances against oligarchy.

In Miletus (in Asia Minor, opposite the island of Samos), Thrasybulus is said to have received a herald sent by his fellow Corinthian reformer Periander in the 7th century BC. Both men were disparagingly called "tyrants" by opponents of their policy of cancelling debts and redistributing land. Herodotus reports that Thrasybulus led the emissary to a field and cut off the highest ears of grain with a scythe.[17] Periander understood this as advice to cut the wealthiest members of Corinth's aristocracy down to size (now called the Tall Poppy Syndrome) by exile or other means.

A similar policy is found in 10th-century Byzantium. When Emperor John I Tzimiskes died in 976, civil war broke out. Bardas Scleros, a general from one of the richest families, sought the throne for himself. Backed by the military aristocracy, he had his troops acclaim him Emperor in 977. Basil II (976-1025) and his court at Constantinople hired Bardas Phocas to defend the city against Scleros, but in 987 (after much fighting), both generals teamed up. Phocas then had Scleros arrested, and marched on Constantinople with his own troops in 988 but died in battle the next year. Scleros's 13-year offensive finally collapsed in 989.

---

[17] Herodotus 5.92. Aristotle (*Politics* 3.1284a26-33 and 5.1311a) reverses the roles, and depicts Periander as sending this advice to Thrasybulus.

In due course Scleros submitted to Basil II, and was assigned a rank second only to the emperor in exchange for promising not to revolt. The 11th-century chronicler Michael Psellus reports that the two leaders held a reconciliation meal in 991, concluding with a long conversation during which Basil asked how his empire "could be preserved free from dissension" in the future.

> Scleros had an answer to this, although it was not the sort of advice one would expect from a general ... 'Cut down the governors who become overproud,' he said. 'Let no generals on campaign have too many resources. Exhaust them with unjust exactions, to keep them busied with their own affairs. ... Be accessible to no one. Share with few your most intimate plans.'[18]

That became Basil's policy. "Whatever happened to contribute to his own (the emperor's) welfare, or to the good of the state, was allowed to remain on the statutes. All those decrees, on the other hand, which referred to the granting of favors or positions of dignity, were now rescinded." Taxing the landed elites helped save smallholders from falling into dependency, leaving them available to serve in the army and pay taxes.

This kind of conflict has changed little today. In Russia, President Putin is seeking to steer the oligarchs to use their wealth to build up the economy, not empty it out and send dividends, interest and capital flight to the West. The legacy of China's Great Revolution created great prosperity, but this inevitably has enabled some families to pull ahead of others and seek to turn their gains into political power. The threat is that a neoliberal-style free market might develop to foster oligarchic kleptocracy and rent extraction.

How should economies cope with this seemingly eternal tendency? Few would advise cutting down all the tall poppies to make everyone equal. The aim should be to create a market structure in which they can gain wealth by playing a productive economic role that enriches the overall community in ways that avoid exploiting others through rent-seeking. The classical ideal is for innovators only to make a profit on their necessary costs of production – payments to labor and for machinery and materials (cost-value) – but not by financial lending and foreclosure, or creation of landlord, creditor or monopoly power relationships charging prices in excess of underlying value.

---

[18] Michael Psellus, *Chronographia* I.29, translated by E.R.A. Sawter as *Fourteen Byzantine Rulers: The Chronographia of Michael Psellus* (London: 1966), p. 43. The word "unjust" no doubt is Psellus's own interpolated value judgment.

A "counter-*rentier*" program

Achieving an equitable growing economy requires a strong state, regulated with a clear distinction between earned and unearned income, and productive and unproductive capital and credit/debt. A "counter-*rentier*" policy program would include the following eleven steps to juxtapose against the neoliberal policy agenda described above (pp. 213-14).

(1)   *Public ownership of natural monopolies*, especially money and credit creation privileges to prevent their monopolization in private hands and resulting rent-seeking.

(2)   *Keep basic infrastructure (in addition to banking) in public hands* to provide essential services such as transportation at subsidized prices or freely to minimize the cost of living. Providing high-quality education and health care as basic human rights will prevent them from being turned into vehicles for monopoly rent-seeking and financialization under private ownership and management.

(3)   *National self-sufficiency* in money and credit creation to protect against other nations' ability to create credit at will, and the political strings that accompany borrowing from the IMF and U.S.-centered international banking systems.

(4)   *Consumer and labor protection* against rent-seeking behavior and exploitative employment conditions.

(5)   *Capital controls* to prevent borrowing or denominating debts in foreign currency. Borrowing foreign currency to spend at home requires the central bank to create domestic credit for use in the local economy in any event. In such cases, foreign currency is not needed, but is simply a liability. When governments need foreign credit to stabilize their exchange rates, a principle of international law is needed to ensure that no government should be obliged to pay foreign debts at the cost of having to impose austerity and economic shrinkage.

(6)   *Taxes should fall mainly on unearned income* (economic rent), which is not a necessary cost of production. Taxing economic rent prevents it from becoming an overhead cost.

(7)   *Progressive taxation* of income and wealth to prevent economic polarization and the resulting instability, and to avoid taxing labor and industry so as to minimize industrial and labor costs.

(8)   *A land tax* to collect the site value that results from public infrastructure spending and general prosperity, not the landlord's own investment. This tax will prevent land's rising rental value from being pledged to banks for credit to bid up real estate prices, and will prevent the emergence of a symbiotic Finance, Insurance and Real Estate sector.

(9)   *Use the economic surplus for tangible capital investment* to raise productivity and improve living standards, and to achieve economic and environmental resilience, not to create financial wealth in the form of claims on the economy.

(10)   *National self-sufficiency in food and other basic needs* so as to protect
the economy from foreign coercive trade and related economic sanctions
as well as from adverse movements in world prices for food and other
essentials.
(11)   *Fiscal and capital controls* to prevent speculative attacks on the
domestic currency, and to prevent capital flight and tax avoidance via
offshore banking centers.

Monetary sovereignty to prevent a *rentier* takeover

An essential element of national sovereignty is to keep banking
and credit as a public utility. Greece's official debts to the IMF and
European Union, along with those of Argentina and other debt-strapped
countries, show the danger of falling into dependency on creditors.
Financial interests claim that anti-labor austerity will make debtors more
competitive and able to "work their way out of debt," but the real aim is
to promote a financial takeover.

To avoid that fate, economies should (as noted above) deter borrowers from denominating domestic debts in foreign currency in order to
obtain a lower interest rate. This raises repayment costs if the domestic
exchange rate weakens. Also to be avoided is borrowing from foreign
banks or bondholders for spending or investment at home. The influx
of foreign credit tends to push up the domestic exchange rate, making
exports more expensive to foreigners and lowering the domestic price of
imports, worsening the trade balance. And such borrowing still obliges
the central bank to create the domestic currency equivalent, while
holding dollar reserves that provide free credit to the U.S. Treasury – in
effect, a global tax enabling America to finance its gunboat diplomacy
simply by its own money creation.

The problem is how to establish a broad principle of international law
to protect national sovereignty in the face of foreign creditor demands.
No nation should be obliged to impose austerity and sell off its public
domain to pay foreign creditors. If that is the only way to pay debts, the
loans should be considered to have gone bad and the creditor should
bear the risk. A modern body of international law along these lines
would be a logical extension of the doctrine of national rights that has
governed the Law of Nations ever since the 1648 Treaty of Westphalia
ended Europe's devastating Thirty Years War.

The United States rejects the sovereignty principle that nations must
not interfere in the government policies of other nations, although it does
not itself submit to international law or other "interference" in its own
internal affairs. It justifies sponsoring coups and other meddling through-

out the world to impose its neoliberal "rules-based order" on the assertion that it is "the exceptional nation." This exceptionalism is at the root
of the political and military strains fracturing today's world economy.

The United States has refused to join any international diplomatic,
judicial or economic institution unless it has veto power to be exempt
from any foreign control over its foreign and domestic policies. That is
why it did not join the League of Nations after World War I, and why
it agreed to join the United Nations only on condition that it have veto
power – which it gained by extending such power to other Security
Council members (Russia, China, Britain and France). Similar U.S. veto
power was achieved in the World Bank and IMF in 1944-45 by setting the
American quota high enough to give it enough votes to block any policy
that U.S. representatives did not feel reflected U.S. national interests.

Being subject to U.S. veto power, the United Nations is unable to
punish American war crimes or stop its biowarfare against countries
(America's use of Agent Orange in Vietnam and similar carcinogenic
poisons in Colombia), its environmental damage (oil spillage and pollution), or its invasions of countries like Iraq whose resources U.S. strategists seek to grab. The resulting self-proclaimed U.S. immunity from the
rules of international law and its breaking of the diplomatic promises
that it has given, has made America, in Vladimir Putin's phrase,
non-agreement-capable.

Indeed, U.S. diplomacy might be called "The Art of Breaking the
Deal." From the early Republic's afore-mentioned land treaties with
Native American tribes to the U.S. promise not to expand NATO if the
USSR would agree to German reunification in 1990, from President
Trump's withdrawal from the Iran agreement to the Paris Climate
Accord, and from U.S. withdrawal from the Eisenhower Adminis-
tration's ballistic missile agreements with Russia for arms parity to
the Anti-Ballistic Missile Treaty in 2002 and the Intermediate-Range
Nuclear Forces Treaty in 2019, the United States does not feel obliged to
live up to any contract that it signs.

It thus hardly can be expected that the United States would agree
to a modern-day Treaty of Westphalia that protects countries from
foreign financial demands to privatize rent-extraction opportunities,
and implicitly outlaws the threat of raids on their foreign-exchange
rates, trade sanctions and other means of economic coercion in pursuit
of these economic demands. Such a principle of national sovereignty
runs contrary to announced U.S. foreign policy. The Project for a New
American Century (PNAC), a think tank backed by the most extreme

U.S. hawks who supported the invasion of Iraq, has celebrated America's basic philosophy of international relations as envisioning

> a strategic confrontation with China, and a still greater permanent military presence in every corner of the world. The objective is not just power for its own sake but power to control the world's natural resources and markets, power to privatize and deregulate the economies of every nation in the world, and power to hoist upon the backs of peoples everywhere – including North America – the blessings of an untrammeled global 'free market.' The end goal is to ensure not merely the supremacy of global capitalism as such, but the supremacy of American global capitalism by preventing the emergence of any other potentially competing superpower.[19]

Backing this imperial evangelism is the dollar-centered financial and monetary system. That system enables Dollar Diplomacy, and indeed Dollar Hegemony, in a way that defines international "adjustment" as imposing austerity to extract rising debt service from the indebted wage-earning populations and businesses of other nations, while inflating their stock, bond and real estate prices by debt-leveraging.

The effect is to deepen inequality among nations, as well as within them. National freedom from this dynamic requires avoiding the use of the U.S. dollar and banks, along with rejection of IMF and World Bank neoliberal demands. That means withdrawing from the Dollar Area's unipolar diplomacy, recognizing that the system is not reformable as it stands. A fresh start is required, as Russian Foreign Minister Sergey Lavrov spelled out in his response to the U.S. demands being forced on the world:

> Realizing that it is impossible to impose their unilateral or bloc priorities on other states within the framework of the UN, the leading Western countries have tried to reverse the process of forming a polycentric world and slow down the course of history.
>
> Toward this end, the concept of the rules-based order is advanced as a substitute for international law. It should be noted that international law already is a body of rules, but rules agreed at universal platforms and reflecting consensus or broad agreement. The West's goal is to oppose the collective efforts of all members of the world community with other rules developed in closed, non-inclusive formats, and then imposed on everyone else. We only see harm in such actions that bypass the UN and seek to usurp the only decision-making process that can claim global relevance. ...

---

[19] Caitlin Johnstone, "If Biden Wins, Russiagate will Magically Morph into China-gate," *Caitlin's Newsletter*, October 26, 2020, quoting Michael Parenti, *Superpatriotism* (2004). https://caitlinjohnstone.substack.com/p/if-biden-wins-russiagate-will-magically.

Another example of the dictatorial methods introduced by the West is the practice of imposing unilateral sanctions without any international and legal grounds, with the sole purpose of punishing "undesirable regimes" or sidelining competitors. ... We believe such efforts to impose totalitarianism in global affairs to be unacceptable, yet we see it more and more from our Western colleagues, above all the United States, the European Union and other allies, who reject all principles of democracy and multilateralism on the global stage. As if to say, either it's our way, or there will be repercussions.

It is striking that Western leaders, while openly undermining international law, do not hesitate to argue that the main task of world politics should be to counter the attempts of Russia and China to "change the rules-based order." ... In other words, there has already been a substitution of concepts: the West is no longer concerned with the norms of international law and now requires everyone to follow its rules and observe its order. What's more, US representatives freely admit that the USA and Great Britain have had the biggest hand in shaping these rules.[20]

Russia is willing to deal with national governments such as Germany, France and Italy on equal terms, Lavrov announced, but has given up trying to deal with Europe via Brussels, whose pan-European policy is committed to supporting U.S. Cold War antagonisms. This rejection of U.S.-directed globalism reflects a radical break from the One World idealism that spread in the wake of World War II. Viewing warfare as a product of nationalism, most people hoped that the antidote would be globalism bringing world peace and mutual economic benefits. It was not expected that globalism would take the form of a self-serving U.S. nationalism imposed globally, as if what is good for its corporations and banks will be good for the world.

There is still a tendency to think of nationalism as a retrograde step. But for foreign countries, breaking away from today's unipolar global system of U.S.-centered financialization is the only way to create a viable alternative that can resist the New Cold War's attempt to destroy any alternative system and to impose U.S.-client *rentier* dictatorships on the

---

[20] Foreign Minister Sergey Lavrov's remarks at the meeting of the UN Security Council, "Maintenance of international peace and security: Upholding multilateralism and the United Nations-centred international system," held via videoconference, Moscow, May 7, 2021, Russian Ministry of Foreign Affairs, *Johnson's Russia List*, May 9, 2021, #24. Lavrov added: "By the way, as soon as we suggest discussing the current state of democracy not just within states but on the international stage with our Western colleagues, they lose interest in the conversation." https://www.mid.ru/en/press_service/minister_speeches/-/asset_publisher/7OvQR5K-JWVmR/content/id/4721942.

world. The international economy is thus far away from having a collective world government.

The most logical alternative is for a grouping of nations to build up a mutual regional prosperity based on their own trade and investment. To achieve this, their governments will need to be in control of their banking and credit creation as a public utility to finance their tangible growth, and have enough foreign currency reserves to withstand speculative attacks by raiders or hostile powers.

To be workable, such a system must organize bilateral balance-of-payments settlements via a region-wide bank empowered to create its own money (as Keynes had proposed with his bancor credit in 1944). Such expansionary region-wide credit is what the Eurozone has failed to create for its member-nation governments, with the resulting fracture between northern European creditor nations and the debt-strapped Mediterranean PIIGS (Portugal, Italy, Ireland, Greece and Spain).

Neither the United States nor Europe and the other Dollar Area satellites are likely to approve of such a region-wide institution. The dollar-centered system requires other Free World countries to acquiesce in privatization sell-offs, anti-labor policies and pro-U.S. trade favoritism (and of course, the free lunch obtained by the Treasury-bill standard of world monetary reserves). The alternative is the classical 19th-century aim of creating a world free of *rentier* overhead. Whether countries will succeed in applying the necessary reforms depends on their ability to create their own de-dollarized alternative institutions.

Part III

The Alternative

12

Reviving the Classical Concepts of Value, Rent and Fictitious Capital

Today's post-industrial economy often is euphemized as well-educated, motivated, productive and efficient, with white-collar labor replacing "unskilled" (meaning low-paid) blue-collar labor. This phenomenon has been called a service economy. The etymological root of "service" is "servile," as in "servant." It connotes a state of dependency. And today's post-industrial service economy is indeed one of dependency – financial dependency, because labor today hardly can survive without running into debt, except for individuals fortunate enough to inherit membership in the emerging *rentier* aristocracy.

This increasingly hereditary aristocracy calls itself a meritocracy, depicting its wealth – and hence, the bifurcated economy's polarization – as a natural result of better education and technology. But the most remunerative "service" is that of collecting interest and rent from an increasingly indebted economy. This revenue is not a technological phenomenon, and it is extractive rather than productive, and is a product of fiscal policy capture, economic deregulation and the creation of legal privilege endowing a self-proclaimed meritocracy of wealth and status.

This is celebrated as a "free market." Like "free trade," it is a euphemism for the status quo dominated by the existing distribution of wealth. Corporate employers have "freed" the U.S. economy from the drudgery of factory labor by moving their production facilities abroad, mainly to Asia. The unemployed are told to learn computer coding, drive Uber taxis or work in home care or other post-industrial services. Despite soaring incomes and wealth for the elite, wages and living standards have not increased for the majority, notwithstanding reported productivity gains (largely from working labor more intensely). What the winners call progress has turned out to be a regression toward oligarchy and its associated exploitation of labor.

With the Covid-19 pandemic having accelerated the debt crisis, the West's 75-year upswing since 1945 is ending in a cascade of bankruptcies and, for the United States, state and local budget shortfalls and a backlog of rent and mortgage arrears leading to looming evictions of renters and mortgage defaulters. The past four decades of neoliberalism since 1980 have enabled the One Percent to turn economies into vehicles to extract land rent, natural-resource rent and monopoly rent by monopolizing control of real estate, industry and hitherto public infrastructure.

The *rentier* class depicts its income and wealth as benefiting society. The generic "trickle-down" image is that of a rising tide raising all boats, as if a larger GDP will make everyone richer. But critics have quipped: "I see the yachts of the stockbrokers, but where are the boats of their customers?" The overgrowth of financial wealth is associated with rising poverty, mainly because financial wealth takes the form of debts claiming interest from corporate business, real estate and individuals, and stockholdings claiming dividends, all at the expense of consumption and fixed capital investment spending. The resulting polarization of income and wealth has led the beneficiaries (and the media) to focus on overall GDP, not on its distribution.

Official GDP and national income statistics depict the U.S. economy as growing, but this growth has accrued entirely to the wealthiest 5 percent since the 2008 bank crash.[1] Millions of evictions followed President Obama's refusal to write down the junk-mortgage debt to realistic valuations when he bailed out Wall Street banks and brokerage houses instead of their victims. In responding to the 2008 crash, and again during the 2020-22 pandemic, the Federal Reserve supported bank liquidity to inflate real estate, stock and bond markets by creating money to lower interest rates (eventually moving to a Zero Interest-Rate Policy, ZIRP). The Fed has even bought, for the first time in its history, junk bonds for its own account, again not spending into the economy to help it revive. Its policy has created unprecedented price gains for the One Percent, who receive 75 percent of today's reported capital gains in the United States. Wealth has soared for the wealthy financial layer even more since the 2020-22 pandemic closed businesses while living standards fell for most of the population.

---

[1] Pavlina Tcherneva of the Levy Institute shows that nearly all the increase in GDP since 2008 has accrued to the wealthiest 5%; GDP has declined for the remaining 95%. http://www.levyinstitute.org/publications/inequality-update-who-gains-when-income-grows. See also Chuck Collins, "U.S. Billionaire Wealth Surges Past $1 Trillion Since Beginning of Pandemic," Institute for Policy Studies, December 9, 2020. https://ips-dc.org/u-s-billionaire-wealth-surges-past-1-trillion-since-beginning-of-pandemic/.

**Chart 12.1 Distribution of U.S. Household Wealth, 2020
Trillions of dollars[2]**

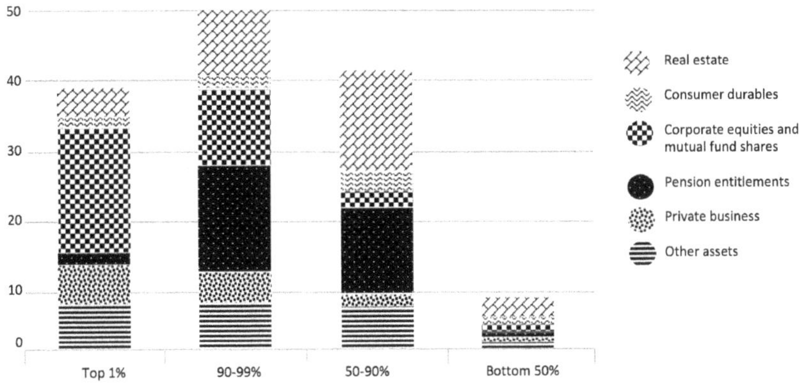

Source: Survey of Consumer Finances and Financial Accounts of the United States

Artificially low interest rates have not helped employment. And they offer personal savers lower safe fixed-income returns, and oblige pension funds to increase their set-asides to meet their retirement-target levels. For businesses, lower interest rates raise the threat of corporate raiders mounting a takeover. This obliges a potential target company to go into debt itself by taking a "poison pill," buying other companies on credit so that raiders cannot load it down with any more debt to pay off their takeover loans from junk-bond buyers. And, of course, near-zero interest rates have encouraged even more borrowing to purchase real estate, stocks and bonds, producing the abovementioned capital gains for the wealthy, along with a tsunami of debt pollution for the overall economy.

The contrast between affluence at the top and deepening distress at the bottom is not new. In 1776, Adam Smith described it as an inherent dynamic of capitalism: "The rate of profit does not, like rent and wages, rise with the prosperity and fall with the declension of the society," he wrote. "On the contrary, it is naturally low in rich and high in poor countries, and it is always highest in the countries which are going fastest to ruin."[3] Today, capital gains are highest while economies are shrinking.

---

[2] Source: Board of Governors of the Federal Reserve System, "Distribution of Household Wealth in the U.S. since 1989." https://www.federalreserve.gov/releases/z1/dataviz/dfa/distribute/chart/#quarter:125;series:Corporate%20equities%20and%20mutual%20fund%20shares;demographic:networth;population:1,3,5,7;units:levels.

[3] Smith, *Wealth of Nations*, Part III, ch. 11, "On the Rent of Land," conclusion of the chapter.

Smith pointed out that the major capitalists of his day (merchants and manufacturers) promoted laws and policies that benefited themselves, not society at large. Their proposals came "from an order of men whose interest is never exactly the same with that of the public, who have generally an interest to deceive and even to oppress the public and who accordingly have, upon many occasions, both deceived and oppressed it."

In today's world the attempt at such deception takes the form of neoliberal "free market" economics. Its defenders argue that making income and wealth equal would hurt the economy, because it is financial capital and property ownership that drives economic growth. The implication is that the wealthy deserve their soaring wealth as a result of their contribution to production, as if they create real output, not extract economic rent.

To support this view, the economics discipline has turned into an abstract and otherworldly attempt to distract attention from the reality that the *rentier* FIRE sector is extractive. Instead, rising capital gains for the wealthy are treated as being not only correlated with rising employment, but implicitly (in good trickle-down fashion) as causing it. This claim formed the basis for the Obama Administration's support of Wall Street. Jason Furman, chair of President Obama's Council of Economic Advisers, blithely commented on what he considered to be the inequality tradeoff: "I don't want to have a lower stock market and higher unemployment." His interviewer commented: "In other words, increasing wealth for the wealthy is an inevitable side effect of keeping interest rates low to support the economy and create jobs."[4]

But the trends have been moving in opposite directions, for reasons that should be obvious as most of the population becomes increasingly indebted to creditors, and home ownership rates fall while stock and bond ownership becomes more highly concentrated in the hands of the wealthiest 10 percent of the U.S. population.

---

[4] Quoted in Allan Sloan and Cezary Podkul, "How the Federal Reserve Is Increasing Wealth Inequality," *Propublica*, April 27, 2021. https://www.propublica.org/article/how-the-federal-reserve-is-increasing-wealth-inequality.

**Chart 12.2 Distribution of U.S. Household Wealth
Corporate Equities and Mutual Fund Shares, 1989-2020
Trillions of dollars[5]**

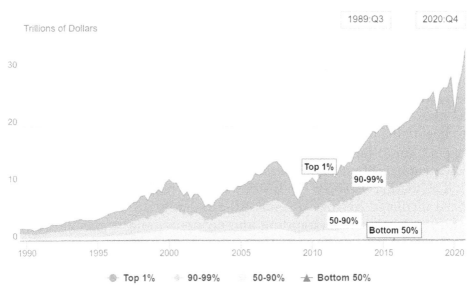

Source: Survey of Consumer Finances and Financial Accounts of the United States

Behind the maldistribution of income in the United States is the concentration of wealth in the hands of a narrowing layer of the population, dominated by *rentiers*. To justify their extractive behavior and support their self-serving mythology, it is necessary for the economy's GDP statistics to depict all income as being earned by making a productive contribution. That was the anti-classical revolution led by John Bates Clark and the Austrian School in the late 19th century, denying the classical distinction between productive and unproductive labor and investment.

Claiming that all income is earned productively implies that all wealth has been fairly obtained as an accumulation of such income – not inflated by financial engineering, debt leveraging and central bank subsidy, or earned in other unproductive ways. To obscure such dynamics, the National Income and Product Accounts (NIPA) and the national balance sheet of asset ownership and debt liability avoid

---

[5] Source: Board of Governors of the Federal Reserve System, "Distribution of Household Wealth in the U.S. since 1989," Corporate equities and mutual fund shares by wealth percentile group. https://www.federalreserve.gov/releases/z1/dataviz/dfa/distribute/chart/#quarter:123;series:Corporate%20equities%20and%20mutual%20fund%20shares;demographic:networth;population:1,3,5,7;units:levels;range:1989.3,2020.4.

drawing the classical distinctions of real wealth from overhead, earned income from economic rent, and productive capital investment from predatory extractive finance.

Plato, Aristotle and other classical Greek writers placed the phenomenon of wealth addiction at the center of their social analysis, as discussed in the introduction. Today's pro-*rentier* academic economics replaces that universal phenomenon with the assumption of diminishing marginal utility – as if the wealthy become as satiated with financial wealth as they would from eating bananas or chocolate cake. But the reality is that as *rentiers* increase their wealth, they do not want to share it. They want to hog it all for themselves and keep making even more. To do this, they oppose government regulatory power to limit their takings or to enact laws that benefit mainly the less affluent 99 Percent.

The tensions between the wealthy and the rest of society have always been mediated by governments. All economies are mixed economies, and the key to understanding any economy, and to designing any national income accounting format, needs to begin with the government's relation to the private sector, and with that sector's division into FIRE "services" and the productive economy that pays economic rent and interest to that FIRE sector. Public policy invariably backs either the wealthy layer at the top or the economy at large. Any pretense by a government to be steering a "middle course" is rarely anything other than a cover for public policies perpetuating a status quo favoring the wealthy, who always have used their wealth to influence and control governments and public policy.

Political democracies have not shown themselves to be very effective in resisting the tendency to turn into financialized oligarchies. Avoiding that fate requires a strong central power not captured by the propertied financial classes. Throughout history, that was achieved only by palace rulers (in the Bronze Age Near East) or today in socialist economies.

I. A model of the economy's sectors

GDP statistics show a rising proportion of GDP as being *rentier* income for banks and bondholders, absentee landlords and monopolists. Their interest charges, penalty fees on debtors, and real estate and monopoly rents, are reported as reflecting a product in the form of "financial services" or the services of landlordship or kindred rent extraction.

These payments leave less disposable income for wage earners and businesses to spend on production and consumption in the "real" economy. That is the phenomenon of debt deflation and rent deflation,

discussed in Chapters 4 and 5. Such payments are thus antithetical to
adding to real product. They are transfer payments from income earners
to *rentiers*.

The government's fiscal role: supplying money to the economy, and taxing it back

A circular flow exists between governments spending money into the
economy and taxing it back. The starting point for analyzing any
modern economy's distribution of income and wealth is this relationship
between government spending money into the economy by providing
basic services and subsidies, and levying taxes to absorb this money.
Accepting it to pay these taxes is what gives money its public value.

Chart 12.3 Economy No. 1, with Government

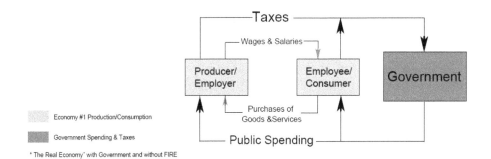

A joke in America is that the United States has a two-party system: a
tax-and-spend party (Democrats), opposed by a borrow-and-spend party
(Republicans). But it is not necessary for governments either to borrow
money or to levy taxes to finance their spending. They can print money.
The effect on prices of doing this is the same as borrowing from wealthy
investors or taxing the public. The money is spent in either case.

However, the fiscal and income effects differ. Borrowing from wealthy
savers does not lead them to cut back their consumption or even production spending, so it does not lower product prices. But paying them
interest is indeed deflationary, to the extent that indebted governments
are obliged to cut back fiscal spending into the economy in order to
meet their interest obligations.

The most important monopoly privilege is that of credit and money
creation, backed by laws governing debt payment and legislating the
rights of creditors relative to general economic welfare. That is why

the money and credit system should be a public utility. As Modern
Monetary Theory (MMT) explains, government money created to cover
deficit spending does not require interest charges, or even repayment.
Keeping the money and credit system in government hands is China's
great advantage over Western financialized economies.

Despite their ability to finance their activities by printing their own
money, there are good reasons for governments to levy taxes. The
classic aim is to minimize economic rent and therefore the economy's
cost structure, by taxes falling mainly on land and natural resource rent,
not on wages and productive capital investment. More modern reasons
include the management of inflation, as well as taxing luxury spending,
pollution and other socially undesirable activities. Rent seeking also can
be averted in sectors that are natural monopolies, such as basic infrastructure, by public investment and pricing instead of letting privatizers
turn these sectors into rent-seeking opportunities.

Bank lobbying against public money creation and public banking

Neoliberal ideology insists that governments forego the advantage of
public money creation and instead rely on private credit creation, borrowing private savings and bank credit at interest rather than financing
budget deficits with their own money. The effect of this financial takeover
of government functions shifts money and credit creation to banks.

The financial sector also advocates lower taxes. Starving public
budgets opens the path for high finance and its clients to take over functions that governments stop supplying – and to extract monopoly rent
from hitherto public infrastructure, seeking to minimize public price
regulation to prevent market manipulation abuses.

To block governments from financing budget deficits by printing
their own money, "Austrian" and Chicago School privatizers claim that
doing so is inherently inflationary. The more extreme lobbyists raise
the red flag of hyperinflation, citing Weimar, Zimbabwe and Venezuela.
But hyperinflations almost always result from currency depreciation,
not from domestic money creation (except in a desperate attempt to pay
foreign debts).[6] Governments cannot create money to obtain foreign
exchange to pay debts owed in foreign currency. Their balance-of-payments deficits may lower the exchange rate, making the debt situation

---

[6] Steven Zarlenga's *The Lost Science of Money* (2002) gives a detailed historical refu-
tation of such accusations.

worse by increasing the domestic cost of imports and hence general price levels.

For that reason, governments should not borrow in currencies that they cannot create. They can save themselves from the threat of bankruptcy by denominating debts in their own currency, because they can always print enough new money to pay what they owe. And to save them from becoming trapped in the way that Germany was in the 1920s, the rules of international finance should adopt the basic principle that no government should be obliged to pay creditors at the cost of imposing austerity and polarizing its economy.

Critics of government money creation sidestep the fact that bank credit is strongly inflationary, but it inflates mainly asset prices, not consumer prices for goods and services. Commercial banks create credit mainly for buyers of assets. About 80 percent of bank loans in the United States and Britain are to buyers of real estate, which is pledged as collateral, with its rents and profits paid as interest to the banks. That is how banks now receive most of the economy's land rent as interest.

Interest charges absorb purchasing power from the economy, just like taxes do. And as will be discussed below, the asset-price inflation resulting from bank credit creation leads to debt deflation in the production-and-consumption sector. Bidding up housing and other asset prices on credit leaves less to spend on production and consumption.

The effect of bank credit thus is different from that of government spending – until recently, when U.S. and Eurozone central banks since 2008 indulged in Quantitative Easing to supply bank reserves to drive interest rates nearly down to zero to support prices for bonds, real estate and stocks. Neoliberal governments discovered that MMT could be used to finance growth of the *rentier* sector, having previously refused to use it to support the industrial economy, the real economy of production and consumption.

II. The rent-extracting FIRE sector vs. the productive value-producing economy

Post-classical ideology avoids acknowledging that the circular flow of wages and profits – the economy of production and consumption – is wrapped in the overlay of the Finance, Insurance and Real Estate (FIRE) sector and its *rentier* siblings – the oil and mining sectors extracting natural-resource rent, and the sectors obtaining monopoly rent. These economic rents are not real "product," but are *transfer payments* extracted from the economy as a result of special privilege (literally "private law").

Charts 12.4 and 12.5 trace the supply of credit and the reciprocal flow of debt service through the government, FIRE sector and "real" economy.

Chart 12.4 Interaction of the "Real" Economy,
The FIRE Sector, and Government

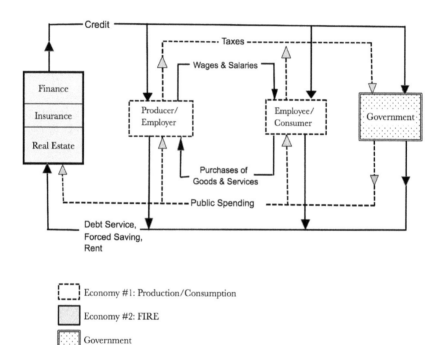

Economy #1: Production/Consumption

Economy #2: FIRE

Government

Chart 12.5 Overall Model of the FIRE Sector, Producers, Consumers and Government

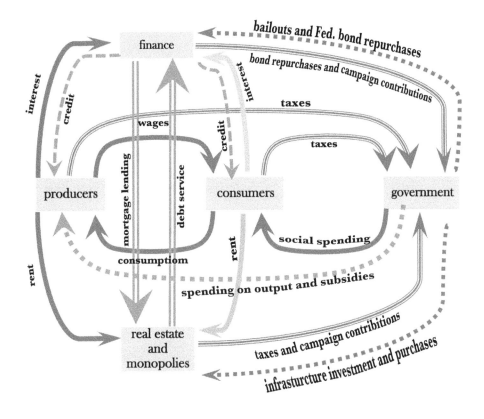

How asset-price inflation causes debt deflation

Running budget deficits spends money directly into the economy. That
may raise prices for goods and services, depending on capacity and
employment constraints. But as described above, banks create credit
for borrowers to buy assets already in place, mostly real estate, stocks
and bonds. Rising debt leverage accelerates the price rise for these
assets. Indeed, price rises for land have far exceeded the rise in GDP or
consumer prices. Wealth is obtained primarily by asset-price ("capital")
gains in the valuation of land and real estate, stocks, bonds and creditor
loans ("virtual wealth"), not so much by saving income (wages, profits
and rents). The magnitude of these asset-price gains dwarfs those of
profits and rental income.

Chart 12.6 Annual Changes in GDP
and the Major Components of Asset Price Gains
(Nominal, $bn)

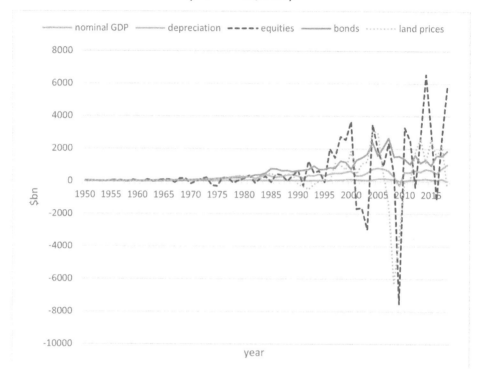

That fact, and the laxity of taxing capital gains, explains why real estate investors are willing to pay most of their rental income as interest to the banking sector. They hope to sell their property at some point for a capital-price gain. Modern finance capitalism focuses on total returns, defined as current income plus asset-price gains.

Inasmuch as a home or other property is worth however much banks will lend against it, wealth is created primarily by financial leverage; by banks lending a rising proportion of the valuation of the assets pledged as collateral. That is what creates a debt-leveraged economy. The fact that asset-price gains are largely debt-financed explains why growth is slowing in the United States and Europe even as stock market and real estate prices are inflated on credit.

By lowering interest rates to near zero, central banks enable financial gains to be made "freely" by arbitrage – borrowing at a low rate to buy an asset yielding a higher return. This has nothing to do with the production and consumption process. The resulting debt leveraging increases "virtual" wealth – prices for financial securities and property claims on the economy – by creating an exponentially growing *rentier* overhead (debt service and rent). The effect is to concentrate ownership of wealth in the hands of creditors and owners of rental real estate, stocks and bonds. Their wealth is based on revenue from debt service and related financial fees, and penalties and overhead imposed on the non-*rentier* economy, as Chapter 2 has noted.

Under these conditions, more bank credit actually tends to reduce consumer prices. Rising debt-leveraged prices for housing require new home buyers and renters to pay a rising proportion of their income to banks as interest on mortgages to buy their homes, or to landlords as rent. These payments to the FIRE sector leave less income to spend on goods and services. Asset-price inflation thus leads to debt deflation as the economy becomes more highly leveraged.

Debt deflation is thus a byproduct of asset-price inflation. Rising housing prices leave less to spend, putting downward pressure on consumer prices, yet the cost of living remains high. That is why governments should aim to keep housing prices down by opposing the FIRE sector's drive to obtain asset-price gains.

A similar deflationary result of asset-price inflation occurs when bank credit is spent on stocks and bonds. That inflates their prices – which means lowering the current yield (*i.e.*, rate of return) of any given asset. When central banks lower interest rates to sustain the asset-price rise (mainly to keep banks solvent), the lower yields on assets increase the amount that pension funds need to set aside to obtain a given current income. So public employers and private corporations are obliged to set aside more revenue to fund pension plans, and thus to spend less on new capital investment, or they themselves speculate in financial markets in search of capital gains.

The housing bubble can continue even as rents are falling because real estate owners hope to pay interest charges by borrowing against the new "equity" created by rising asset prices – capital gains inflated on credit. To sustain the solvency of indebted landlords and speculators, central banks keep flooding the asset markets with new credit, enabling bank customers to "borrow their way out of debt." An exponential increase in the rate of such lending to pay debt service is required to keep the financial system from collapsing. That is the mathematical dynamic inherent in the "magic of compound interest." The only way to keep financialized economies solvent is to turn them into Ponzi schemes, attracting new inflows of credit. That requires central bank aiding and abetting.

III. Relations between the federal government and local state and city budgets

Many countries are suffering a common problem: a fiscal squeeze. States and cities cannot create money. Only the central government can do that. Only national government can create money. Local governments are obliged to balance their budgets by levying taxes or borrowing when their spending exceeds their fiscal revenue. They either must live within the constraints of balanced budgets, borrow against future tax revenue, sell off public property or, if they are fortunate, receive grants-in-aid from their national government.[7]

The way in which states and localities deal with this fiscal problem often determines their economic fate for many years to come. Many U.S. cities have felt obliged to sell future tax revenues to the financial sector under distress conditions. A notorious example occurred when Chicago sold off 75 years of its street parking-meter rights to Wall Street.

> Mayor Richard M. Daley in 2008 struck a deal with the investment consortium Chicago Parking Meters LLC, or CPM, that included Morgan Stanley, Allianz Capital Partners and, yes, the Sovereign Wealth Fund of Abu Dhabi, to privatize our meters. The price of parking – and the intensity of enforcement – skyrocketed. ... City Council members got two days to study the billion-dollar, seventy-five-year contract before signing off on it. An early estimate from the Chicago inspector general was that the city had sold off its property for about half of what it was worth. Then an alderman said it was worth about four times what the city had been paid. Finally, in 2010, Forbes reported that in fact the city had been underpaid by a factor of ten.[8]

Such privatization sharply raised the cost of driving in Chicago. Neighboring Indiana has turned the state's main roads into toll roads. The financial firms acquiring tollbooth rights raised tolls so high that much traffic chose to take slower side roads. "In 2014, the private operators of the Indiana Toll Road, one of the best-known public-private partnerships (PPPs), filed for bankruptcy after demand dropped, due at least in part

---

[7] Strapped cities have long sought emergency local currency, such as Germany's *Notgeld* or "need-money" in the early 1920s. They are accepted locally to the extent that local governments accept them in payment of taxes and other public services. The problem is that there is little acceptance of such *Notgeld*, except by store owners or other businesses who can use this emergency money to pay for taxes or for goods and services provided by the locality.

[8] Rick Perlstein, "On Privatization's Cutting Edge," *The Nation*, September 5, 2013. http://www.thenation.com/blog/176043/privatizations-cutting-edge#.

to rising toll rates. Other high-profile PPP bankruptcies have occurred in San Diego, California and Richmond, Virginia, and in Texas."[9]

China's rural areas and small towns have experienced a similar budget squeeze. Many localities have sold public land on long-term leases to real estate developers. These contracts are often for periods as long as 75 years, and prevent the locality from raising land taxes to reflect the land's rising rental income and valuation. As Wen Tiejun summarizes:

> Fiscal constraint had been a long-term problem for many local governments except some developed provinces and municipalities. ... The economic lockdown in early 2020 further worsened the problem. The national fiscal revenues dropped by 21.4% and 26.1% in February and March 2020 year on year, the worst numbers since 2008. ... The local budget deficits might reach 56% in the first season of 2020.[10]

The way to alleviate this problem is for the central government to extend funding to localities. That has long been done in U.S. revenue-sharing arrangements between the federal government and the states. Kindred proposals are being pressed for the European Central Bank to help finance the national and local budgets of Eurozone members. Without such central-government aid there often seems little alternative but to resort to distress sales of the major local asset: land. As Wen describes the economy-wide effect of this fiscal problem:

> To release local governments from over-relying on land revenues, it is pivotal to reform the taxation system which after all functions as the wealth-redistribution mechanism of a society. Land revenues are usually generated at the expense of transferring rural land resources to the urban sector. Inflationary land prices imply an implicit land tax on lower and middle classes as their costs of living and commerce are also being inflated. China's current taxation system mainly taxes personal income, goods trading (value-added tax) and services. Such a system discourages involvement in the real economy and motivates people to speculate. It results in an unfair burden among classes. According to estimates, the richest class who own over 50% of the total wealth in China have

---

[9] William Mallett, "Indiana Toll Road Bankruptcy Chills Climate for Public-Private Partnerships," National Council for Public-Private Partnerships, 29 September 2014, http://www.ncppp.org/wp-content/uploads/2013/02/CRS-Insights-, quoted in Ellen Brown, *Banking for the People: Democratizing Money in the Digital Age* (Democracy Collaborative, Washington, DC: 2019), p. 282.

[10] Wen Tiejun, *Ten Crises - The Political Economy of China's Development (1949-2020)* (London: 2021), Chapter 5. He notes that: "Only 8 out of 31 provinces and municipalities recorded a revenues/expenditures ratio over 50% in 2019."

contributed less than 10% of personal income tax while 60% is paid
by wage earners. The current practice apparently fails to redistribute wealth among different classes in an equitable manner. A
sensible taxation system should keep tax rates low on earned incomes
from the real economy, including salaries and profits from manufacturing and commerce. It should instead tax non-productive unearned
income (rent-seeking) of the *rentier* class and capital gains, such as by a
property tax or asset-holding tax. Only through conversion of the current
pro-speculation tax structure can China prevent its economy from being
hollowed out and orient its society toward wealth redistribution in favor
of the lower and middle classes.

National revenue sharing or direct subsidy would save localities from
having to relinquish the public domain to privatizers "enclosing the
Commons" and levying rent charges as access fees. Apart from such
central government subsidy to save localities from having to lease or sell
land and tax rights under distress conditions, the other way to prevent
a *rentier* class from gaining power over local governments is to tax away
rents and land-price gains.

IV. Problems to avoid in creating post-*rentier* economies

The interest of governments in taxing away *rentier* gains that are not
earned by providing a productive service is inherently opposed to the
implicit business plan of commercial banking – namely, to lend and
charge interest up to the point where it absorbs all the land and natural-resource rents and monopoly rents.

The higher the tax rate on these rents, the less leeway the banking
system will have to expand the market for debt. From the vantage point
of banks and other creditor institutions, the aim is to increase the loan
market by loosening credit terms, with high debt/income and debt/
asset ratios. The resulting debt leveraging inflates prices for housing and
other *rentier* assets, while holding the rest of the economy in deepening
debt to banks, as well as bondholders (*e.g.*, via junk bonds) and other
creditors. That cuts into fiscal revenue and also ends up slowing the
economy while enriching a *rentier* class.

The most obvious way to avoid this proliferation of debt and its associated asset-price inflation is to keep money and credit creation in the
public domain, in the national Treasury or at least firmly under its regulatory control. The second, equally obvious way, is to limit the financialization of economic rent by taxing that rent away at its source. Whatever
the tax collector relinquishes is left available to be paid to the bank; and
whatever is taxed leaves less to be capitalized into bank loans. Such a

tax would reverse the rollback of taxes on economic rent since the 1920s, which has left this rent available to be pledged to banks as interest.

Keeping land, natural resources and natural monopolies in the public domain is the traditional way to minimize rent-seeking. Although China's government is the nominal owner of all its land, it does not collect all the land rent. That is why housing and other real estate prices have risen so high. Leaving economic rent uncollected – privatizing it – threatens to raise the overall economy's cost structure. That occurred in Britain under Margaret Thatcher and Tony Blair, resulting in soaring prices for housing, busses and railways, water and public needs.

Even when land and future tax rights have been sold in advance, the federal government can pass a windfall ("capital gains") tax on the rising valuation of the leasehold. To help recapture the "free lunch," the government could construct a land-price and rental-value map, establishing uniform land and rental tax rates to prevent localities from competing in a race to the bottom in their attempt to attract business from other jurisdictions.

Such civic rivalry has become a serious problem in the United States, where cities offer tax breaks to large corporations to persuade them to relocate and employ local labor. New York City offered so enormous a tax exemption to Amazon if it would relocate to Long Island City in 2018 that public demonstrations were mounted to stop the giveaway. Entire states are played off against each other to extract special local tax holidays and related incentives. This race to the bottom has led many corporations to locate their head offices in Delaware, with its corporate-friendly deregulatory laws and absence of income taxation. Likewise, credit-card companies have incorporated in South Dakota, from where they are able to charge high interest rates hitherto blocked by local anti-usury laws.[11]

The result of permitting such localism is to create a legacy of giveaways that weigh down a nation's present and future development. If China lets contractual leases at low land taxes or rents run their course for another 60 years or so, it will forego growth while *rentiers* will gain political leverage and try to make their favorable status quo permanent.

Any successful alternative to today's neoliberal attempt to create a unipolar diplomacy extending creditor power and that of international banks and financial institutions such as the IMF, World Bank and

---

[11] See for instance Ann Sullivan and National Journal, "How Citibank Made South Dakota the Top State in the U.S. for Business," *The Atlantic*, July 10, 2013, on that state's lax banking laws.

U.S. A.I.D. requires replacing the pro-*rentier* assumptions of neoliberal orthodoxy with a more reality-based economics, reviving the classical doctrine of value, rent and fictitious capital. The most important characteristic of any economic model should be to show the tendency of economies to polarize and become unbalanced. That is the dynamic that should inform governments as to what needs to be done to restore balance when it is destroyed.

IV. The need for a Clean Slate to restore economic balance

The major dynamic polarizing and unbalancing society is the exponential growth of debt. As noted earlier, this growth results from the dynamics of compound interest – implying a doubling time – and from accruals of unpaid bills in general, and endogenous new bank credit. This dynamic is self-destructive in the long run, because the rising debt overhead leads to debt deflation that slows economic growth, leaving the economy unable to pay its carrying charges, not to mention paying off the principal itself.

The fiction underlying *rentier* economies in their Ponzi stage is that loans can be paid, if only banks will keep lending more – backed by the debt-inflated rise in the price of the assets pledged as collateral. A related belief is that creditors cannot lose, because they can seize the real estate and other collateral of debtors in case of the debtors' insolvency. In addition, the capture of central banks by creditors enabled them to save themselves in the face of the tidal wave of foreclosures of 2009-16. While making the victims of junk-mortgage lending homeless, the Obama bank bailouts and Federal Reserve support made creditors and private-equity property investors such as Blackstone rich.

By the time the Covid-19 pandemic hit in 2020, the U.S. and Eurozone economies already had reached the end of their post-1945 expansion and were entering an epoch of debt deflation. Economies suffering such financial austerity are unable to "grow out of debt," because existing claims on income do not leave enough economic surplus for new direct investment. That leaves only one way out: cancel the bad-debt overhead.

The economy's net worth does not change with a debt cancellation. Lower debt on one side of the balance sheet wipes out an equal volume of creditor claims on the asset side. The net worth of debtors recovers, while that of creditors is rolled back toward the levels that existed prior to the explosion of bad loans, takeover loans and related financial overhead.

Wiping out the savings (creditor claims) on the asset side of the balance sheet is politically difficult, because of the power wielded by the vested creditor interests. China has minimized this difficulty by keeping the financial system as a public utility. It is easy to write down debts when you are the creditor. It has regularly written down debts to troubled companies deemed to be in the public interest, rather than closing them down.

Even after economies have their balance restored, the natural tendency is for the polarization process to begin again – the exponential growth of debt at compound interest, with interruptions of business activity and personal income causing arrears. The adverse effects of these economic phenomena can be held in abeyance by a tax policy that falls mainly on *rentier* income, with the ultimate creditor being the national government and its banks.

Countries owing debts to foreign creditors do not have this option. Governments can only wipe out debts within their own national economy. They are blocked from wiping out debts owed to or protected by official international organizations. The pro-creditor rules of IMF central planners and other bureaucratic enforcers of U.S. diplomacy still follow the model used ever since the 1920s to squeeze debt service out of indebted countries, without regard for their ability to pay. The guiding idea is to impose austerity on debtor countries, shrinking the domestic market by taxing labor and industry heavily, in the expectation that this will free output for export.

The reality is that such austerity programs discourage new capital formation and erode educational, health and living standards. That increases dependency on foreign suppliers and creditors, impairing rather than helping the balance of payments. A downward spiral ensues. This policy continues to be imposed with the same result over and over again. That has been the case ever since German reparations in the 1920s, when the financial austerity doctrine was refuted and shown to be fatally disastrous.

The fact that this anti-labor austerity continues to be applied after a century's demonstration of its effects, and after decades of "IMF riots" by its victims, shows that it is a deliberate policy of financial conquest. Its predatory and destructive effect remains central to mainstream economic policy as perhaps the most successful policy "error" of the 20th century.

It is not an "error" for predatory banks and bondholders, to be sure. The destruction of Third World economies is not a bug in the program; it's a feature. That makes the IMF, World Bank and U.S. A.I.D. unreformable, at least while they remain subject to U.S. control and wedded to the neoliberal orthodoxy on which their destructive policies are based.

13

The War against Governments Strong Enough to Check Oligarchs

Is China's market intervention to promote industrial growth and raise living standards an autocratic road to serfdom, or a classical policy of prosperity that is rapidly outstripping the West's de-industrialization, economic polarization and road to debt peonage? Neoliberals accuse public enterprise, protective tariffs and subsidies to check rent seeking and reduce economic inequality of being less efficient than "free markets." The question that needs to be asked is: "Efficient at *what*?"

Rentiers look to efficiency at maximizing economic rent, and measure economic success by their own fortunes and those of the One Percent. Financial and property investors would like to siphon off China's economic surplus as interest, rents and dividends. That aim has led George Soros to urge U.S. firms to boycott investing in China to protest against President Xi's Common Prosperity aim "to reduce inequality by distributing the wealth of the rich to the general population," because putting the people's interests first "does not augur well for foreign investors."[1] In his view, *rentier* income can be maximized by preventing wages and living standards from rising.

Also deemed unacceptable is China's policy of subsidizing public services to minimize its living costs and the market prices for its industrial exports. Arguing for "fair trade" and a "level playing field," American diplomats complain that providing low-cost support for basic needs in this way is an unfair mode of trade competition. Yet this was the policy that the United States and Europe followed in their own industrial takeoffs. China simply is doing what the United States did in the late 19th and early 20th centuries, and indeed what the social democracy of that era was expected to achieve in the West. China's "interference" with markets follows the classical aim of minimizing *rentier* "free lunch" income. It has achieved its remarkable growth in capital investment, productivity and living standards largely by public investment and

---

[1] George Soros, "BlackRock's China Blunder," *Wall Street Journal*, September 7, 2021.

regulatory shaping of its economy ("the market"), above all by keeping money, bank credit creation and other key infrastructure as public utilities instead of privatizing them for profit and rent extraction.

U.S. trade diplomats blame China for de-industrializing America. But even if China didn't exist, there seems little way for the United States to regain its former industrial dominance. The aim of the Clinton Administration's NAFTA trade agreement with Mexico and Canada in 1994, followed by its invitation to China to join the WTO in 2001, was to facilitate the offshoring of U.S. manufacturing to countries with lower wages. De-industrialization was inevitable as privatizing education, health care and other basic infrastructure, alongside a debt-financed real estate bubble, has made the U.S. cost of living so high that industrial employers have little choice but to shift their employment and production abroad.

It hardly is China's fault that the United States has rejected the 19th-centrury American School's policy of public infrastructure investment that fueled the nation's rise to power, instead leaving investment and economic returns to a "market" controlled by the *rentier* class and the monopolies it has created. However, the need for a mixed public/private industrial economy is again being recognized in the United States. On May 27, 2021, the U.S. House of Representatives passed a 470-page bill, "Ensuring American Global Leadership and Engagement Act" (EAGLE). Supported by the U.S. business community, the Senate moved to back this public subsidy to industry. As *The New York Times* summarized:

> the ideological orthodoxies ... have been swept away by the realities of how China funds its 'national champions' like Huawei, the telecommunications giant that is wiring nations around the world with 5G networks capable of directing traffic back to Beijing. ... Senator John Cornyn, a conservative Texas Republican who has been critical in the past of government funding of industry, said of the semiconductor funding, "Frankly, I think China has left us no option but to make these investments." ...
>
> The bill is gaining support after years in which the United States has objected to government subsidies for private industry — whether it was Airbus in France or Huawei in China. "We're making an attempt to punish China and their bad industrial policies," said Sage Chandler, the vice president of international trade at the Consumer Technology Association, a trade group. "But rather ironically, we punish them and then start to copy exactly what they're doing in a number of ways."[2]

---

[2] David E. Sanger, Catie Edmondson, David McCabe and Thomas Kaplan, "Senate Poised to Pass Huge Industrial Policy Bill to Counter China," *The New York Times*, June 7, 2021.

While such recognition of the need for public investment is welcome, the problem is that the most remunerative ways to obtain wealth in the United States and most other Western economies are no longer by industrial capital formation. Fortunes are acquired financially, mainly by capital gains as bank credit inflates prices for real estate, stocks and bonds bought on credit, that is, by debt leveraging that loads down the economy with interest charges, and by companies raising their stock prices by using profits and rents for stock buybacks and high dividend payouts instead of for new tangible capital investment, research and development. Financialized wealth is further increased by monopoly rent extraction obtained by privatizing public infrastructure.

This financialization and rent overhead is deterring capital investment and effective public subsidy to lower the economy's cost structure. The U.S. government does indeed undertake its own research and development and provides this at a low price, but to private pharmaceutical, information-technology and other campaign contributors to extract monopoly rents from the economy at large.

The effect of all this has been to de-industrialize the U.S. and other Western economies while concentrating wealth in the hands of a *rentier* elite.

Contrasting this de-industrialization and polarization in the West with China's economic success leads to the obvious question: Should governments limit private rent-seeking (as classical free-market economists urged) or support it (as neoliberals demand), and what kind of social system will emerge dominant? This question is the basic issue that shapes today's rivalry between the United States and China.

The conflict is not an industrial trade competition, but a fight between opposing economic systems. Burdening family budgets and industrial companies with debt service, land rent and monopoly rent is not something that China seeks to "do better" by creating more *rentier* billionaires. Its policy makers view the U.S. economy as an object lesson in what to avoid, not what to emulate.

Financialized markets produce austerity, not prosperity

Neoliberalism presents itself as a free-market opposition to centralized planning, but its aim is precisely to use control of credit to concentrate resource allocation in the hands of the major financial centers. There is still Big Government, but its role is to protect the wealth of the One Percent *from* public regulation and taxation of *rentier* income, not to raise prosperity for the economy at large. The financial sector's aim is to promote *rentier* oligarchies in which bankers play the dominant role, wielding their wealth to control national politics much as landed aristocracies did down through the 19th century.

The Clinton Administration (1993-2000) epitomized this philosophy by backing Boris Yeltsin's turning over of Russia's natural-resource crown jewels to the "Seven Bankers" in 1994. Russia's government endowed these banker-insiders with deposits in their banks. The banks then lent this money back to the government – which redeposited the checks in the banks that had written them. In effect, this was a free giveaway. The aim of this charade was for the government to pledge oil and gas, nickel and other assets as collateral, which it forfeited when its central bank was persuaded by Western advisors to refrain from simply printing the money to pay the loans on schedule.

The forfeited collateral began to be sold off to U.S. and other foreign investors – the only ones with money to buy shares in the privatized rent-extraction companies. The effect was to enable U.S. banks, investors and official creditors to become Russia's new central planners, and they organized a bonanza of asset grabs. Dysfunctional state planning became even more dysfunctional privatized financial planning. U.S. officials applauded this carve-up as being the alternative to centralized planning. But the planners had simply left government to become bankers.

The bankers' aim dovetailed with that of U.S. Cold War strategists, whose dream for Russia's post-Soviet economy was summarized by Senator John McCain's quip disparaging Russia as "a gas station with atomic weapons." The plan was for this weaponry to be dismantled, by buying out the military's major industrial suppliers and closing them down, and by breaking up the old Soviet Union's far-flung supply system.

U.S. advisors helped the new oligarchy's members cash out by selling their takings to foreigners and keep their gains safely abroad out of the government's reach. Natural-resource rents from oil and gas, nickel and land, and monopoly rents from public utilities, were to be paid to stockholders as dividends and to bondholders as interest, not to the government to restructure the post-Soviet economy. U.S. investors had similar neoliberal dreams for China's economy upon its admission to the WTO in 2001.

In the United States itself, the 2008 junk-mortgage crash led to a wave of evictions reducing U.S. home ownership rates, and has been capped by the 2020-22 Covid pandemic leading to what threatens to be a new wave of evictions of renters and defaulting mortgage debtors. Millions of employees who lost their jobs are falling behind in their rents and mortgage payments, and have been left debt-strapped and in danger of losing their homes. Evictions were temporarily frozen to prevent a home-lessness crisis, but the day of reckoning is looming for 2022. U.S. housing prices rose by 20 percent in large metropolitan areas from August 2020 to August 2021 as buy-to-rent investors increased their share of U.S. housing. The result is that the U.S. home ownership rate is plunging (as it is in Britain) as housing is turned into a rental investment vehicle.

Meanwhile, the wealthiest One Percent in the United States gained $1 trillion in their stock and bond holdings in the twelve months after the virus began. The upshot has been a K-shaped economy – up for the One Percent, down for the 99 Percent. Homeowners and stockholders imagine that not only themselves but the overall economy is growing richer when housing and stock market prices rise. However, U.S. home ownership rates have fallen since 2006, and mortgage debt now exceeds owners' equity for U.S. housing as a whole. Banks capitalize rising rents into larger bank loans at rising debt-to-price ratios, fueling rising prices by lending more and more for housing. Debt-financed inflation of real estate prices has made banks and speculators rich, but has left most homeowners only with a minority claim on their home's market valua-tion while debt deflation intensifies.

State and local budgets also have suffered instead of sharing in the rise in real estate prices. Public investment in transportation and other amenities has been increasing the rent-of-location for real estate owners along the routes and in favored neighborhoods, but this windfall gain has not been recaptured by a tax on rent-of-location to recover the public cost of making the civic improvements that increase these rents. Land ownership has been turned into an investment vehicle and a market for bank credit to extract rent instead of serving as a public need for living and shelter at minimum cost.

The *rentier* problem has become endemic. Financializing U.S. educa-tion has created a student-debt treadmill to debt dependency even before one enters the labor force, effectively blocking the traditional way to achieve upward mobility through higher education. University degrees have become a financialized commodity, paid for by running up student debt instead of education being provided freely as a public right. Labor and its employers share the high cost of privatized health insurance, in contrast to "socialized medicine" abroad. A self-proclaimed meritocracy is emerging, based largely on the merit of inheriting wealth via trust funds, along with the associated oligarchic mutual-aid educational and employment networks.

Financialization of basic needs for housing, education and health care has raised the cost of living so high that even if all Americans were given their physical consumer goods for free – their food, clothing and so forth – they still could not compete with China or other countries that have minimized the *rentier* charges that burden finance capitalism.

How China has avoided the American financial disease

1. Instead of privatizing natural monopolies and key infrastructure, China has kept its "commanding heights" in the public domain, headed by banking as the most important public utility. The central bank, the Peoples' Bank of China, provides credit for tangible investment in high-speed railroads, schools, transportation systems and research laboratories to keep down the cost of living and doing business.

2. China has pursued an Economy of High Wages policy by providing high-quality education and health standards to make its labor more productive and thus able to undersell low-wage but less productive labor and that of high-overhead *rentier* economies.

3. As a socialist economy, China has aimed to free itself from rent seeking and usurious banking by government regulation strong enough to prevent an independent financial oligarchy from emerging with its own self-seeking *rentier* agenda. Still to be achieved is a progressive tax policy falling mainly on *rentier* income, headed by land rent.

4. To protect themselves from U.S. and other trade and financial sanctions and related attempts at disruption, China and Russia are creating an alternative international payments system to avoid using the U.S. dollar and the SWIFT bank-payments clearing system. The policy of de-dollarizing their monetary systems, foreign trade and investment includes securing their own self-sufficiency in food production, technology and other basic needs.

U.S. defense of *rentier* privilege and opposition to foreign reforms

Neoliberalism attacks the classical and Progressive Era ideology formerly advocated throughout the West. Viewing fiscal and regulatory checks on rent-seeking as posing an existential threat to the *rentier* takeover of national economies, the United States seeks to isolate China and other countries resisting financialization and privatization.

1. The essence of the Thatcher and Reagan privatizations of the 1980s was a giveaway of the public domain at low prices that afforded opportunities for capital gains and enormous underwriting fees for investment bankers, deriving ultimately from monopoly rents charged to labor and

its employers. In the 1990s, neoliberals obtained a free hand in Russia and other post-Soviet republics to endow a kleptocratic pro-Western oligarchy with natural resources, real estate and public infrastructure. Regulatory capture of government agencies throughout the West has blocked enforcement of anti-trust laws and other constraints on predatory monopoly rents resulting from privatizations.

2. Wages and living standards in the United States have been kept stagnant since the 1980s by weakening labor rights, declining unionization and ending defined-benefit pension plans. Indebted workers fear to strike or make any other form of protest that might cause them to be fired and therefore miss their rising debt and rent obligations and lose their employer-sponsored health care. Wage earners are being turned into self-employed "gig" workers such as Uber drivers, lacking corporate responsibility for health care and Social Security contributions, vacations and overtime payments.

To distract attention from this deterioration in U.S. wage and workplace conditions in the face of rising FIRE-sector expenses, identity politics based on racial, ethnic, gender and religious categories has replaced the common identity of being wage earners.

3. Classical fiscal policy was supposed to tax away land and natural-resource rent, while anti-trust regulation and keeping natural monopolies in the public domain was to minimize monopoly rent. But Progressive Era tax and regulatory reforms have been reversed, creating a neoliberal counter-reform era.

The major markets for U.S. high finance are lending against assets already in place (headed by real estate), corporate raiding, buying and selling companies, privatizing public asset selloffs, and stock market speculation. The banking sector's major market consists of lending against rent-yielding assets pledged as collateral, to the point where rents have been almost fully pledged to pay interest. Any move to restore taxation or re-regulate rent-seeking threatens to reduce prices for these assets, most notably stocks, bonds and real estate. That would crash the debt superstructure that is supporting asset prices.

Classical reformers spent the 19th century trying to free economies from *rentiers*. Yet their effort failed in the West. Democratic reforms proved unable to prevent *rentiers* from dominating electoral politics and political parties, having co-opted the liberal-leaning middle class, whose members hold *rentier* aspirations for themselves and shy from taxing away or limiting economic rent seeking. Proposals to gradually enact classical tax and regulatory reforms are unlikely to work, because banks and other *rentiers* would have time to wield the political power that they have built up during their counter-revolution against the classical economic reforms to limit rent-seeking.

The degree to which central banks and treasuries have been captured by the financial sector was demonstrated after the 2008 financial crash. The U.S. Federal Reserve and European Central Bank pursued Quantitative Easing to subsidize debt-leveraged financial and real estate speculation. Then, responding to the 2020-22 Covid crisis, they re-inflated asset prices by near-zero interest rates for financial borrowers. Restoring interest rates to normal levels, or taxing the rents now being paid to the financial sector, would crash prices for real estate, stocks and bonds, threatening insolvency for debt-leveraged investors and banks. So housing and other asset prices remain high.

4. Claiming to spread democracy, America's foreign interventions have been to promote Chicago-style free-market fundamentalism, as in Pinochet's military dictatorship in Chile, spreading its terror squads throughout Latin America. Foreign alternatives to *rentier* finance capitalism are to be deterred by sanctions and, where deemed necessary, by force to impose a neoliberal "free market" for finance capital and its rent-seeking clientele. Blaming China for the deteriorating U.S. economy, American diplomats have escalated military confrontation and sanctions against it and its Shanghai Cooperation Organization allies.

The New Cold War against countries resisting neoliberal takeover

What seemed to be the inherent logic and destiny of the Industrial Revolution, creating economies free from unearned income, required tax and regulatory policies that have now been reversed by U.S. demands that countries privatize their infrastructure and relinquish economic planning to U.S. and other banks, polarizing their economies at the hands of a *rentier* class backed internationally by the U.S. "rules-based order."

To neoliberals a "free market" means letting the *rentier* class become the economy's planning agency. Governments are accused of being "autocracies" if they resist this takeover. It is as if the label "democracy" cannot be applied to such a nation – as if letting the *rentier* One Percent monopolize economic gains is a natural and even efficient post-industrial stage of economic evolution. This is the ground on which neoliberalism presents itself as an evangelistic drive for global conquest against nations that resist its takeover.

But China's industrial success shows that financialization, privatization and monopoly rent are not natural laws, and that debt deflation, privatization of basic needs and the associated polarization of wealth and income do not have to occur. Perception that nations do not have to follow the *rentier* lead is what ultimately threatens the U.S.-based world order. Isolating strong governments opposing *rentier* control of their own natural-resource rents and monetary and credit systems is therefore the essence of today's New Cold War trade and financial sanctions and related moves against China, Russia and other nations rejecting the U.S.-sponsored "rules-based order."

Such nations are not only to be isolated by economic sanctions but destabilized by "color revolutions" in the hope that this will lead to dissident regime change, such as the destabilization attempts that the United States has sponsored along Russia's southern and western flanks, and in China's west and Hong Kong. To cap matters, U.S. officials have brought pressure on Europe to reverse the trade agreements negotiated with China at the end of 2020, hoping to lock Europe into economic and political dependency on the United States.

But the cost of this confrontation is so high that for many counties the dollar, sterling and euro are losing their status as acceptable international currencies because they are seen to be arms of U.S. Cold War diplomacy. A Russian commentator on the hostility of the EU Parliament in Brussels pointed out that as a result of its subordinate satellite position leading to threats to cut off Russia from the SWIFT bank-clearing system: "The EU is losing the opportunity to strengthen and promote the role of the euro as a more desirable instrument for international payments."[3] And as for sterling, Britain's role as an international financial haven was shaken when the Bank of England seized Venezuela's gold reserves and gave them to a U.S.-designated opposition nominee.

To protect themselves against such ploys, China and Russia are de-dollarizing their trade and investment relations. Russia's Foreign Minister Sergey Lavrov summarized matters at year-end 2020, announcing that Russia would maintain relations with individual European governments but not with Brussels, given its support for U.S.-NATO confrontation with Russia. He concluded:

> We are pursuing our own foreign policy, which has taken shape over the past two decades. ... Attempts to destroy external opportunities that can be used to promote Russia's growth continue unabated, but, in any

---

[3] Ivan Timofeev, "Disconnecting From SWIFT? No, We Did Not Hear About It," *Valdai Discussion Club*, April 30, 2021, in *Johnson's Russia List*, May 5, 2021. See also Gabriel Gavin, "'Vicious' sanctions are hurting Russia, but Moscow has plan to ditch US dollar & axe dependency on West,' Foreign Ministry tells RT," www.rt.com, May 3, 2021, in *Johnson's Russia List*, April 4, 2021, #17.

case, there's more to the world than the West. In the 1990s, after the collapse of the Soviet Union, we wanted to become part of something, but we now realize that there isn't much we can become part of. At least, the West is not building anything of its own. ...

If we take Western development models, we have no place to fit in. The coronavirus, as if everything else wasn't enough, showed it very convincingly. We need to build something ourselves. This is a fairly ambitious and complex goal, but it calls for immediate action.[4]

Promoting a coercive pro-*rentier* "rules-based order" at gunpoint, U.S. diplomacy continues to back the world's most oppressive governments and the most violent and intolerant jihadist movements, as it has done for many decades. It is a strange kind of democracy and human rights that euphemizes kleptocratic insider grabbing enforced by client oligarchies as a "free market." Installing warlords and military dictatorships has led to waves of refugees pouring out of Honduras, Guatemala and Ecuador, and America's alliance with Saudi Arabia has backed Salafi jihadist forces in Syria, Iraq and Afghanistan. As Chris Hedges has summarized:

> There is not a single case since 1941 when the coups, political assassinations, election fraud, black propaganda, blackmail, kidnapping, brutal counter-insurgency campaigns, US sanctioned massacres, torture in global black sites, proxy wars, or military interventions carried out by the United States resulted in the establishment of a democratic government. ...
>
> The idea that America is a defender of democracy, liberty, and human rights would come as a huge surprise to those who saw their democratically elected governments subverted and overthrown by the United States in Panama (1941), Syria (1949), Iran (1953), Guatemala (1954), Congo (1960), Brazil (1964), Chile (1973), Honduras (2009) and Egypt (2013). And this list does not include a host of other governments that, however despotic, as was the case in South Vietnam, Indonesia, or Iraq, were viewed as inimical to American interests and destroyed, in each case making life for the inhabitants of these countries even more miserable.[5]

---

[4] Foreign Minister Sergey Lavrov's opening remarks at the 28th Assembly of the Council on Foreign and Defence Policy, Moscow, December 10, 2020. https://www.mid.ru/en/foreign_policy/news/-/asset_publisher/cKNonkJE02Bw/content/id/4478752.

[5] Chris Hedges, "The Unraveling of the American Empire," *Consortium News*, April 19, 2021.

The oligarchic fight to limit the power of democracies

From Rome to the modern world, the main source of oligarchic power has been financial. What is euphemized as "security of property" actually is an *insecurity* of the property rights of debtors, leading to foreclosure or forced sale of *their* property. Backed ultimately by the rule of force, that is how oligarchies through the ages have gained control of land and its rent, and have indebted labor to make it dependent on creditors.

Western democracies have not been able to protect citizens from the power of creditors, landowners and monopolists to create an underclass of debtors and rental tenants. Preventing that fate would require governments to make the monetary and credit system a public utility, supported by credit laws to protect the indebted population at large.

Rejecting such governmental control, oligarchies seek to restrict the meaning of "democracy" to the political sphere of letting all citizens vote but limiting just what they are permitted to vote on. Classical Athens empowered a pre-boule to limit just what laws and policies the popular assembly could discuss and vote on. Rome's constitution let all enrolled citizens vote in its popular assembly, but weighted voting groups according to their property holding.

Even if a populist leader could be elected or popular reforms approved by citizens, oligarchies historically have had fallback positions to nullify voting (not to mention using violence against reformers). Roman senators claimed to find religious omens to suspend or nullify the voting. Today that quasi-religious function is filled in the United States by the Supreme Court, empowered to nullify Congressional reforms, much as it blocked passage of an income tax for many decades before 1913.

As Chapters 8 and 9 have described, the oligarchic U.S. system permits private funding of political campaigns as a form of "free speech" (the result of the Supreme Court's Citizens United ruling in 2010). Electoral candidates for the Republican/Democrat political duopoly win nomination according to how much money they can raise from donors. This enables the Donor Class to negate meaningful democracy in practice by effectively letting it veto candidates who would tax and regulate the *rentier* sector's financialization and rent seeking. The effect is to limit what citizens can vote on. That always has been the essential feature of political democracies controlled by oligarchies.

Political democracy overshadowed by economic oligarchy

The seemingly most obvious way to determine whether a society is democratic is to ask whether voters are able to get enacted the policies that they want. Recent opinion polls in the United States show a strong preference for public health care and forgiveness of student debt, but no political party is backing these policies. These are beyond the permitted range of options open to democratic choice. Nominal political democracy has faltered at legislating policies that would benefit most of the population by limiting *rentier* power.

Western democracies tend to polarize into oligarchies composed of creditors, landlords and monopolists, who win support from middle-class voters who fear radical policies threatening their aspiration to make *rentier* gains for themselves as small investors and property owners. Werner Sombart characterized this bourgeoisie as the most ambitious layer of the 99 Percent, "floating like globules of fat on the rich soup of the economy."[6] Some professionals, innovators and artisans are able to save up and make gains in housing and the stock market. Their feet are in the wage-earning class, but they are reaching up to the asset-holding class as its advocates, enablers and entertainers.[7]

The One Percent views the role of this layer of the well-to-do as being to co-opt ordinary wage earners, encouraging the dream that enough opportunities for upward mobility exist to raise living standards for the population at large, as if wealth will trickle down instead of extracting yet more income from the economy below it. Recognizing this ploy, the philosopher John Dewey ridiculed "the belief that those who have privilege and power will remedy the breakdown they have created," and characterized American politics as "the shadow cast on society by big business."[8]

Oligarchies oppose strong government power unless they control it themselves. Greek oligarchs feared "tyrants" because the reformers of Corinth, Megara and other city-states in the 7th and 6th centuries BC gained popular support by canceling debts and redistributing land. Sub-

---

[6] Werner Sombart, *Der Bourgeois* (Munich and Leipzig: 1913).

[7] In the United States the Democratic Party has today reached the stage that in seeking the votes of this class, it openly dismisses even the need to win working class votes. As New York senator Chuck Schumer put it, "For every blue-collar Democrat we lose in western Pennsylvania, we will pick up two moderate Republicans in the suburbs in Philadelphia," by which he means upper middle-class housewives hoping to rise in society via *rentier* wealth.

[8] John Dewey, "The Need for a New Party" (1931), reprinted in Dewey, *The Later Works, 1925-1953* (Carbondale, Illinois: 1985), p. 163, cited in Jake Johnson, "Dewey was Right: American Politics is Merely the Shadow Cast by Big Business," *Common Dreams*, July 21, 2016.

sequent critics accused these reformer-tyrants of being prone to power lust, but most Greek philosophers warned that the main social danger was the tendency of the wealthy to succumb to addictive money-lust and resort to violence to protect their takings.

Rome never was a democracy. Its legendary kings are credited with having kept wealthy families in check, but the oligarchic coup against them in 509 BC led to five centuries of civil warfare over debt cancellation and land redistribution. The Senate oligarchy killed the most threatening and viable reformers, accusing them of "seeking kingship." That was the accusation made against Julius Caesar, fearing that his popularity might enable him to cancel Roman debts, as Catiline had sought to do a generation earlier before he and most of his followers were killed. The Gracchi brothers had been killed a century earlier for advocating land redistribution, and Sulla killed the followers of the popular general Marius who sought land for his troops.

Western civilization's unwillingness to check *rentier* dominance

Greek and Roman citizens wanted liberty from debt and its associated clientage to creditors. The refusal by their oligarchies to cancel debts and redistribute land led their economies to polarize and collapse into a Dark Age. Subsequent Western democracies have not been able to prevent economies from succumbing to a similar dynamic, polarizing and impoverishing their economies by the combination of debts growing at compound interest and the concentration of land and wealth resulting from economic rent seeking.

To reduce the privileges that the landlord class had inherited from feudal times, 19th-century reformers extended voting rights to a broader constituency. But the legacy of Rome's pro-creditor ethos and legal system remains intact throughout today's Western world. It has been left to socialist economies to resist the power of finance capital to capture the state, rolling back *rentier* power by restoring control of money, credit, land tenure and basic infrastructure to governments.

This socialist effort is closing a long historical loop. For thousands of years it was normal for Bronze Age Near Eastern rulers to prevent wealthy families from becoming an independent oligarchy able to resist royal protection of indebted smallholders. Byzantine rulers of the 9th and 10th centuries AD also succeeded in this aim. Clean Slates cancelled the debts of smallholders, liberated debtors from bondage and restored land they had lost.

This was a pragmatic policy, not utopian. It aimed to regulate credit relations and land tenure in ways designed to stabilize economic self-reliance, the flow of fiscal receipts and the supply of goods to the rest of the economy. To save subjects from having to pay their crop surpluses to creditors and work for them instead of for the palace, Clean Slates asserted the priority of subjects paying taxes, working on public construction projects and performing the military duties normally attached to their land tenure.

There was no Milton Friedman to argue that land and labor should be made part of a "free market" or that market efficiency should permit the wealthy to expropriate smallholders who fell into debt. Any realm that adopted such a policy would have become depopulated from flight of its population, or conquered or overthrown, or experienced a revolution. Restoring liberty to smallholders could not have been achieved if rulers had left debt and land-tenure relations to "the market." Strong authority was needed to regularly roll back the credit and debt dynamics that drove smallholders into bondage and transferred land to creditors.

Roman law's support for "property rights" transmogrified this term to mean the right for creditors to expropriate the property of debtors. This has been a defining feature of Western civilization ever since. Only strong governing powers, such as Babylonian and Byzantine rulers or 20th-century socialist governments, have been able to check financial and other *rentier* interests. Opposing such power, today's neoliberal antagonism toward China resembles Rome's hatred of kingship or civic government not firmly under oligarchic control. From antiquity to today's world, kings, tyrants and revolutionary governments have been the only powers able to successfully cancel oppressive debts and promote widespread land tenure. Yet such authorities are called autocratic, as if the tyranny of debt has not been even more oppressive throughout history.

Table 13.1 shows the kinship between modern socialism and pre-classical monarchies in their ability to block a *rentier* financial class from taking control.

Table 13.1

Ancient, Oligarchic and Socialist Economic Relations		
Bronze Age Near Eastern Monarchies	Western Democracy / Oligarchy	Socialism
The market is regulated by the palace administering land tenure, credit terms and interest rates. But trade and other activities are delegated to merchants. The result is a palace-dominated mixed economy.	Financial and landlord oligarchies unseat kings and minimize state power, public spending and regulation. Economies polarize as the state serves the wealthy at the expense of overall prosperity.	A state-regulated economy administers basic prices and public services, leaving opportunity for business innovation to create personal fortunes within limits, but not letting wealthy families monopolize national growth and prosperity.
Land is a public utility, allocated in standardized lots with holders owing corvee labor, service in the armed forces, and in some cases sharecropping payments to the palace. The aim is to preserve smallholders as viable taxpayers, free from debt bondage.	Land becomes "commodified" as the crop surplus is concentrated in the hands of absentee landlords becoming an entrenched oligarchy. *Latifundia* are farmed by tenant labor (initially working off their debts), slaves and later by serfs. Housing becomes debt-financed and its price inflated on credit.	State ownership of land manages it as a public utility, but may lease it. Owner-occupancy is promoted by a land-rent tax that discourages absentee ownership and debt financing that turns rent into interest payments instead of tax revenue.
Citizens are self-supporting on the land, but pay debts by working for their creditors and turning over crops.	Pro-creditor laws force debtors into clientage, leading to debt bondage and ultimately to serfdom.	Citizens receive basic needs as a human right without a need for debt financing for housing, health care and education.
Money is developed to denominate debts, public services and taxes, above all to the palace and temples, by standardizing prices for products designated for such payments.	Monetary fortunes and hence credit shift to private owners. Silver money is still given value by being accepted as taxes and tribute.	The state creates money and credit as a public utility. Its central bank extends credit for public purposes, not for financial speculation.

Major prices are administered for payment of taxes and other transactions between the community and the palatial economy.	Prices may be controlled for basic needs such as food. But most services and prices are privatized, leading to monopoly rents and profits.	Basic needs and services are provided freely or at subsidized prices. The aim is not to make a profit but to subsidize widespread growth.
Debts and their associated clientage to creditors are reversible, being cancelled by new rulers taking the throne or in times of economic disruption or warfare.	Debts are irreversible as they accumulate over time. Advocates of debt cancellation are denounced by oligarchies and often killed. Modern bankruptcy laws only cancel debts on a case-by-case basis.	Debts are written down when that is needed to avoid major close-downs and economic disruption.
The palace and temples are the major early creditors. Hence, royal Clean Slates are cancelling debts mainly to the palatial economy itself.	Credit is privatized, and debts are cancelled only by civil war. Debt dependency, clientage and forfeiture of land become irreversible.	The state is the major creditor via its public banks, and treats credit as a public utility to finance tangible investment and growth.
"Divine kingship" is sanctified by rulers being subordinate to their patron deities and the ethic of justice and equity protecting the weak (widows and orphans) from the strong and powerful (creditors).	Monetary fortunes and money-love (wealth addiction) break "free" of public regulation, as the wealthy gain control of ideology and religion. Private charity replaces public social welfare spending.	The state and its officials are committed to protect overall prosperity and restrict the power of wealthy individuals to act in ways adverse to public policy and prosperity.
Restoring widespread self-support and viability preserves a resilient economy. Royal Clean slates and palace regulation prevent an independent creditor-landlord power base from emerging more than temporarily.	Social resilience is lost as a creditor-landlord oligarchy gains control of the state to enact pro-creditor laws, administer its courts and prevent debt cancellations and land redistribution.	Resilience is achieved by subordinating personal wealth-seeking, above all in finance and land tenure, to social objectives. Wealthy individuals remain subject to public oversight.
The palace is the major customer and also creditor for merchants. Unlike the grain debts of smallholders, mercantile silver-debts are not cancelled by Clean Slates.	States and localities become net debtors to a creditor oligarchy, which privatizes tax collecting and mobilizes state power to enforce its claims on debtors.	The state organizes money and credit as a public utility, adjusting debt service to the ability to pay without causing economic disruption.

Circular time: Rulers intervene from outside "the market" by proclaiming Clean Slates to restore economic balance as an idealized *status quo ante*. That reverses the buildup of debts, bondage and forfeiture of land for debt arrears.	Linear time: Economic inequality, debt bondage and loss of land rights become cumulative and irreversible as debts and financial savings grow exponentially. The resulting economic polarization is only reversed by revolution.	State-sponsored stability prevents a financial debt cycle from emerging. Debts may be written down to save individuals or firms threatened by insolvency when that would disrupt the economy.

Credit and debt regulation as a natural public utility

When the basic economic elements of markets were being put in place in the third millennium BC in Mesopotamia and Egypt, almost all transactions during the crop year took place on credit, from farming inputs to drinking beer at the public ale house. The palatial sector developed the monetary and credit system to facilitate fiscal account-keeping and resource allocation, and leased land on tenure arrangements that obliged its holders to provide corvée labor to build public infrastructure and serve in the military.

Money was innovated as an administrative device to allocate the flow of labor, crop production, temple handicrafts and foreign trade, not as a commodity to enable its holders to disrupt this economic order. Harvest time was the occasion for smallholders to settle the debts that they had run up during the crop year. These debts were denominated in grain, and were paid on the threshing floor, the point at which actual money payment was required. Most agrarian debts were owed to the palace and temples, as well as to officials acting on their own account.

Silver was the unit of account for merchants, who typically paid debts at the end of their contracted voyage or trading venture (typically five years). The palace for its part kept unified economic accounts by setting a unit of grain equal to a unit of silver for keeping balance sheets of its relations with the rest of the economy. This created a common denominator to consolidate its various operations, track income and spending, and calculate overall institutional surpluses and deficits.

Agrarian debtors who could not pay enough grain or other crops to settle their debts at harvest time usually had to pay the remaining debt balance by performing labor services for their creditors. This caused a fiscal tension between the palatial economy and individual creditors. Early societies could not afford to leave private creditors with a "free" right to enserf the population and take crops for themselves at the expense of the palace's need for this labor and produce, nor a right to in time monopolize the land and its yield by appropriating the debtor's land tenure rights. For thousands of years, rulers restored economic balance by cancelling personal grain debts, liberating bond-servants and returning self-support land to its customary former owners. That made archaic economies resilient instead of letting creditors foreclose and permanently turn land, labor and interest-bearing credit into choke points for private ownership to extract the economic rent that was the original fiscal base.

These redistributive and fiscal principles are the basis of modern socialism but not of Western economies. Ever since classical Greece and Rome stopped the Near Eastern practice of Clean Slates, Western economies have not been able to save themselves from polarizing between creditors and debtors, landlords and tenants, patrons and clients. Today, the neoliberal reaction against social democracy has ensured such polarization, first by letting debts grow faster than the ability to be paid and hence concentrating wealth in the hands of creditors, and second by advocating that basic public utilities be privatized and run by financial managers, not provided as a human right.

The financialization and privatization of hitherto public functions have gone together, with rent-seeking and asset-price gains being the essence of today's finance capitalism. The United States leaves education, banking and other privatized monopolies that control basic needs to "the market." Housing is the largest financialized sector, followed by privatized health care that enables pharmaceutical companies to charge monopoly rents and even to block the government from bargaining over prices for drugs to reduce monopoly rent charges. Health Management Organizations meanwhile monopolize medical treatment for profit (or more accurately, for monopoly rent).

Can the West achieve resilience by debt writedowns and de-privatization?

Today's Western economies face a choice between shrinking into financialized austerity or taking the seemingly unthinkable step of writing down the debts that are polarizing their distribution of wealth and income, and taking the further step of ending the dominance of *rentier* unearned income.

What is blocking these reforms are the political, legal and informational blocks that the *rentier* interests have put in place, and their willingness (even enthusiasm) to protect their privileges by force against any political movements or governments that resist neoliberal privatization and financialization. *Rentiers* and exploiters have almost always shown a much greater willingness to defend their takings with violence than victims are willing to fight to protect themselves or achieve substantive reform.

This is the essence of U.S. support for client oligarchies in Latin America and elsewhere in today's world, as it was of Rome's oligarchy throughout ancient history. Faced with the mobilization of police, the military, politicians and the courts by the vested interests to block reform, victims are confronted with the fact that throughout history the *rentier* class and its defenses have been so strong that it has taken a political revolution to establish an alternative to *rentier* domination.

Today, the willingness and even evangelistic eagerness of the United States to engage in military and economic aggression against countries seeking an independent path explains the need for such countries to create a countervailing power by investing in their own military overhead to avoid the fate of countries like Libya, Iraq and Syria, and to decouple their economies from reliance on foreign food and other basic needs so as to defend themselves against U.S. sanctions aimed at destabilizing their economies, such as those imposed on Iran, Russia and China.

The alternative to U.S.-centered Western finance capitalism

China's economic success in resisting the *rentier* revival and takeover has led U.S. officials to declare that nation to be an existential enemy. The idea of having a public sector that administers money and credit creation, debtor rights and creditor practices, land tenure, educational and health-care systems to meet human needs instead of turning them into rent-extracting choke points is treated as aggression against today's U.S.-sponsored financialized economic system.

U.S. diplomats and politicians accuse nations that put in place public restrictions against monopoly and related rent-seeking of being autocratic and authoritarian if they defend their economies against privatization and the associated American attempt at financial takeover. As U.S. Secretary of State Antony Blinken asserted rhetorically in August 2021: "The Chinese and Russian governments, among others, are making the argument in public and in private that the United States is in decline so it's better to cast your lot with their authoritarian visions for the world than with our democratic one."[9]

---

[9] "Blinken urges investment at home to compete with China," *Yahoo News*, August 9, 2021. https://sg.news.yahoo.com/blinken-urges-investment-home-compete-194036906.html. "Blinken cited a World Economic Forum study that the

That assertion is an Orwellian rhetorical attempt to obscure the most important economic issue dividing the world: Which offers more real democracy in the sense of reflecting what most people want: a strong independent state engaging in public regulation and social investment to make its economy prosperous and less unequal by keeping the *rentier* sector in check (defamed as "autocracy" by its opponents), or oligarchic quasi-democracy (nominally political but not real economic democracy) in which financial and *rentier* power prevents governments from protecting debtors, employees, consumers and renters?

As matters were coming to a head in August 2021, not long after Secretary of State Blinken's rhetorical assertion, China's President Xi Jinping expressed his view on this basic global issue: "At present, income inequality is a prominent issue around the globe. The rich and the poor in some countries are polarized with the collapse of the middle class. This has led to social disintegration, political polarization, and rampant populism ... Our country must resolutely guard against polarization, drive common prosperity, and maintain social harmony and stability."[10]

And in October 2021, Russia's President Vladimir Putin framed this contrast as the main crisis facing today's world. The crisis, he said, is "conceptual and even civilization-related. This is basically a crisis of approaches and principles that determine the very existence of humans on Earth." Despite claims in recent decades "that the role of the state was outdated and outgoing," he emphasized that only strong nation-states can resist the economic carve-up and immiseration of the planet. "Globalization supposedly made national borders an anachronism, and sovereignty an obstacle to prosperity. ... This ... was said by those who attempted to open up other countries' borders for the benefit of their own competitive advantages."[11]

United States ranks 13th in infrastructure and said that China was spending three times as much and also investing more in research and development."

[10] Xi Jinping, "To Firmly Drive Common Prosperity" (translated by Adam Ni), published in *Qiushi*, available at https://www.neican.org/p/to-firmly-drive-common-prosperity.

[11] President Vladimir Putin's remarks at the plenary session of the 18th Annual Meeting of the Valdai Discussion Club in Sochi, October 22, 2021: "Global Shake-Up in the 21st Century: The Individual, Values, and the State." https://valdaiclub.com/events/posts/articles/vladimir-putin-meets-with-members-of-the-valdai-discussion-club-transcript-of-the-18th-plenary-session/.

The age-old conflict between broad economic welfare and *rentier* wealth-grabbing

Today's global crisis is repeating the fight that characterized the Western takeoff in classical antiquity. The Free World/NATO alignment has no state power corresponding to ancient "divine kingship" or what is reported for Roman and Spartan kings whose interest lay in preventing a *rentier* oligarchy from emerging to use financial and rent-extracting power to reshape the economy in its own narrow interests. In today's neoliberalized world, autocratic governments are strongest in the most highly financialized oligarchies and their client protectorates. Money-lords, U.S. clients and military *caudillos* have become the new rulers in the West, denying the majority of citizens an opportunity to elect governments whose policies reflect what they most want. That leaves nominal political democracy with little real meaning.

This problem has been endemic since antiquity. For century after century, during the entirety of Rome's Republic, 509-27 BC, the system of voting by wealth cohorts gave electoral power to Rome's One Percent. This voting system was imposed by Rome's oligarchy after it overthrew the kings and blocked popular cries for debt cancellation and land distribution. The resulting autocracy was in sharp contrast to the policy of providing for basic needs that Rome's kings are reported to have promulgated to attract immigrants to Rome to fuel the city's remarkable early growth.

Debt relief protecting smallholders had been proclaimed for thousands of years by Near Eastern "divine kingship." Clean States restoring economic order were proclaimed because rulers were strong enough to prevent oligarchies from emerging and irreversibly expropriating debtors from their self-support land. Similar protection is promised today by socialist movements in China and other countries. However, American diplomats characterize any nation seeking to provide widespread economic resilience as "autocratic."

Regulation to limit *rentier* power is deemed antithetical to U.S.-style democracy, whose idea of a "free market" turns out in practice not to promote universal values, but rather to mean central planning by Wall Street financial managers politically empowering themselves as the Donor Class. At issue is who will get the benefit of rising economic and productivity growth. In the Orwellian vocabulary of finance capitalism, a free market means whatever the wealthy *rentier* class wants to charge for access to the land, financial credit creation and monopoly rights that it has appropriated. The neoliberal ideal of today's finance capitalism is epitomized by what the Chicago Boys were able to impose at gunpoint in Chile under the Pinochet "free market" dictatorship of the 1970s, and what U.S. neoliberals and neocons created in Russia under President Yeltsin in the 1990s.

Militarizing neoliberal *rentier* ideology

Neoliberal ideology has taken on an evangelistic dimension in Western elite society and its mass media. And just as religious fights often have been settled by violence and armed force, so today the United States has militarized its attempt to force other countries to abandon their drives for financial and commercial self-reliance and even for social democracy not under the free-market patronage of U.S. financial investors and planners.

Russia succumbed to neoliberal mythology in 1990-91 because President Mikhail Gorbachev and other leaders were enamored at the prospect of ending the Cold War. The dream was to create an era of international peace among the world's most highly militarized nations. How it was dashed has been explained by Vladimir Putin, most recently in his above-mentioned Valdai Club speech of October 2021:

> Humanity entered into a new era about three decades ago when the main conditions were created for ending military-political and ideological confrontation. ... We were looking for this support but must say that we did not find it, at least so far. ... Where are the humanitarian fundamentals of Western political thought? It appears there is nothing there, just idle talk. ... The attempt to create [an extremely favourable precedent] after the end of the Cold War on the basis of Western domination failed, as we see. The current state of international affairs is a product of that very failure, and we must learn from this.

Since the 1980s, Western leaders have insisted on the Chicago School free-market claim that neoliberal economies are naturally self-regulating and more productive than mixed economies with government regulation and ownership of basic infrastructure. Friedrich Hayek proclaimed that such government "interference" is the road to serfdom. That was the Orwellian rhetoric that so entranced Margaret Thatcher and American libertarian free marketers and deregulators, and which underlies much of the New Cold War's hyperbole. A "market" with public "interference" is accused of "violating" economic "liberty" – by which is meant the liberty of the wealthy to deprive debtors, clients and consumers of their *own* economic and personal freedom. The two thousand years of historical experience since classical Rome shows that such liberty or "free markets" for the wealthy lead to oligarchy, and that oligarchies literally are the road to serfdom.

Today's civilizational fork in the road

There are essentially two types of society: mixed economies with public checks and balances, and oligarchies that dismantle and privatize the state, taking over its monetary and credit system, the land and basic infrastructure to enrich themselves but choking the economy, not helping it grow. The lesson of history is that privatized oligarchies polarize and become failed states. Mixed economies with governments strong enough to protect their society and people from predatory *rentier* exploitation are successful and resilient.

A mixed economy in which governments aim to combine economic progress with social stability can only survive by resisting the attempt by the wealthiest families to gain control of public power and put themselves in the government's place. Recognizing the dangers that result from not resisting such an oligarchy, China's President Xi pointed out in his August 2021 article cited above that: "Some developed countries have been industrializing for hundreds of years, but due to their social systems, they have not solved the problem of common prosperity and, in fact, the problem of disparity between the rich and the poor has worsened." To avoid this fate, China "must maintain the public ownership system as the mainstay ... While we should allow some people to get rich first, it should be emphasized that those who become rich first [shall] lead and assist those who are not yet rich."[12]

Neoliberal Cold Warriors deem China to be an existential enemy for having taken this position. What they oppose is China's ability to prevent the U.S.-centered *rentier* interests from extracting exorbitant amounts of wealth at its expense, and its demonstration that there is a highly successful alternative to neoliberal finance capitalism, potentially leading countries away from the U.S. policy orbit.

The threat posed to society by *rentier* interests is the great challenge of every nation today: whether its government can restrict the dynamics of finance capitalism and prevent an oligarchy from dominating the state and enriching itself by imposing austerity on labor and industry. So

---

[12] Xi concluded by emphasizing the most important potentially destabilizing dynamic that his nation – and in fact, every nation throughout history – has had to address: "We must improve the housing supply and support systems, and insist on the position that housing is for living in and not for speculation."

far, the West has not risen to this challenge. Financialization and rent seeking remain the dominant features of today's Western economies, which have put in place a Potemkin village of political democracy as window dressing for *rentier* oligarchy.

That is the West that Putin and other Russians speak of rejecting. It might be argued that Western Europe itself has rejected what made it the "West" in the time of Peter the Great and the 19th-century Progressive Era of classical political economy and parliamentary reform that aimed at strengthening the power of social-democratic governments over the *rentier* class inherited from feudalism.

Today's New Cold War is thus a clash of economic systems, confronting the world with an either/or conflict between the resurgence of *rentier* wealth and privileges, and the ability of governments to resist this anti-progressive counter-revolution. Rosa Luxemburg described the choice a century ago as one of barbarism or socialism. Today it is a choice between financialized austerity on the one hand, and a recovery of society's ability to put its overall prosperity and growth above that of special interests gaining wealth by extractive means.

Western finance capitalism is being dragged down by financialization, privatization and debt deflation. But the decline of the West is not necessary or historically inevitable. It is the result of choosing policies dictated by its *rentier* interests. Failed states emerge when *rentier* oligarchies are allowed to prevail and dismantle government regulatory and taxing power on the basis of the false logic that their rent extraction is payment for productive activity, and that their *rentier* wealth adds to society's prosperity rather than being an overhead burden to the rest of the economy. Embracing this flawed logic has seen austerity and polarization throughout the West.

Perhaps China's successful state-sponsored development may inspire the United States and other Western nations to recover what used to be their own industrial dynamic. The 19th-century flowering of classical political economy developed the concepts of value, price and rent to distinguish earned and unearned income. The Progressive Era's alternative to rent extraction was to make money creation a public utility, and to supply health, education and other basic public services as human rights. These were long the social-democratic ideals of Europe and North America when industrial capitalism seemed to be evolving into socialism.

Today, it is through these ideals that China's socialist government seeks to realize the traditional economic aim associated with democracy: preventing a *rentier* oligarchy from polarizing and indebting society by extracting income (economic rent) that has no productive role. This aim was precisely that of the West's long 19th-century fight by classical political economists to free economies from a hereditary landlord class, predatory banking and privatized monopoly privileges. But this drive failed in the West. By the early 20th century the landlords, monopolists and bankers – whose rent-yielding privileges the classical economists hoped to democratize, by nationalization (or at least taxing away) – fought back by promoting a post-classical economics that swept aside the concept of economic rent as unearned "free lunch" income.

The result is that the economic reform movement that started out as a democratic revolution has failed in the West. Today's economic ideology is basically the Economics of the One Percent, erasing the classical distinction between productive and unproductive income and credit. *Rentier* gains are now reported as if they add to national output (as measured by GDP), not as extracting overhead rents *from* the rest of society as "transfer payments." The result is not democratic; it is oligarchic.

The question is: Can the West recover its former progressive path by a revival of democratic reform, or must that "final" reform require a revolution – which does not look likely, to be sure. So where does that leave the Western economies?

Failure to restrain today's *rentier* dynamics threatens to impose debt-ridden and rent-ridden austerity on the Western neoliberalized economies. Their future in this case would be to limp along in a slow crash, weighed down by their financial and privatization overhead paid to the now politically entrenched *rentier* layer at the top.

America's response to its declining industrial and economic power at home has been to tighten its control over Europe and other client economies by military force and political sanctions. The result is a new Iron Curtain aiming to block these allies from expanding their trade and investment with the Russian and Chinese economies in the rising Eurasian core. Forcing nations to choose which geopolitical block they will belong to is driving many out of the dollarized trade and investment orbit with remarkable speed.

Postword:

After I completed writing this book, the New Cold War became hot in Ukraine. The result is that the world is now quickly dividing into two blocs.[13] The U.S. seizure of Venezuela's, Afghanistan's and Russia's

---

[13] The war that began in Ukraine in February 2022 has dramatically accelerated the process of de-dollarization and global fracture, impelling the creation of a new

gold and foreign exchange reserves has ended the dollar-centered trade
and financial system that was put in place in 1945. Despite this system's
benefit to the U.S. economy – by making its Treasury bonds and bank
debts the basis for foreign countries' monetary reserves – the Biden
Administration (2021-24) has taken the lead in ending this globalization
of American power.

---

world order much faster than anyone had anticipated. For my initial writings on
these events see "America's real adversaries are its European and other allies,"
February 8, 2022, "America Defeats Germany for the Third Time in a Century,"
February 28, 2022, and "The American Empire self-destructs. But nobody thought
it would happen this fast," March 6, 2022. At https://michael-hudson.com/2022/02/
americas-real-adversaries-are-its-european-and-other-allies/, https://michael-hudson.
com/2022/02/america-defeats-germany-for-the-third-time-in-a-century/, and https://
michael-hudson.com/2022/03/the-american-empire-self-destructs/, respectively.

Summary of Michael Hudson's Intellectual Contributions

1. In 1972, Michael Hudson gained renown for his book *Super Imperialism: The Economic Strategy of American Empire*, the first explanation of how going off gold would strengthen rather than weaken the United States' ability to finance its military spending abroad. It demonstrated how the U.S. Treasury-bill standard provides an international free lunch to the United States as the key-currency nation, obliging foreign countries to recycle their dollar inflows into new loans to the U.S. Treasury. The effect is for the military-induced balance-of-payments deficit to help finance the domestic U.S. federal budget deficit. That analysis prompted the State Department to do everything it could to block foreign attempts to resist Dollar Diplomacy.

2. Without government protection the international economy tends to polarize rather than converge. Hudson's critical history of international trade theory, *Trade, Development and Foreign Debt*, shows that this awareness was the basis of mercantilism and early free-trade imperialism, whose advocates realized that reality is the opposite of the Factor-Price Equalization Theorem rationalized by Paul Samuelson and similar free traders.

   Hudson's analysis also shows how IMF austerity programs are based on the blind spot that characterized the bank spokesman David Ricardo's "free finance" logic two centuries ago. That logic assumes that payments of debt service to creditors will be spent back into the debtor's economy, enabling all debts "automatically" to be paid, so there can be no monetary deflation. Hudson showed how this logic was refuted in the 1920s in the German reparations debate, yet continues to be retained as a tool of financial aggression against indebted Global South economies, above all to prevent their public spending domestically by earmarking government spending to pay foreign debt service, not for investment in public infrastructure and related social programs.

3. Financing domestic spending by domestic money creation is no more inflationary than borrowing, and certainly is less inflationary than borrowing foreign currency. Hudson's analysis in *Canada in the New Monetary Order* applied what later would become Modern Monetary Theory to the balance of payments and international credit and debt:

When money is borrowed abroad to spend locally, the central bank has
to create the domestic money for use in the local economy in any case.
Why then is foreign credit needed at all, except to pay for imports or
military spending?

4. The FIRE sector is a form of *rentier* overhead, and as such, its
economic rents should not be treated as a contribution to GDP. *Killing
the Host* and numerous scholarly articles outline Hudson's reformulation
of the National Income and Product Accounts (NIPA) to revive the classical concept of economic rent as price without value, and hence income
without an economically necessary cost of production. The *Financial
Times* credited Hudson with using this analysis to forecast the 2008
financial crash and its aftermath.

5. *Killing the Host* and numerous articles by Hudson explain the tendency
of interest-bearing debt to grow in excess of the community's ability
to pay, and why this results in debt deflation. The more credit that
banks create – meaning debts owed by their customers – the larger the
phenomenon of debt deflation becomes. This led Hudson to explain
a dynamic that is the opposite of the mainstream monetarist theory.
Contrary to the assumption that newly created credit (debt) is spent on
goods and services (causing proportional inflation in consumer prices,
wages and other current costs), and the related assumption that new
lending to business borrowers finances new direct investment in means
of production and hiring, Hudson shows that most bank credit/debt
is taken on to buy real estate or other existing assets, bidding up *their*
prices, not goods and services for consumption or industrial use. What
is inflated are asset prices, not commodity prices.

The effect of increased bank credit on these commodity prices and
economic activity is in fact *deflationary*. That is because more credit
means more debt, whose carrying charges siphon off purchasing power
from the economy. Paying debt service leaves households and businesses
with less income available to spend on goods and services. Hudson's
analysis shows how debt (and hence, the "savings" of creditors) grows
exponentially at compound interest, leading to debt deflation that slows
the "real" economy's expansion, tending to deflate consumer prices
and, at a point, leading to austerity. Financial crashes occur when these
exponentially expanding debts cannot be paid, forcing bankruptcies
and foreclosures transferring assets from debtors to creditors. And to
cap matters, this debt and related FIRE-sector overhead has priced
American labor and industry out of world markets, and hence is largely

responsible for post-industrializing the U.S. economy and eroding its former competitive advantage in international markets.

6. Ever since antiquity, attempts to impose public regulation and control over creditor claims have been fought, often violently, by emerging financial and landowning oligarchies. The resulting conflict between a mixed public/private economy and a privatized and financialized "free market" oligarchy is the major fight characterizing today's global economic and military conflict.

Hudson has traced the analysis of this public/private tension back through history. One result of this historical analysis has been to show that interest-bearing debt originated in the Bronze Age Near East in the third millennium BC, and was brought to Greece and Rome only in the 8th century BC (*"... and forgive them their debts,"* and his forthcoming *The Collapse of Antiquity*). But unlike the ancient Near East, classical antiquity had no palace rulers nor their tradition of debt cancellation and land redistribution (Clean Slates). Creditor oligarchies emerged and ultimately prevailed against reformers, monopolizing the land and most monetary wealth on the road to the Roman Empire's eventual collapse into feudalism. The resulting pro-creditor body of post-Roman law has distinguished Western civilization from others.

A related contribution has been to show that money and debt did not originate out of barter, but as an accounting device in Bronze Age Mesopotamia and Egypt, above all to denominate fiscal debts owed to the palatial economy in diverse commodities (by setting a gur of grain equal to a shekel of silver). From the outset, money has been a legal phenomenon, not a commodity. *Creating Economic Order* and numerous articles in scholarly journals regarding this palatial origin of money creation has led the mainstream of Assyriologists and anthropologists to reject the Austrian individualistic (anti-government) theory of money that imagines it to have evolved out of barter with no role of government even as minter of monetary metals and overseer of standardized weights, measures and quality.

7. Given the tendency of interest-bearing debt to grow in excess of the community's ability to pay, Clean Slates are needed to avoid the economic polarization that results from foreclosure and transfer of assets from indebted families, businesses and governments to the financial sector. However, financial oligarchies seek to limit the power of governments to implement oversight policies that aim to restore economic stability and revive economic growth. These oligarchies seek to shift the tax burden off themselves onto the rest of the economy, and to replace

public spending with private charity and private ownership of basic infrastructure and administration.

8. *The Bubble and Beyond* and *The Destiny of Civilization* explain how most wealth in finance-capital economies is achieved by asset-price inflation for real estate, stocks and bonds, not by saving up profits or wages. In contrast to industrial capitalism, the dynamics of finance capitalism are based on financing the privatization of rent-extracting assets and seeking finance-capital gains, which far exceed current net income. Adding these "capital gains" to current income provides a measure of "total returns" that traces the degree to which the inequality of wealth exceeds income inequality.

9. Mainstream economic theory inverts the classical concept of a free market as one free *from* economic rent into one free *for rentiers* to extract such rent. *Killing the Host* traces the 20th century's reversal – involving advocacy for tax privileges and a dismantling of government regulation to make economies free *for* rent-extractors – largely to J. B. Clark in the 1890s and the Austrian anti-socialist school. This anti-classical body of economic theory denies that any income or wealth is unearned. The pretense is that whatever produces income or wealth is, by definition, productive (and hence an addition to GDP), not extractive land rent, natural-resource rent or monopoly rent. The resulting economic theory does not aim at explaining how economies work in the real world, but serves as special-interest pleading by the vested interests. *J is for Junk Economics* seeks to untangle today's vocabulary of economic deception.

10. *The Destiny of Civilization* explains how democratic politics tends to end up promoting the interests of the middle class striving to join the *rentier* class instead of those of wage-earners as a whole. Playing on middle-class aspirations and opposing policies that would tax or limit *rentier* gains in real estate and finance, oligarchs translate their economic power into political co-option of social-democratic and labor parties. The result is to shift and centralize economic planning and tax policy away from government to the financial centers (Wall Street, the City of London, etc.).

11. International trade, finance and related economic relations reflect a conflict of economic systems. U.S.-NATO diplomacy supports neoliberal *rentier* economies in which the top One Percent monopolize wealth, mainly in the form of financialized economic rent from absentee real estate ownership, natural resources, monopolies, debt-inflated housing and other real estate prices, and privatized banking and finance. The great fear of this diplomacy is that socialist economies may succeed

in minimizing *rentier* income, above all by keeping money and credit creation as public utilities. Public control of credit allows socialist economies to create credit to increase productivity and advance other social aims, and also to write down bad debts that threaten to polarize their economies.

Finance capitalism is de-industrializing the U.S. economy and that of its allied NATO satellites. *The Destiny of Civilization* explains that the resulting international diplomacy is not a competition for markets (as the Western economies already are de-industrializing as a byproduct of financialization and capital's war against wage labor), nor a conflict between democratic freedom and authoritarianism, but rather a conflict of economic systems juxtaposing the *rentier* economics of debt deflation and austerity to socialist state-subsidized growth protecting the 99 Percent by keeping the One Percent in check.

12. The irony is that only mixed public/private economies with strong public regulatory sectors can promote economic democracy. What usually are thought of as political democracies turn out to be economic oligarchies – just as Aristotle noted was the case in classical antiquity.

Most economic practices – money, interest-bearing credit, standardized prices and contractual profit agreements – were developed by the palaces and temples of the ancient Near East for their interaction with the economy at large. Greece and Rome had no such central institutions, and hitherto public functions were privatized in the hands of an economic oligarchy from the outset in the West. It took until the 19th century for political pressure to develop a program of socializing finance, real estate and natural infrastructure monopolies in public hands.

That was the aim of classical political economy. But World War I untracked that reform program. Its failure explains why the Western economies are suffering austerity and debt deflation as a result of the *rentier* recapture of economic and political power, sponsored mainly by U.S. diplomacy. The remarkable growth of China suggests that civilization is now reaching the other side of the Mobius strip of history's long spiral, by seeking to restore a balanced public/private economy steered in the interests of the population at large, not by a narrow and increasingly predatory and self-destructive *rentier* class seeking gains at the expense of the rest of the economy.

Selected Bibliography

Super Imperialism: The Economic Strategy of American Empire, 1972 (2nd ed. 2003; 3rd ed. 2021)

Global Fracture – The New International Economic Order, 1977 (2nd ed. 2005)

Economics and Technology in 19th Century American Thought: The Neglected American Economists, 1975

Canada in the New Monetary Order, 1978

Creating Economic Order, 2004, and its companion volumes *Debt and Economic Renewal in the Ancient Near East* (2002), *Land Ownership and Urbanization in the Ancient Near East* (1999), *Privatization in the Ancient Near East and Classical Antiquity* (1996), and *Labor in the Ancient World* (2015), with assyriological co-editors. Hudson's collected articles on these topics are scheduled to be published in *Temples of Enterprise* (2022).

Trade, Development and Foreign Debt, 1992 (2nd ed. 2010)

Finance Capitalism and its Discontents, 2012

The Bubble and Beyond, 2012

Killing the Host: How Financial Parasites and Debt Destroy the Global Economy, 2015

J is for Junk Economics: The Vocabulary of Economic Deception and Reality, 2017

"... and forgive them their debts": Lending, Foreclosure and Redemption from Bronze Age Finance to the Jubilee Year, 2018

The Destiny of Civilization, 2022

The Collapse of Antiquity, in press for 2022

Subject Index

A

Afghanistan 262, 277
Africa 108, 118-9, 139
arbitrage 29, 98, 121, 244
agriculture 129-36
    agricultural chemistry 74, 130-32
    differential agricultural land rent
    72-9
    and environmental destruction
    131-3
    and free trade 131-3
    fertilizers 78, 130-1, 143
    financial, marketing & transport
    monopolies 78, 133-7
    plantation monocultures 56-7,
    107, 113, 119, 129, 131-3, 136, 143
    productivity (increasing returns)
    4, 130
    protectionism 17, 57, 73, 79-81,
    131, 148-9, 199
    and U.S. imperialism & trade
    policy 56-9, 136, 199
        sanctions 121-2
the **Alternative** to neoliberal finance
capitalism *see* **post-*rentier* society &
economy**
Amazon, the 135, 145, 147-8
Argentina 135-6, 190, 197-8, 226
aristocracy
    ancient 223
    European landed 6, 19, 25, 71,
    73, 80, 83, 85, 101, 130, 153, 157,
    170-2, 255-6
    new financial 6, 19, 22, 25, 83,
    85, 101, 171-2, 178, 233-4, 255-6
    post-Soviet Russian 209
ASEAN 150
Asian Crisis of 1997-98 217
asset prices 43-4
    central bank support of 29-30
        see also central banks; Quan-

        titative Easing
    discounted earnings 29, 97-8
    P/E (price/earnings) ratios 29
asset-price inflation ("capital gains")
xii-xiii, xvi-xvii, xxii, 29-30, 33-6, 38-9,
43-4, 90-8, 104, 241, 243-5, 248, 270, 282
    and bank lending & credit
    creation 29-30, 33, 66-8, 90-4
    and central banks *see* central
    banks; Quantitative Easing
    and debt deflation viii, 33-6, 44,
    91-7, 243-5
    see also debt; debt deflation; finance
    capitalism; neoliberalism
austerity
    austerity programs (IMF) 100,
    118, 251, 279
    as deliberate policy of financial
    conquest 251
    see also economic polarization;
    IMF; neoliberalism; finance capi-
    talism
Australia 122, 143-4, 148, 150, 176-7
Austria-Hungary 153, 157
autocracy
    as invective of U.S. propaganda
    45, 59-60, 121, 125, 218, 253, 260,
    266, 271-3
    neoliberal *rentier* autocracy 103, 273
    autocratic governments represent-
    ing oligarchies 129, 271, 273
automatic stabilizers 1, 3, 13

B

Baltic states 59, 61, 199, 215, 216
Bandung Conference 57, 62
bankruptcy
    modern laws 268
    bankruptcy for profit 28, 58
    national or local bankruptcies 67,
    99, 241

282-3
against countries resisting
neoliberal takeover 229-30,
260-2
China as existential threat to
rentier capitalism 125-6, 216-22,
258, 271-2, 275
not mere trade rivalry 218
Russia as existential threat to U.S.
finance capitalism 221-2, 271-2
parallels & contrasts with ancient
Greece 47-50
parallels with Rome 50-2, 123
sanctions & economic isolation
46, 121-6, 137, 140-2, 201, 205, 216,
221-2, 229, 258, 260-1, 271, 277
U.S. destabilization activities
201-2, 221
sponsorship of dissidents 261
Ukraine War 277-8
see also coups; United States,
coups; de-dollarization; China;
global fracture; Nord Stream 2;
Russia; Shanghai Cooperation
Organization
New Deal 164
New World - conquest of 71, 209
New Zealand 146, 150
90 Percent, the 13, 15
99 Percent, the 15, 22, 35, 45, 68, 98,
153, 155, 173, 176, 238, 257, 264, 283
Nobel Economics Prize 167, 175, 177
Non-Aligned Movement 52, 57, 62, 221
Nord Steam 2 46, 137, 141-2, 216, 221
Norman Invasion 71-2, 209
North American Free Trade Act
(NAFTA) 115, 149, 254
Norway 129-30, 139
nuclear weapons 61
U.S. policy on first use 60, 124
treaties & agreements 227

O

offshore banking centers
tax avoidance through xii, xiv, 32,

55-6, 121, 130, 135, 138, 198, 213,
226
U.S. promotion of to attract hot
money xiv
oil & gas Ch. 7 (137-42)
oil-exporting countries - recycling
export earnings to U.S. & other
foreign financial & arms markets
139, 186, 196
oil industry 137-42, 194
pollution & environmental
damage 138-9, 146-8, 227
rent extraction & financialization xxi, 89, 113, 129-30,
137-8, 241
tax avoidance xii, xiv, 32,
56, 130, 135, 137-8
U.S. control of oil trade 137,
141-2
backing client oligar-
chies 54-6, 58-9, 117,
215-6
isolating independent
producers 139-42, 216
oil grabs 117, 139-40,
205-6
oligarchy 2, Chs. 11 & 13 (passim), 281-3
and democracy 62, 153, 170
Aristotle on 283
oligarchic fight to limit the
power of democracies 31,
263-5
oligarchic political strategy
in nominal democracies 282
U.S. oligarchic two-
party duopoly 6-7, 46,
169, 263
financial & *rentier* oligarchy v, xix,
6, 16, 31
finance as main source of oligarchic power xvi, 22, 263
war against strong independent government (the basic
conflict of *rentier* oligarchy
vs. mixed economy) 103,
218-24, 238, Ch. 13 (esp.

Name Index

A

Allende, Salvador 58, 142
Amazon.com, Inc. 150, 249
American Enterprise Institute 53, 177
American International Group (A.I.G.)
85
American Tobacco Company 153
Americans for Prosperity 177
Anaconda Copper Mining Company
58, 142
Andersen, James 75
Apple 32, 56, 124
Aramco 210
Arbenz, Jacobo 56
Archer-Daniels-Midland (ADM) 78,
135-7
Armas, Carlos Castillo 57
Aristotle
    on democracy & oligarchy 49, 51,
    283
    on cutting down aristocratic
    wealth 223
    on interest & money 85-6, 172, 174
    on wealth addiction 2, 238
Attlee, Clement 54

B

Badian, Ernst 51
Bair, Sheila 40
Baker, James 60, 215
Ball, George 180-1
Biden, Joe 45-6, 124, 126, 150, 182-3,
205, 218, 278
Blackstone 250
Blair, Tony 165, 169, 172, 249
Blankfein, Lloyd 14
Blinken, Antony 201, 271-2
Black, William K. xvi, 28
Bosch, Carl 131
Brecht, Bertolt 180
Brzezinski, Zbigniew 206, 216, 218

British Petroleum (Anglo-Persian Oil)
54-5, 138
British Telecom 89, 169
Browder, Bill 216
Brown & Williamson Tobacco 189
Buchanan, David 75
Buchanan, James M. 162, 166, 178
Bunge 135-6
Burnham, James 31
Burns, George 166
Bush, George H. W. 53, 60, 215

C

Cargill 78, 134-5
Carlyle, Thomas 156
Carter, Jimmy 206
Cerro de Pasco Corporation 142
Champion, George 193
Chase Manhattan Bank xii, 193
Chevron 147-8
Chiang Kai-Shek 163
Chodorov, Frank 162
Chunying, Hua 46
Churchill, Winston 54
Clark, John Bates 167-8, 237, 282
Cleveland, Grover 111
Clinton, Bill 59-60, 115, 164, 169, 172,
215, 254, 256
Clinton, Hillary 58, 115, 139, 149, 182,
205
Cobden, Richard 79-80
Connally, John 195

D

Damaschke, Adolph 162
Davis, Norman 188
de Gaulle, Charles 193
Deng Xiaoping 125, 144, 207, 216
Desai, Radhika 41
Dewey, John 264
Disraeli, Benjamin 19

Milton Keynes UK
Ingram Content Group UK Ltd.
UKHW031819120224
437723UK00011B/986